Indiana

interactive SCIENCE

A raccoon's paws are highly sensitive. especially when they get wet.

Glenview, Illinois • Boston, Massachusetts • Chandler, Arizona • Upper Saddle River, New Jersey

Authors

You are an author!

You are one of the authors of this book. You can write in this book! You can take notes in this book! You can draw in it too! This book will be yours to keep.

Fill in the information below to tell about yourself. Then write your autobiography. An autobiography tells about you and the kinds of things you like to do.

My Photo

Name ....

School ....

Town, State ....

Autobiography ....

....

....

....

....

....

....

Credits appear on pages EM23–EM25, which constitute an extension of this copyright page.

ON THE COVER
A raccoon's paws are highly sensitive, especially when they get wet.

ISBN-13: 978-0-328-52094-7
ISBN-10: 0-328-52094-2
4 5 6 7 8 9 10 V011 19 18 17 16 15 14 13 12

Program Authors

DON BUCKLEY, M.Sc.
Information and Communications Technology Director,
The School at Columbia University, New York, New York
Mr. Buckley has been at the forefront of K–12 educational technology for nearly two decades. A founder of New York City Independent School Technologists (NYCIST) and long-time chair of New York Association of Independent Schools' annual IT conference, he has taught students on two continents and created multimedia and Internet-based instructional systems for schools worldwide.

ZIPPORAH MILLER, M.A.Ed.
Associate Executive Director for Professional Programs
and Conferences, National Science Teachers Association,
Arlington, Virginia
Associate executive director for professional programs and conferences at NSTA, Ms. Zipporah Miller is a former K–12 science supervisor and STEM coordinator for the Prince George's County Public School District in Maryland. She is a science education consultant who has overseen curriculum development and staff training for more than 150 district science coordinators.

MICHAEL J. PADILLA, Ph.D.
Associate Dean and Director, Eugene P. Moore School of
Education, Clemson University, Clemson, South Carolina
A former middle school teacher and a leader in middle school science education, Dr. Michael Padilla has served as president of the National Science Teachers Association and as a writer of the National Science Education Standards. He is professor of science education at Clemson University. As lead author of the *Science Explorer* series, Dr. Padilla has inspired the team in developing a program that promotes student inquiry and meets the needs of today's students.

KATHRYN THORNTON, Ph.D.
Professor and Associate Dean, School of Engineering
and Applied Science, University of Virginia,
Charlottesville, Virginia
Selected by NASA in May 1984, Dr. Kathryn Thornton is a veteran of four space flights. She has logged more than 975 hours in space, including more than 21 hours of extravehicular activity. As an author on the *Scott Foresman Science* series, Dr. Thornton's enthusiasm for science has inspired teachers around the globe.

MICHAEL E. WYSESSION, Ph.D.
Associate Professor of Earth and Planetary Science,
Washington University, St. Louis, Missouri
An author on more than 50 scientific publications, Dr. Wysession was awarded the prestigious Packard Foundation Fellowship and Presidential Faculty Fellowship for his research in geophysics. Dr. Wysession is an expert on Earth's inner structure and has mapped various regions of Earth using seismic tomography. He is known internationally for his work in geoscience education and outreach.

Understanding by Design® Author

GRANT WIGGINS, Ed.D.
President, Authentic Education,
Hopewell, New Jersey
Dr. Wiggins is coauthor of *Understanding by Design®* (UbD), a philosophy of instructional design. UbD is a disciplined way of thinking about curriculum design, assessment, and instruction that moves teaching from content to understanding.

Planet Diary Author

JACK HANKIN
Science/Mathematics Teacher,
The Hilldale School, Daly City, California
Founder, Planet Diary Web site
Mr. Hankin is the creator and writer of Planet Diary, a science current events Web site. Mr. Hankin is passionate about bringing science news and environmental awareness into classrooms.

Activities Author

KAREN L. OSTLUND, Ph.D.
Advisory Council, Texas Natural Science
Center, College of Natural Sciences,
The University of Texas at Austin
Dr. Ostlund has more than 35 years of experience teaching at the elementary, middle school, and university levels. Previously Dr. Ostlund served as the Director of WINGS Online (Welcoming Interns and Novices with Guidance and Support) and the Director of the UTeach | Dell Center for New Teacher Success with the UTeach program in the College of Natural Sciences at the University of Texas at Austin. She also served as the Director of the Center for Science Education at the University of Texas at Arlington, President of the Council of Elementary Science International, and on the Board of Directors of the National Science Teachers Association. As an author of the *Scott Foresman Science* series, Dr. Ostlund was instrumental in developing inquiry activities.

ELL Consultant

JIM CUMMINS, Ph.D.
Professor and Canada Research Chair,
Curriculum, Teaching and Learning
Department at the University of Toronto
Dr. Cummins's research focuses on literacy development in multilingual schools and the role technology plays in learning across the curriculum. *Interactive Science* incorporates research-based principles for integrating language with the teaching of academic content based on Dr. Cummins's work.

Reviewers

Program Consultants

WILLIAM BROZO, Ph.D.
Professor of Literacy, Graduate School of Education, George Mason University, Fairfax, Virginia.
Dr. Brozo is the author of numerous articles and books on literacy development. He co-authors a column in The Reading Teacher and serves on the editorial review board of the Journal of Adolescent & Adult Literacy.

KRISTI ZENCHAK, M.S.
Biology Instructor, Oakton Community College, Des Plaines, Illinois
Kristi Zenchak helps elementary teachers incorporate science, technology, engineering, and math activities into the classroom. STEM activities that produce viable solutions to real-world problems not only motivate students but also prepare students for future STEM careers. Ms. Zenchak helps elementary teachers understand the basic science concepts, and provides STEM activities that are easy to implement in the classroom.

Content Reviewers

Paul Beale, Ph.D.
Department of Physics
University of Colorado
Boulder, Colorado

Joy Branlund, Ph.D.
Department of Earth Science
Southwestern Illinois College
Granite City, Illinois

Constance Brown, Ph.D
Atmospheric Science Program
Geography Department
Indiana University
Bloomington, Indiana

Dana Dudle, Ph.D.
Biology Department
DePauw University
Greencastle, Indiana

Rick Duhrkopf, Ph. D.
Department of Biology
Baylor University
Waco, Texas

Mark Henriksen, Ph.D.
Physics Department
University of Maryland
Baltimore, Maryland

Andrew Hirsch, Ph.D.
Department of Physics
Purdue University
W. Lafayette, Indiana

Linda L. Cronin Jones, Ph.D.
School of Teaching & Learning
University of Florida
Gainesville, Florida

T. Griffith Jones, Ph.D.
College of Education
University of Florida
Gainesville, Florida

Candace Lutzow-Felling, Ph.D.
Director of Education
State Arboretum of Virginia & Blandy Experimental Farm
Boyce, Virginia

Cortney V. Martin, Ph.D.
Virginia Polytechnic Institute
Blacksburg, Virginia

Sadredin Moosavi, Ph.D.
University of Massachusetts Dartmouth
Fairhaven, Massachusetts

Klaus Newmann, Ph.D.
Department of Geological Sciences
Ball State University
Muncie, Indiana

Scott M. Rochette, Ph.D.
Department of the Earth Sciences
SUNY College at Brockport
Brockport, New York

Karyn Rogers, Ph.D.
Department of Geological Sciences
University of Missouri
Columbia, Missouri

Laurence Rosenhein, Ph.D.
Dept. of Chemistry and Physics
Indiana State University
Terre Haute, Indiana

Sara Seager, Ph.D.
Department of Planetary Science and Physics
Massachusetts Institute of Technology
Cambridge, Massachusetts

William H. Steinecker, Ph.D.
Research Scholar
Miami University
Oxford, Ohio

Paul R. Stoddard, Ph.D.
Department of Geology and Environmental Geosciences
Northern Illinois University
DeKalb, Illinois

Laurence Rosenhein, Ph. D.
Department of Chemistry
Indiana State University
Terre Haute, Indiana

Janet Vaglia, Ph. D.
Department of Biology
DePauw University
Greencastle, Indiana

Ed Zalisko, Ph.D.
Professor of Biology
Blackburn College
Carlinville, Illinois

Built especially for Indiana

Indiana *Interactive Science* covers 100% of Indiana's Academic Standards for Science without extraneous content. Built on feedback from Indiana educators, *Interactive Science* focuses on what is important to Indiana teachers and students, creating a personal, relevant, and engaging classroom experience.

Indiana K-8 Science Teacher Advisory Board

Jodi Allen
Glen Acres Elementary School
Lafayette, IN

Rick Dubbs
Monrovia Middle School
Monrovia, IN

Margaret Flack
Vincennes University
   Jasper Campus
Jasper, IN

Michael Gibson
New Haven Middle School
New Haven, IN

Jill Hatcher
Spring Mill Elementary School
Indianapolis, IN

Jamie Hooten
Lincoln Elementary School
Bedford, IN

Jamil Odom
Mary Bryan Elementary School
Indianapolis, IN

Mike Robards
Franklin Community Middle School
Franklin, IN

Richard Towle
Noblesville Middle School
Noblesville, IN

K-8 National Master Teacher Board

Tricia Burke
E. F. Young Elementary School
Chicago, IL

Lisa Catandella
Brentwood UFSD
Brentwood, NY

Karen Clements
Lynch Elementary School
Winchester, MA

Emily Compton
Park Forest Middle School
Baton Rouge, LA

Pansy Cowder
Lincoln Magnet School
Plant City, FL

Georgi Delgadillo
East Valley School District
Spokane, WA

Dr. Rick Fairman
McGregor School of Education
Antioch University
Yellow Springs, OH

Joe Fescatore
Green Elementary School
La Mesa, CA

Mimi Halferty
Gorzycki Middle School
Austin, TX

Christy Herring
Prairie Trace Elementary School
Carmel, IN

Treva Jeffries
Toledo Public Schools
Toledo, OH

James Kuhl
Central Square Middle School
Central Square, NY

Dr. Patsy Latin
Caddo Public School District
Shreveport, LA

Greg Londot
Hidden Hills Elementary School
Phoenix, AZ

Stan Melby
Sheridan Road Elementary
Fort Sill, OK

Bonnie Mizell
Howard Middle School
Orlando, FL

Dr. Joel Palmer
Mesquite ISD
Mesquite, TX

Leslie Pohley
Largo Middle School
Largo, FL

Susan Pritchard
Washington Middle School
La Habra, CA

Anne Rice
Woodland Middle School
Gurnee, IL

Adrienne Sawyer
Chesapeake Public Schools
Chesapeake, VA

Richard Towle
Noblesville Middle School
Noblesville, IN

Dr. Madhu Uppal
Schaumburg School District
Schaumburg, IL

Maria Valdez
Mark Twain Elementary School
Wheeling, IL

Viv Wayne
Montgomery County Public Schools
Rockville, MD

Indiana

Indiana Unit A
Science, Engineering, and Technology

⬤ Indiana Unit A
Science, Engineering,
and Technology 1

Chapter 1

The Nature of Science

Scientists may study the amount of water pollution in a marsh.

⬤ **myscienceonLine.com**

Untamed Science
Watch the Ecogeeks as they learn about the nature of science.

Got it? ⏱ 60-Second Video
Watch and learn about the nature of science.

Envision It!
See what you already know about the nature of science.

Explore It! Animation
Watch a nature of science lab online.

⬤ **I Will Know...**
See how the key concepts of the nature of science come to life.

Design and Function

Technology can make work easier and solve problems.

 myscienceonline.com

Untamed Science™
Ecogeeks answer your
questions about design and
function.

Got it? 60-Second Video
Review lessons about design
and function in 60 seconds!

 my planet diary
Learn some fun facts about
design and function.

Envision It!
See what you already know
about design and function.

Memory Match
Mix-and-match design and
function vocabulary.

Indiana Unit B
Physical Science

Properties of Matter

*Gold has properties that
determine how it can be used.*

ⓘ **mYscienceonLine.com**

UntamedScience™
Ecogeeks answer your
questions about properties of
matter.

Got it? **60-Second Video**
Review lessons about
properties of matter in
60 seconds!

🌐 **mY planeT DiaRY**
Learn some fun facts about
properties of matter.

Investigate It! Virtual Lab
Investigate new ways of
separating mixtures.

Memory Match
Mix-and-match properties of
matter vocabulary.

Indiana Unit B Summary

Physical and Chemical Changes

Colorful products can form in a chemical change.

◐ myscienceonline.com

🦎 **UntamedScience™**
Watch the Ecogeeks as they learn about physical and chemical changes.

Got it? ⏱ **60-Second Video**
Watch one-minute videos for every physical and chemical changes lesson.

Envision It!
Interact with science to find out what you know about physical and chemical changes.

▶ **Explore It!** Animation
Explore physical and chemical changes in a new way!

❓ I Will Know...
See what you have learned about physical and chemical changes.

Indiana

Chapter 5

Indiana Unit C
Earth Science

The Solar System

*When the Western
Hemisphere is facing the sun,
it is day in Indiana.*

⏰ **myscienceonline.com**

UntamedScience
Ecogeeks answer your
questions about the solar
system.

Got it? ⏱ **60-Second Video**
Review lessons about the
solar system in 60 seconds!

MY PLANET DIARY
Clear up your misconceptions
about stars.

Envision It!
See what you already know
about the solar system.

Vocabulary Smart Cards
Mix-and-match solar system
vocabulary online

Chapter 6

Ecosystems

The Cooper's hawk is at the top of some food chains in Indiana.

myscienceonLine.com

Untamed Science
Ecogeeks answer your questions about ecosystems.

Got it? 60-Second Video
See each ecosystems lesson reviewed in one minute!

Explore It! Animation
Explore ecosystems in a new way!

I Will Know...
See how the key concepts about ecosystems come to life.

Vocabulary Smart Cards
Hear and see your ecosystems vocabulary words online.

Indiana

Chapter 7

Human Body

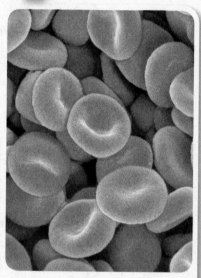

Red blood cells carry oxygen to other cells in the body.

myscience**online.com**

Untamed Science™
Watch the Ecogeeks as they learn about the human body.

Got it? **60-Second Video**
Watch one-minute videos for every human body lesson.

Explore It! Animation
Explore the human body in a new way!

I Will Know...
See what you have learned about the human body.

my planet diary
Learn some amazing science stats about mammals.

Videos that bring Science to life!

Go to **MyScienceOnline.com** to watch exciting Untamed Science videos!

The Untamed Science team has created a unique video for every chapter in this book!

"This is your book. You can write in it!"

interactive SCIENCE

 Big Question

At the start of each chapter you will see two questions—an **Engaging Question** and a **Big Question.**
Just like a scientist, you will predict an answer to the Engaging Question. Each Big Question will help you start thinking about Indiana's Big Ideas of science. Look for the symbol throughout the chapter!

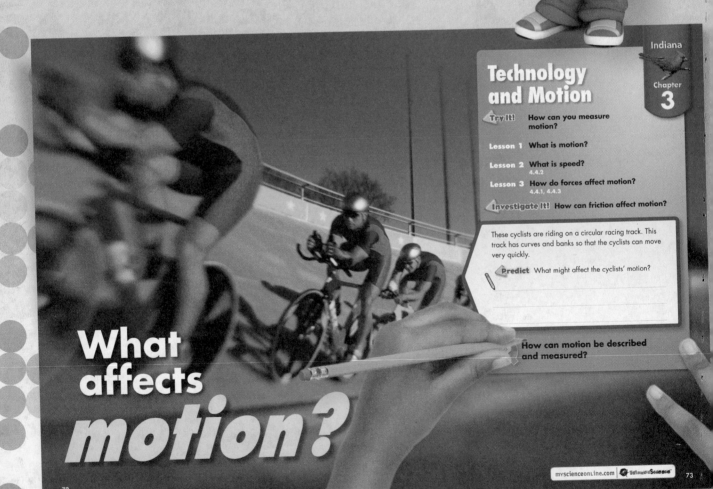

Indiana

Technology and Motion

Chapter 3

Try It! How can you measure motion?

Lesson 1 What is motion?

Lesson 2 What is speed?
4.4.2

Lesson 3 How do forces affect motion?
4.4.1, 4.4.3

Investigate It! How can friction affect motion?

These cyclists are riding on a circular racing track. This track has curves and banks so that the cyclists can move very quickly.

Predict What might affect the cyclists' motion?

_____

_____

How can motion be described and measured?

What affects motion?

72

73

Let's Read Science!

You will see a page like this toward the beginning of each chapter. It will show you how to use a reading skill that will help you understand what you read.

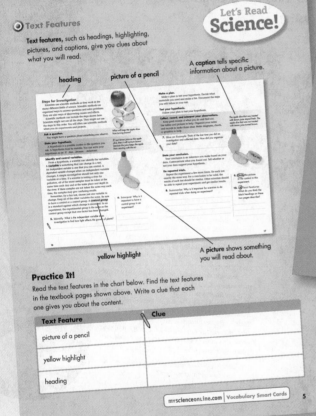

Practice It!

Read the text features in the chart below. Find the text features in the textbook pages shown above. Write a clue that each one gives you about the content.

Text Feature	Clue
picture of a pencil	
yellow highlight	
heading	

myscienceonline.com | Vocabulary Smart Cards   5

Vocabulary Smart Cards

Go to the end of the chapter and cut out your own set of **Vocabulary Smart Cards.** Write a sentence, draw a picture, or use a vocabulary strategy to learn the word. Play a game with a classmate to practice using the word!

Look for **MyScienceOnline.com** technology options.
At MyScienceOnline.com you can immerse yourself in virtual environments, get extra practice, and even blog about current events in science.

interactive SCIENCE

Envision It!

At the beginning of each lesson, at the top of the page, you will see an **Envision It!** interactivity that gives you the opportunity to circle, draw, write, or respond to the Envision It! question.

Lesson 4

How do organisms get and use energy?

Observe and classify common Indiana organisms as producers, consumers, decomposers, predator and prey based on their relationships and interactions with other organisms in their ecosystem. (Also ...)

Envision It!

Tell how you think plants get the energy they need to live.

UNLOCK

I will know how plants use energy from the sun.

Words to Know

photosynthesis
cellular respiration

my planet diary
for Indiana

DISCOVERY

What comes to mind when you think of corn? You might think of corn on the cob, popcorn, or cornbread. However, corn is not just food. Scientists have discovered that it can also be used to produce a liquid fuel called ethanol. Ethanol is a type of biofuel. Biofuels are fuels made from living things. Other plants used to make biofuel are soy and sugarcane. Biofuels are more environmentally friendly than other fuels, such as gasoline. Because gasoline-powered vehicles produce air pollution, using biofuels instead might help preserve Earth's environment.

How do you think biofuels might affect your life?

mvscienceonline.com   my planet diary   254

Energy Sources

What is your favorite type of green salad? You might like one made of spinach. Perhaps you choose iceberg lettuce or crispy romaine lettuce. Spinach, iceberg lettuce, and romaine lettuce are all types of leaves. A leaf is a major plant part. Unlike animals, plants make their own food. Most of the food that a plant makes is made in the plant's leaves.

When you eat spinach or lettuce leaves, your body gets their energy. Your body cells need this energy to carry out its many functions. The energy you get is stored in the leaves. Where did the leaves get this energy? It came from the sun in the form of sunlight. The sun is Earth's primary energy source. The plant used the sunlight's energy to make its food, which it uses to grow. This form of energy passes on to you when you eat the leaves.

1. **Identify** Where does the stored energy in these cabbage leaves come from?

2. **Explain** How does a plant get its food?

cabbage

mvscienceonline.com   **Envision It!**   255

---

my planet diary

My Planet Diary interactivities will introduce you to amazing scientists, fun facts, and important discoveries in science. They will also help you to overcome common misconceptions about science concepts.

After reading small chunks of information, stop to check your understanding. The visuals help teach about what you read. Answer questions, underline text, draw pictures, or label models.

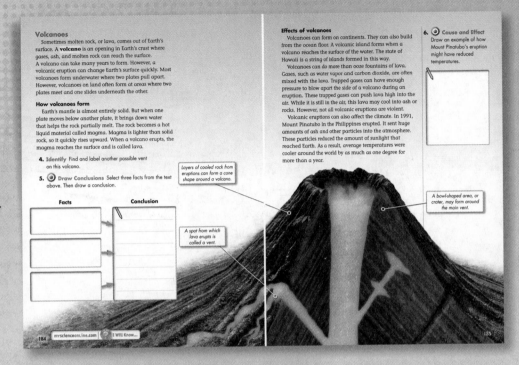

Volcanoes

Sometimes molten rock, or lava, comes out of Earth's surface. A **volcano** is an opening in Earth's crust where gases, ash, and molten rock can reach the surface. A volcano can take many years to form. However, a volcanic eruption can change Earth's surface quickly. Most volcanoes form underwater where two plates pull apart. However, volcanoes on land often form at areas where two plates meet and one slides underneath the other.

How volcanoes form

Earth's mantle is almost entirely solid. But when one plate moves below another plate, it brings down water that helps the rock partially melt. The rock becomes a hot liquid material called magma. Magma is lighter than solid rock, so it quickly rises upward. When a volcano erupts, the magma reaches the surface and is called lava.

4. Identify Find and label another possible vent on this volcano.

5. Draw Conclusions Select three facts from the text above. Then draw a conclusion.

Facts

Conclusion

Layers of cooled rock from eruptions can form a cone shape around a volcano.

A spot from which lava erupts is called a vent.

Effects of volcanoes

Volcanoes can form on continents. They can also build from the ocean floor. A volcanic island forms when a volcano reaches the surface of the water. The state of Hawaii is a string of islands formed in this way.

Volcanoes can do more than ooze fountains of lava. Gases, such as water vapor and carbon dioxide, are often mixed with the lava. Trapped gases can have enough pressure to blow apart the side of a volcano during an eruption. These trapped gases can push lava high into the air. While it is still in the air, this lava may cool into ash or rocks. However, not all volcanic eruptions are violent.

Volcanic eruptions can also affect the climate. In 1991, Mount Pinatubo in the Philippines erupted. It sent huge amounts of ash and other particles into the atmosphere. These particles reduced the amount of sunlight that reached Earth. As a result, average temperatures were cooler around the world by as much as one degree for more than a year.

6. Cause and Effect Draw an example of how Mount Pinatubo's eruption might have reduced temperatures.

A bowl-shaped area, or crater, may form around the main vent.

Velocity and Acceleration

Some objects change speed *and direction*. **Velocity** is both the speed and the direction an object is moving. Some words that describe direction are *north, south, east,* and *west*. Others are *left, right, up,* and *down*.

Any change in the speed or direction of an object's motion is acceleration. Starting, speeding up, and slowing down are accelerations. The roller coaster accelerates as it speeds up or slows down. It is changing speed. A roller coaster on a curved path accelerates even if its speed does not change. That is because it changes direction as it moves around the curve.

7. Decide Which of the following is NOT an example of an acceleration?
a. An airplane moving at the same speed in the same direction
b. An airplane slowing its speed and moving down to land
c. An airplane slowing its speed and moving in the same direction

8. Summarize What are two things that must be measured in order to find an object's velocity?

9. Illustrate Look at the roller coaster on the opposite page. Draw a solid arrow where the roller coaster slows down, and a dotted arrow where the coaster speeds up.

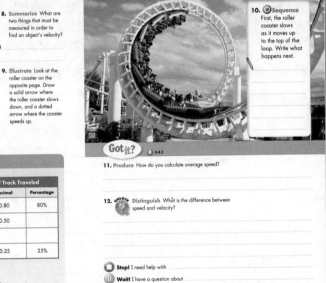

Got it? 4.4.2

11. Produce How do you calculate average speed?

12. Distinguish What is the difference between speed and velocity?

Stop! I need help with

Wait! I have a question about

Go! Now I know

10. Sequence First, the roller coaster slows as it moves up to the top of the loop. Write what happens next.

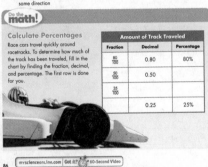

Calculate Percentages

Race cars travel quickly around racetracks. To determine how much of the track has been traveled, fill in the chart by finding the fraction, decimal, and percentage. The first row is done for you.

Amount of Track Traveled

Fraction	Decimal	Percentage
$\frac{80}{100}$	0.80	80%
$\frac{50}{100}$	0.50	
$\frac{35}{100}$		
	0.25	25%

Scientists commonly use math as a tool to help them answer science questions. You can practice skills that you are learning in math class right in your Interactive Science Student Edition!

Got it?

At the end of each lesson you will have a chance to evaluate your own progress! After answering the **Got it?** questions, think about how you are doing. At this point you can stop, wait, or go on to the next lesson.

"Have fun! Be a scientist!"

Try It!

At the start of every chapter, you will have the chance to do a hands-on inquiry lab. The lab will provide you with experiences that will prepare you for the chapter lessons or may raise a new question in your mind.

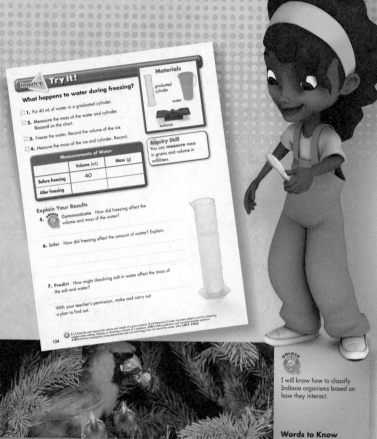

Inquiry · Try It!

What happens to water during freezing?

☐ **1.** Put 40 mL of water in a graduated cylinder.

☐ **2.** Measure the mass of the water and cylinder. Record on the chart.

☐ **3.** Freeze the water. Record the volume of the ice.

☐ **4.** Measure the mass of the ice and cylinder. Record.

Materials

graduated cylinder

water

balance

Measurements of Water

	Volume (mL)	Mass (g)
Before freezing	40	
After freezing		

Inquiry Skill
You can measure mass in grams and volume in milliliters.

Explain Your Results

5. Communicate How did freezing affect the volume and mass of the water?

6. Infer How did freezing affect the amount of matter? Explain.

7. Predict How might dissolving salt in water affect the mass of the salt and water?

With your teacher's permission, make and carry out a plan to find out.

124

Lesson 3

How do some Indiana organisms interact?

Observe and classify common Indiana organisms as producers, consumers, decomposers, predator and prey based on their relationships and interactions with other organisms in their ecosystem. (Also ___)

Envision It!

Tell how these organisms are interacting.

I will know how to classify Indiana organisms based on how they interact.

Words to Know
deciduous plant
evergreen plant

Inquiry · Explore It!

How do food webs show relationships?

☐ **1.** Choose a card. Hold it so it can be seen. Stand in a circle with your group. Look for organisms that your organism eats or that eats you. Toss the ball of yarn to one of them but hold onto the end of the yarn.

☐ **2.** Take turns until everyone is connected. You have made a **model** of a food web.

☐ **3.** Lay down the yarn and the cards. Using the names of the organisms, draw your food web in the space to the right.

Materials

Food Web Cards

yarn

Explain Your Results

4. Interpret Data Look at your food web. Explain the relationships the web shows. Give examples.

248   mysciencenLine.com   **Explore It! Animation**

S.NS.3 Plan and carry out investigations as a class, in small groups or independently, often over a period of several class lessons. (Also 5.NS.7)

Indiana Organisms

When you look around outside, what sort of organisms do you see? Indiana is home to many organisms that are common in many parts of the United States. Some common Indiana plants, such as the tulip poplar, are deciduous trees. A **deciduous plant** loses all of its leaves for a part of the year. In Indiana, deciduous plants lose their leaves in the winter. Another Indiana tree is the eastern hemlock. This tree is an example of an **evergreen plant**, or a plant that keeps green leaves on its branches all year. Other plants that are found throughout the state include the serviceberry, common buttonbush, dogwood, goldenrod, and aster.

Of course, in addition to plants, Indiana is also home to many animals. Fish, such as the northern pike and yellow perch, and mammals, such as the red fox and Indiana bat, all live in Indiana. Just as in other ecosystems, the plants and animals of Indiana interact with one another in food chains, food webs, competition, and symbiotic relationships.

1. ◉ Main Idea and Details Read the first paragraph above. **Underline** the main idea of the paragraph. **Circle** three details.

mysciencenLine.com   **Envision It!**   249

Explore It!

Before you start reading the lesson, **Explore It!** activities provide you with an opportunity to first explore the content!

Design It!

STEM activities are found throughout core and ancillary materials.

The **Design It!** activity has you use the engineering design process to find solutions to problems. By identifying the problem, doing research, and developing possible solutions, you will design, construct, and test a prototype for a real world problem. Communicate your evidence through graphs, tables, drawings, and prototypes and identify ways to make your solution better.

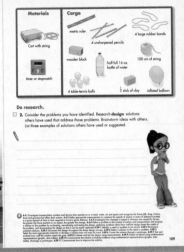

Investigate It!

At the end of every chapter, a Directed Inquiry lab gives you a chance to put together everything you've learned in the chapter. Using the activity card, apply design principles in the Guided version to Modify Your Investigation or the Open version to Develop Your Own Investigation. Whether you need a lot of support from your teacher or you're ready to explore on your own, there are fun hands-on activities that match your interests.

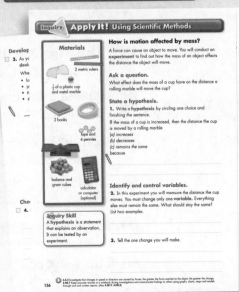

Apply It!

At the end of every unit, an Open Inquiry lab gives you a chance to explore science using scientific methods.

"Go online anytime!"

interactive SCIENCE

Here's how you log in...

1 Go to www.myscienceonline.com.

2 Log in with your username and password.

Username: _____

Password: _____

3 Click on your program and select your chapter.

Check it out!

Watch a Video!

Untamed Science™ Join the Ecogeeks on their video adventure.

Got it? 60-Second Video Review each lesson in 60 seconds.

Go Digital for Inquiry!

Explore It! Simulation Watch the lab online.

Investigate It! Virtual Lab Do the lab online.

Show What You Know!

Got it? Quiz Take a quick quiz and get instant feedback.

ISTEP+ Practice Prepare for the "big test."

Writing for Science Write to help you unlock the Big Question.

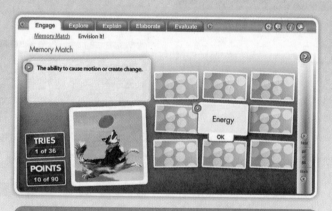

Get Excited About Science!

The Big Question Share what you think about the Big Question.

my planet diary Connect to the world of science.

Envision It! Connect to what you already know before you start each lesson.

Memory Match Play a game to build your vocabulary.

Get Help!

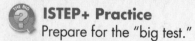 **my science coach** Get help at your level.

Indiana

Unit

A

Science, Engineering, and Technology

Chapter 1
The Nature of Science

THE BIG ? What is science?

Chapter 2
Design and Function

THE BIG ? How does technology affect our lives?

What is she trying to DISCOVER?

The Nature of Science

Scientists use a variety of skills and tools to discover new things about the world around them.

Explain How is this young scientist using tools to learn more about her world?

....

....

THE BIG ? What is science?

Inquiry ▶ Try It!

What questions do scientists ask?

Scientists ask questions about objects, organisms, and events. Good scientific questions can be answered by making observations and measurements.

☐ **1.** Work in a group. Cut apart the questions.
Classify the questions into 2 piles.
Pile 1 Good Scientific Questions

Pile 2 Not Good Scientific Questions

☐ **2.** Discuss how you made each sorting decision.

Explain Your Results

3. Draw a Conclusion
Pick one question from Pile 1. Letter of question: _____
Explain why it is a good scientific question.

....

....

4. Pick one question from Pile 2. Letter of question: _____
Explain why it is not a good scientific question.

....

....

5. UNLOCK THE BIG **?** Pick another question from Pile 2. Letter of question: _____
Rewrite it to make it into a good scientific question.
Then explain why it is a good scientific question.

....

....

Materials

Scientific or Not?

✂ scissors

Inquiry Skill
You **classify** when you sort things into groups.

5.NS.1 Make predictions and formulate testable questions. **5.NS.3** Plan and carry out investigations as a class, in small groups or independently, often over a period of several class lessons.

Text features, such as headings, highlighting, pictures, and captions, give you clues about what you will read.

heading   **picture of a pencil**   A **caption** tells specific information about a picture.

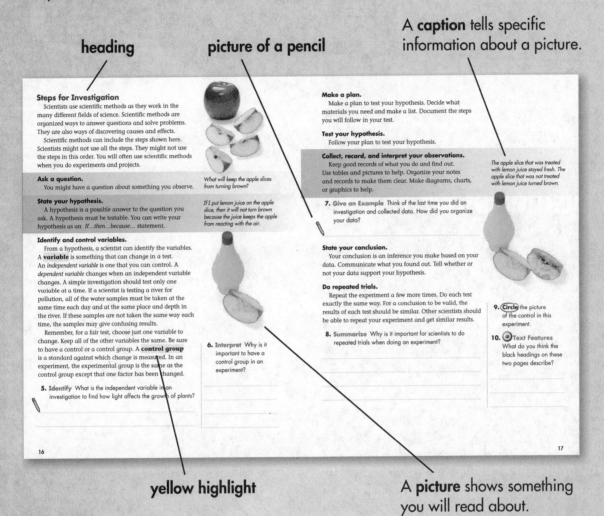

Steps for Investigation
Scientists use scientific methods as they work in the many different fields of science. Scientific methods are organized ways to answer questions and solve problems. They are also ways of discovering causes and effects.
Scientific methods can include the steps shown here. Scientists might not use all the steps. They might not use the steps in this order. You will often use scientific methods when you do experiments and projects.

Ask a question.
You might have a question about something you observe.

State your hypothesis.
A hypothesis is a possible answer to the question you ask. A hypothesis must be testable. You can write your hypothesis as an *If...then...because...* statement.

Identify and control variables.
From a hypothesis, a scientist can identify the variables. A **variable** is something that can change in a test. An *independent variable* is one that you can control. A *dependent variable* changes when an independent variable changes. A simple investigation should test only one variable at a time. If a scientist is testing a river for pollution, all of the water samples must be taken at the same time each day and at the same place and depth in the river. If these samples are not taken the same way each time, the samples may give confusing results.
Remember, for a fair test, choose just one variable to change. Keep all of the other variables the same. Be sure to have a control or a control group. A **control group** is a standard against which change is measured. In an experiment, the experimental group is the same as the control group except that one factor has been changed.

5. Identify What is the independent variable in an investigation to find how light affects the growth of plants?

What will keep the apple slices from turning brown?

If I put lemon juice on the apple slice, then it will not turn brown because the juice keeps the apple from reacting with the air.

6. Interpret Why is it important to have a control group in an experiment?

Make a plan.
Make a plan to test your hypothesis. Decide what materials you need and make a list. Document the steps you will follow in your test.

Test your hypothesis.
Follow your plan to test your hypothesis.

Collect, record, and interpret your observations.
Keep good records of what you do and find out. Use tables and pictures to help. Organize your notes and records to make them clear. Make diagrams, charts, or graphics to help.

7. Give an Example Think of the last time you did an investigation and collected data. How did you organize your data?

State your conclusion.
Your conclusion is an inference you make based on your data. Communicate what you found out. Tell whether or not your data support your hypothesis.

Do repeated trials.
Repeat the experiment a few more times. Do each test exactly the same way. For a conclusion to be valid, the results of each test should be similar. Other scientists should be able to repeat your experiment and get similar results.

8. Summarize Why is it important for scientists to do repeated trials when doing an experiment?

The apple slice that was treated with lemon juice stayed fresh. The apple slice that was not treated with lemon juice turned brown.

9. Circle the picture of the control in this experiment.

10. ● Text Features What do you think the black headings on these two pages describe?

16   17

yellow highlight   A **picture** shows something you will read about.

Practice It!

Read the text features in the chart below. Find the text features in the textbook pages shown above. Write a clue that each one gives you about the content.

Text Feature	Clue
picture of a pencil	
yellow highlight	
heading	

What do scientists do?

Envision It!

5.NS.1 Make predictions and formulate testable questions. 5.NS.9 Compare the results of an investigation with the prediction.

Tell what you think this scientist is learning about the ocean.

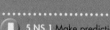 my planet diary

 FunFact

Deep in the ocean lies a world that is almost completely unexplored by humans.

2,600 meters below the ocean's surface, animals such as the giant tubeworm live in extreme conditions. That far below the surface there is extremely high pressure and not very much oxygen or light. Structures called hydrothermal vents are near volcanoes and release very hot water. The water temperature can be more than 400°C!

Giant tubeworms can grow to be up to 2.5 meters long and 10 centimeters wide. They do not have mouths. Instead, giant tubeworms absorb nutrients made by tiny bacteria that live inside of them!

giant tubeworm

Describe What might a scientist do to find out how giant tubeworms interact with their environment?

....

....

....

I will know how scientists use inquiry to learn about the world around them.

Words to Know

hypothesis
observation

Problems, Decisions, and New Ideas

How deep is the ocean? What creatures live in its depths? The world around us is filled with things that are still unknown. To better understand the world, scientists first define a problem and then try to find answers.

Scientific investigation begins with a testable question. Almost every part of your life has been improved in some way by science or by something science made possible. Science can help you get the information you need to make good decisions too. Should you snack on a banana or a soda? What can you do to avoid catching a cold? Scientists can help people answer questions, solve problems, and form new ideas through the use of scientific processes.

1. ◉ **Text Features** Complete the chart to explain the text features on this page.

This instrument shows water temperature and depth. It is used in fishing.

2. **Predict** Tell what problem you think the tool above might help solve.

Text Feature	Clue
photograph	shows an example of a tool used to find depth
blue heading	

Scientific Research and Knowledge

After scientists define a problem, they begin their investigation with research. Scientists need to use a variety of appropriate reference materials to do research. The reference materials they use need to be sources of information that scientists have agreed upon. Scientists cannot draw valid conclusions from information that cannot be verified by other scientists. For example, a scientist researching ocean water cannot simply find information from a random Internet source and use it in an investigation. The source must be reliable, and the information must have been reviewed and verified by other scientists.

Examples of appropriate reference materials may include books and scientific journals. Scientists may use articles in the scientific journals to do their research. These articles are written by scientists and reviewed by other scientists before they are published. Many of these journals can be found in libraries and on the Internet. Sometimes, information even from reliable sources can change. New findings might cause scientists to rethink old ideas.

3. **Analyze** The scientists below found information on the Internet in a blog. Could they use this piece of information to answer a scientific problem they have defined? Explain.

Predict and Make Hypotheses

Scientists use a problem they have defined and research from appropriate sources to form a prediction, or a hypothesis. A **hypothesis** is a statement of what you think will happen during an investigation. It is often written in the form of an *if... then... because* statement. Scientists use experience and what they have found in their research to predict what they think will be a solution to the problem.

Look at the picture above. One example of a hypothesis that the scientist might have made is, *If the level of water pollution increases, then the population of manatees will decrease because the plants they eat cannot live in highly polluted water.*

4. **Compose** You have read one possible hypothesis about manatees. Write an example of a different hypothesis the scientist could have formed.

....

....

....

....

Go Green

A Bright Invention
Through research and careful observation, scientists often find solutions to everyday problems. Think about your community. Define a pollution problem that affects it. What are some ideas you can think of to solve this problem? Share your ideas with others.

Make Observations

Scientists use many skills and processes to find answers to problems. One of these is making observations. An **observation** is something you find out about objects, events, or living things by using your senses. Scientists make observations very carefully. In this way, they can be sure that the information they gather is reliable. Scientists often use tools, such as thermometers, to extend their senses. Scientists are also good at organizing their observations. When scientists have collected their information, they analyze and evaluate it to draw conclusions. They also share their findings with other scientists, who can then see if their own results are similar.

For example, scientists may have observed that a group of sea turtles returns to the same beach every year to lay eggs. The scientists want to find out what causes the turtles to return and where they go between the yearly beach visits. Scientists used identification tags and radio transmitters to observe that a sea turtle might travel thousands of kilometers in one year and return to the same beach.

5. Analyze The scientist below is observing a sea turtle. What problem might the scientist define, and how might she find answers to the problem?

myscienceonline.com | Got it? 60-Second Video

Draw Conclusions

Scientists use their observations to draw conclusions. When they draw a conclusion, they summarize what they have learned by analyzing their observations. For example, a scientist may observe that some populations of birds that eat certain fish are decreasing. The scientist may then observe that the fish have been dying. By testing the properties of soil samples from the riverbed, the scientist may be able to observe qualities of the soil, such as the presence of pollution. Using this observation, the scientist might conclude that pollution in the river is causing the living things there to be unhealthy and to die or move away.

These scientists are testing for pollution.

6. Describe Tell how scientific testing helps scientists draw conclusions.

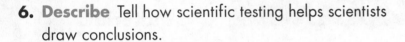

Got it? 5.NS.1, 5.NS.9

7. Explain What are four things that scientists do?

....

....

8. Explain How can people solve problems?

....

....

9. Draw Conclusions Why should you use a variety of sources when you do research for an investigation?

....

⬛ **Stop!** I need help with ....

⏸ **Wait!** I have a question about ....

▶ **Go!** Now I know ....

How do scientists investigate?

5.NS.1 Make predictions and formulate testable questions. 5.NS.2 Design a fair test. (Also 5.NS.3, 5.NS.4)

Envision It!

Tell how you think scientists use this wind tunnel to build better cars.

Inquiry ## Explore It!

Which method keeps bread freshest?

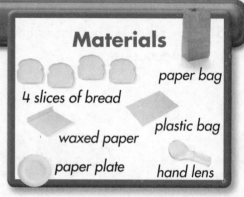

Materials

4 slices of bread

waxed paper

paper plate

paper bag

plastic bag

hand lens

☑ **1.** Put 2 slices of bread on a plate. **Observe** with a hand lens. **Record.** Cover 1 slice with waxed paper.

☑ **2.** Put another slice in a paper bag. Close the bag. Put another slice in a plastic bag. Seal the bag.

☑ **3.** Wait 5 days. Observe the slices. Record your observations on the chart.

Bread Observations				
	Waxed Paper	**Plastic Bag**	**Paper Bag**	**Uncovered Slice**
Day 5				

Explain Your Results

4. Interpret Data Compare the freshness of the bread slices after 5 days.

5. Infer How could you combine methods to keep bread fresh longer?

5.3.2 Investigate the action of different decomposers and compare the role they play in an ecosystem with that of producers and consumers. 5.NS.3 Plan and carry out investigations as a class, in small groups or independently, often over a period of several class lessons. (Also 5.NS.8)

myscienceonline.com | **Explore It!** Animation

I will know how scientists investigate problems in many different ways.

Words to Know

experiment   control group
variable   procedures

Scientific Investigation

Scientific investigation usually begins with an observation. Someone observes that cars with a certain shape are more fuel efficient. Scientists then ask a question about the observation and collect data to answer their question. One important way to find reliable answers is to do an experiment. An **experiment** is the use of scientific methods to test your hypothesis. Remember that a hypothesis is a statement of what you think will happen in an investigation.

There is no single "scientific method" for finding answers. Biologists study living things with different methods than astronomers use to study the stars. For both types of scientists, however, it is important to observe, collect information, test ideas, make predictions, and share their findings with other scientists who can disagree with or confirm the findings.

However, it is not always possible to manipulate variables in a way that can answer scientific questions. Sometimes you have to design an investigation to test a hypothesis without doing a controlled experiment. In addition to controlled experiments, three types of investigations that scientists use are models, surveys, and sampling. These often help scientists test hypotheses.

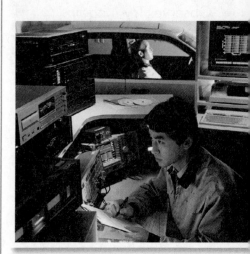

1. **Predict** Write a possible hypothesis that this scientist is thinking about as he does his experiment.

....

....

....

....

At-Home Lab

Falling Water
Carefully make a hole 2 cm from the top of a cup. Make an identical hole 5 cm below the first one. Hold your fingers over the holes. Fill the cup with water. Predict what will happen when you let go. Try it. Hold the cup high over a sink or tub. Observe. Try it again. State your conclusion.

Models

Scientists often use models to learn more about the world or to test designs and materials. Models are objects or ideas that represent other things. They show how something is constructed or how it works. Models are often used to study things that are very large, have many parts, or are difficult to observe directly.

The car model in the picture below is a computer-generated model. Testing a computer model of a car has some advantages over testing real cars. For example, it is easier to control parts of the experiment, such as driving conditions, in a computer model. Once a computer-generated model car has been tested virtually, a machine is used to carve the car out of clay. The physical model can be used to help scientists learn more about how an actual car will work.

Models are helpful tools. However, they are not the actual objects. Testing different models or the real car, for example, may give different results. Scientists may have to do more research and testing to find more information about the cars. Even so, models are valuable tools that help scientists understand the world around them.

2. Give an Example What is another advantage of using a computer-generated model of a car?

....

....

....

These models help scientists study cars.

Surveys and Sampling

Scientists do investigations in many different fields of science. Sometimes the best way for a scientist to investigate is by using a survey. Surveys can be questionnaires that are given to a number of people whose answers are recorded and then analyzed. Sometimes people are interviewed in person or on the phone. For example, if a number of people became ill at a picnic, doctors would want to know what each person ate and drank. They would also want to know who got sick and who did not. The answers will help them find the source of the illness.

Scientists also use sampling to collect data. Scientists examine random individuals from a population. For example, doctors may examine a few people from the picnic and see how healthy they are. Doctors can then generalize their results to all the people at the picnic. This may also help the doctors find the source of the illness.

3. **Evaluate** Write one question that the doctor could be asking the patients in the picture below in his survey.

....

....

4. CHALLENGE How could a scientist use sampling to investigate the health of the deer population in a forest preserve?

....

....

....

....

....

....

....

....

Steps for Investigation

Scientists use scientific methods as they work in the many different fields of science. Scientific methods are organized ways to answer questions and solve problems. They are also ways of discovering causes and effects.

Scientific methods can include the steps shown here. Scientists might not use all the steps. They might not use the steps in this order. You will often use scientific methods when you do experiments and projects.

Ask a question.

You might have a question about something you observe.

What will keep the apple slices from turning brown?

State your hypothesis.

A hypothesis is a possible answer to the question you ask. A hypothesis must be testable. You can write your hypothesis as an *If...then...because...* statement.

If I put lemon juice on the apple slice, then it will not turn brown because the juice keeps the apple from reacting with the air.

Identify and control variables.

From a hypothesis, a scientist can identify the variables. A **variable** is something that can change in a test. An *independent variable* is one that you can control. A *dependent variable* changes when an independent variable changes. A simple investigation should test only one variable at a time. If a scientist is testing a river for pollution, all of the water samples must be taken at the same time each day and at the same place and depth in the river. If these samples are not taken the same way each time, the samples may give confusing results.

Remember, for a fair test, choose just one variable to change. Keep all of the other variables the same. Be sure to have a control or a control group. A **control group** is a standard against which change is measured. In an experiment, the experimental group is the same as the control group except that one factor has been changed.

5. Identify What is the independent variable in an investigation to find how light affects the growth of plants?

6. Interpret Why is it important to have a control group in an experiment?

Make a plan.

Make a plan to test your hypothesis. Decide what materials you need and make a list. Document the steps you will follow in your test.

Test your hypothesis.

Follow your plan to test your hypothesis.

Collect, record, and interpret your observations.

Keep good records of what you do and find out. Use tables and pictures to help. Organize your notes and records to make them clear. Make diagrams, charts, or graphics to help.

The apple slice that was treated with lemon juice stayed fresh. The apple slice that was not treated with lemon juice turned brown.

7. Give an Example Think of the last time you did an investigation and collected data. How did you organize your data?

State your conclusion.

Your conclusion is an inference you make based on your data. Communicate what you found out. Tell whether or not your data support your hypothesis.

Do repeated trials.

Repeat the experiment a few more times. Do each test exactly the same way. For a conclusion to be valid, the results of each test should be similar. Other scientists should be able to repeat your experiment and get similar results.

8. Summarize Why is it important for scientists to do repeated trials when doing an experiment?

9. (Circle) the picture of the control in this experiment.

10. ⊙ **Text Features** What do you think the black headings on these two pages describe?

Document Procedures

Meaningful scientific results come from experiments that can be replicated. In order for a scientific experiment to be replicated, the procedures must be thoroughly explained, or documented. **Procedures** are step-by-step instructions for completing a task.

Procedures are important when experimenting but also when doing things such as making certain foods or playing games.

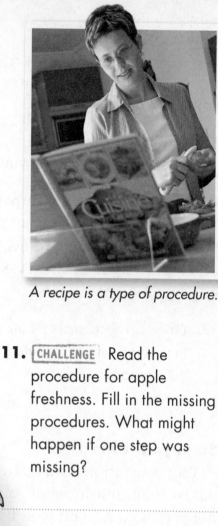

A recipe is a type of procedure.

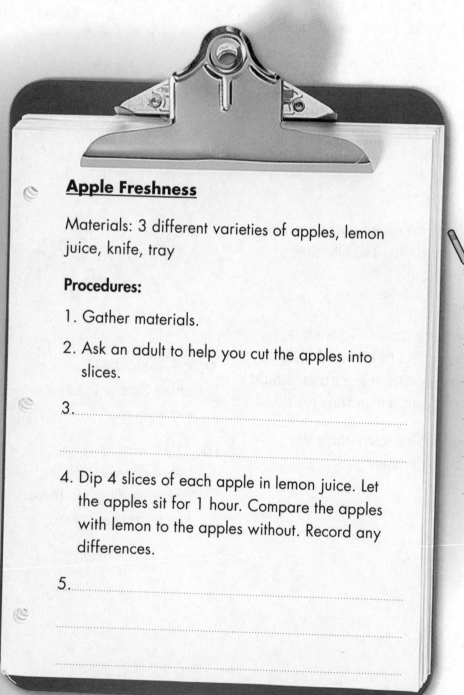

Apple Freshness

Materials: 3 different varieties of apples, lemon juice, knife, tray

Procedures:

1. Gather materials.

2. Ask an adult to help you cut the apples into slices.

3. ....

....

4. Dip 4 slices of each apple in lemon juice. Let the apples sit for 1 hour. Compare the apples with lemon to the apples without. Record any differences.

5. ....

....

....

11. CHALLENGE Read the procedure for apple freshness. Fill in the missing procedures. What might happen if one step was missing?

....

....

....

....

....

....

....

myscienceonline.com | Got *it*? 60-Second Video

When you design an experiment, it is important to write your procedures so that someone who reads them can follow them and repeat your experiment. If you leave out details, your procedure may not be followed exactly. The experiment may then give unintended results. This means the original experiment was not repeated and the conclusion may be different.

12. Evaluate Look at the procedures for the Apple Freshness experiment again. What might you change about the procedures to make it easier for others to follow?

....

....

....

Got it? 🕐 5.NS.1, 5.NS.2, 5.NS.3, 5.NS.4

13. Explain Why would a scientist use a model in an investigation? Write two reasons.

....

....

14. Describe What are some ways you can use to investigate different types of questions?

....

....

⬛ **Stop!** I need help with ....

⏸ **Wait!** I have a question about ....

▶ **Go!** Now I know ....

Lesson 3

How do scientists collect and interpret data?

5.NS.5 Use measurement skills and apply appropriate units when collecting data.
5.NS.8 Identify simple patterns in data and propose explanations to account for the patterns.

Tell how scientists studying strong storms could help people stay safe.

Inquiry Explore It!

Why do scientists use thermometers?

☑ **1. Record** the air temperature of the room.

☑ **2.** Pour room-temperature water into Cup A. Pour warm water into Cup B. Pour slightly warm water into Cup C.

☑ **3.** Feel the water in each. Record *cool, warm,* or *neither.* **Measure** the temperatures in °C and °F. Record.

Materials

3 plastic cups   thermometer

room temperature water

warm water   slightly warm water

Comparing Temperatures			
	Temperature		
	Feels (warm, cool, neither)	**° C**	**° F**
Cup A (room-temperature water)			
Cup B (warm water)			
Cup C (slightly warm water)			

Explain Your Results

4. Interpret Data Compare how warm the water felt with your **measurements.**

5. Draw a Conclusion Discuss why scientists use thermometers to **collect** temperature **data.**

myscienceonline.com | **Explore It!** Animation

5.NS.4 Perform investigations using appropriate tools and technology that will extend the senses.

I will know that scientists collect and interpret data using many different kinds of tools in a safe way.

Words to Know

data   accuracy
precision   inference

Data Collecting

Tornadoes can be very dangerous. In a tornado, winds can gust to more than 100 miles per hour, lift up objects, and cause very serious damage. What makes a tornado form? Scientists have done a great deal of research to try to understand the causes of tornadoes, but there is still a lot to learn in order to predict when tornadoes will happen.

In order for scientists to be able to predict tornadoes more successfully, they need to collect large amounts of data. **Data** are information from which a conclusion can be drawn or a prediction can be made.

For example, scientists can collect data about the air temperature before a tornado forms. These data can be connected to information they already know about other weather patterns during that time. It is important that each type of data is collected consistently and recorded in a useful way. Scientists can find relationships among data and possibly make predictions about how a tornado forms.

1. **Decide** You collect data about the type of weather your town has been experiencing. Can you use the data to draw conclusions about all other areas in the state? Explain.

....

....

....

2. (Circle) what scientists need to do to understand how tornadoes form.

Doppler radar towers track weather patterns and help scientists collect data to predict future storm patterns.

Precision and Accuracy

When collecting data, scientists try to control their experiments. This means they avoid having things happen that might interfere with good data collection. Data from a controlled experiment are consistent and precise.

Precision is the ability to consistently repeat a measurement. **Accuracy** is the ability to make a measurement that is as close to the actual value as possible. Look at the targets in the example below. In science, valid data are data measured with precision and accuracy.

This target shows high precision because the marks are very close to one another. It shows low accuracy because the marks are not at the center of the target.

This target shows high accuracy because the marks are close to the center of the target. It shows low precision because the marks are not very close to one another.

3. Demonstrate Draw marks on the target to the right to represent data that are both accurate and precise.

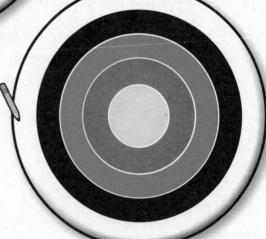

4. ◉ **Text Features**
What does the yellow highlighting tell you about the words on this page?

....

....

....

....

....

....

....

....

Tools

Scientists use many different kinds of tools to collect data. The tool used depends on the task. You can use tools to help you see things that you normally could not see. If something is very small or very far away, a tool can help you see it in more detail.

Tools also help you measure things and gather information. You can measure volume, temperature, length, distance, mass, time, and more with the proper tools. Tools can help you gather information and analyze your data. Scientists share their findings. Because they do, tools can help you find information collected by others.

5. Describe Underline four things that tools help you do.

6. Infer Why should you look at a graduated cylinder at eye level when reading the scale?

7. Infer Scientists use tools in addition to the ones on this page. What tool could help you gather information, analyze data, and find information collected by others?

A microscope makes objects appear much larger.

You can use a balance to measure mass.

You use a thermometer to measure temperature. Many thermometers have both Fahrenheit and Celsius scales.

A spring scale is used to measure force.

You can use a stopwatch or timer to measure elapsed time.

Scientists use a meterstick to measure length and distance.

A calculator helps you analyze data easier and faster than you could with paper and pencil.

A graduated cylinder is used to measure volume.

Safety

Scientists know they must work safely when doing experiments. You need to be careful when doing science activities too. It is important to keep yourself and other people safe. Care must be taken to make sure all living organisms, including plants and animals, are handled properly. Follow these safety rules.

Tie long hair back and avoid wearing loose clothing.

Wear safety goggles when needed.

Never taste or smell any substance unless directed to do so by your teacher.

Listen to the teacher's instructions. Ask questions.

Use chemicals carefully.

Help keep the plants and animals that you use safe.

Read the activity carefully before you start.

Handle sharp items and other equipment carefully.

8. Explain Why might it be important to ask questions after your teacher gives instructions?

....

....

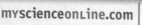

myscienceonline.com   THE BIG ?   I Will Know...

Organize Data

When scientists use tools to make observations, they collect data. In order to be useful, data must be organized. Organizing data allows a scientist to more easily recognize patterns that may be present. Data can be organized in many ways, including tables, graphs, charts, and graphics.

Tables and Graphs

One way that scientists organize data is by using a table. Look at the table below. It shows that scientists have collected data on the frequency of tornadoes in various states and have organized the information.

Once the information has been organized into a table, it may be displayed in a graph, such as the bar graph below. Graphs can help scientists see mathematical relationships in their data. The information in both the table and the graph is the same, but it is shown in different ways.

9. Compute Use data in the table to complete this bar graph.

10. Infer Based on the table and graph, what might land descriptions tell you about tornadoes and where they are most likely to occur?

....

....

....

....

....

....

....

....

....

Number of Tornadoes in One Year for Selected States

State	Number of Tornadoes	Land Description
Florida	55	flat
Indiana	22	flat
Louisiana	27	flat
New York	7	hilly
Oregon	2	hilly

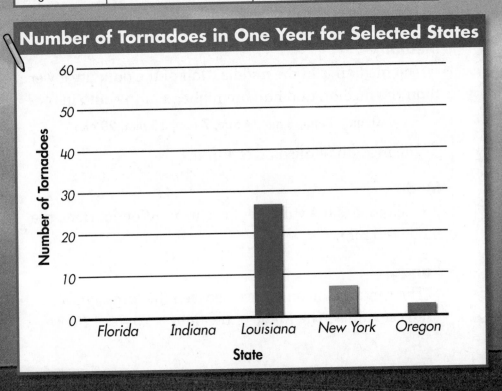

Number of Tornadoes in One Year for Selected States

Number of Tornadoes (y-axis: 0, 10, 20, 30, 40, 50, 60)

State (x-axis: Florida, Indiana, Louisiana, New York, Oregon)

Lightning Lab

Estimate and Measure

Scientists estimate and measure. Estimate the length, width, or height of an object in your classroom. Measure the object with a meterstick or metric ruler. Make a chart to record your data. Do this with 5 objects in the room. Compare. Did your estimates get more accurate with practice?

11. **Calculate** Look at the table on the previous page. What is the median number of tornadoes for the five states in the table and graph? What is the mean?

Interpret Data

When scientists interpret data, they look at the information they have collected by using tools safely to observe, measure, and estimate. Then they try to find patterns in those data. Patterns may help them make predictions. Weather forecasts are predictions that may help people better prepare for severe storms.

Scientists use values such as the mean, median, mode, and range when they interpret data. These values can help scientists determine the quality and usefulness of data. This analysis may help scientists decide whether they have enough information or whether they should collect more data.

Mean

The mean is the average. You find the mean by adding the data together and then dividing by the number of data. Rainfall measurements were taken daily for one week and the following data were obtained:

0 mm, 4 mm, 15 mm, 7 mm, 20 mm, 3 mm, 0 mm

mean = sum of data ÷ number of data

Step 1: Find the sum.

$0 + 4 + 15 + 7 + 20 + 3 + 0 = 49$

Step 2: Divide the sum by the number of data to find the mean.

$49 ÷ 7 = 7$

The mean of the data is 7 mm.

Median

The median is in the middle. Half of the data are lower than the median and half are higher. Put the data in order:

0 mm, 0 mm, 3 mm, 4 mm, 7 mm, 15 mm, 20 mm

The median of the data is 4 mm.

Mode

The mode is the value that occurs most often. Here, the mode is 0 mm.

Range

The range is the difference between the largest and smallest values. The range of the data is 20 – 0 = 20 mm.

Make Inferences

Science deals with observations and facts. Imagine that you hear a dog barking in the distance. This is a scientific observation because anyone listening to and looking at the dog would agree that the dog is barking. Data and observations are facts. For example, the statement *Dogs bark* is a fact.

Scientific observations are different from opinions. An opinion is a personal belief and is not always based on facts. An example of an opinion in this case would be *The dog is a bad dog*. A scientist uses facts and observations to draw conclusions and make inferences. An **inference** is a conclusion based on observations. An example of an inference is *The dog is barking because it sees a rabbit*. In science, for a conclusion to be valid, it must be based on observations and sound reasoning, not on opinion.

12. Infer Look at this picture of a dog. Write a statement that is an observation. Write a statement that is an inference.

Got it? 🎵 **5.NS.5, 5.NS.8**

13. Describe Why is it important to organize data with consistency and precision?

14. UNLOCK THE BIG ? How are data used in science?

⬜ **Stop!** I need help with

⏸ **Wait!** I have a question about

▶ **Go!** Now I know

Lesson 4

How do scientists support their conclusions?

Envision It!

5.NS.6 Test predictions with multiple trials.
5.NS.7 Keep accurate records in a notebook during investigations and communicate findings to others using graphs, charts, maps and models through oral and written reports.

Tell what you can conclude about these birds' beaks based on your observations.

Inquiry **Explore It!**

Which towel absorbs the most water?

☑ **1.** Pour 100 mL of water into a cup. **Measure** carefully. Wad up one Brand A towel. Dip it completely into the cup and remove it. Measure and **record** the water left in the cup.

☑ **2.** Repeat twice using the same brand of towel.

☑ **3.** Repeat Steps 1 and 2 with each of the other brands.

Paper Towel Testing			
Trial	Water Left in Cup (mL)		
	Brand A	Brand B	Brand C
1			
2			
3			
Total			

Explain Your Results

4. Draw a Conclusion
Which towel absorbed the most?

....

5. How did carrying out repeated trials help you trust your conclusions?

....

Materials

plastic cup

graduated cylinder

3 sheets each of 3 different brands of paper towel

water

For each trial, dip your towel the same way.

28 mysienceonline.com | **Explore It!** Animation

5.NS.3 Plan and carry out investigations as a class, in small groups or independently, often over a period of several class lessons. 5.DP.9 Present evidence using mathematical representations (graphs, data tables). (Also **5.NS.5**, **5.NS.8**)

I will know how scientists draw conclusions and support them using evidence.

Word to Know

evidence

Draw and Defend Conclusions

After analyzing the information that has been collected, scientists draw conclusions about what they have discovered. Scientists defend those conclusions by using the observations they made during their investigations. Sometimes, different conclusions can be drawn from the same set of data. Other scientists may question the methods that the scientists used to draw their conclusions, and the evidence from the investigations must be researched and reviewed.

For example, the behavior of some types of birds is not well known. Scientists must continue to collect and interpret data in order to understand the different behavior of the birds, such as their migration patterns, diet, and shelter preferences. Scientists have drawn conclusions about these bird behaviors, but the scientists' conclusions must be defended with appropriate scientific observations.

1. Give an Example
What is one way a scientist may defend a conclusion? **Underline** a statement in the text to support your answer.

....

....

These scientists are collecting data about bird behavior by placing identification bands around the birds' legs.

myscienceonline.com | **Envision It!**

Evidence

One way for scientists to ensure that their work is valid is to share their results with others. Each of their investigations must be replicable, or repeatable, by other scientists. In addition, the conclusions that the scientists drew about their experiments must be based on evidence. **Evidence** are observations that make you believe that something is true. When scientists have testable experiments that are based on evidence, they are able to give their results to other members of the scientific community.

During a scientific investigation, evidence may show results that are unexpected. The evidence may not support a scientist's hypothesis. However, this does not mean the experiment was not useful. The unexpected findings can lead to a new understanding of a scientific concept or cause scientists to experiment further.

Sometimes, scientists may misinterpret evidence from an investigation. They may come to an incorrect conclusion. This is why it is important for scientists to communicate with and accept feedback from one another.

2. **Justify** This scientist is testing a sample of ice from Antarctica. Do you think other scientists will be able to replicate this experiment? Why or why not?

This scientist may be able to use his data as evidence to support his hypothesis.

Lightning Lab

Coin Flip
Scientists gather evidence to make valid conclusions. How often do you think a coin will come up heads? Flip a coin ten times. How often did it come up heads? Have your partner repeat your experiment. Did the results change? Draw a conclusion and explain it.

mysienceonline.com | Got it? | 60-Second Video

Review and Retest

Scientists must describe exactly what they did in an experiment and how they did it. This allows other scientists working in the same field to replicate the experiment to see if the results are the same. They may also ask questions about the experiment and point out problems.

In science, communication is important. Scientists must describe their procedures and report their findings honestly. They must answer questions. Although some variation in results is acceptable, the results from different scientists should be similar. If results are not consistent, then the experiment must be done again.

3. List two things these scientists may be talking about. **Underline** a statement in the text that supports your answer.

....

....

....

....

Got it?

🅘 5.NS.6, 5.NS.7

4. Contrast Explain the difference between an observation and an inference.

....

....

5. UNLOCK THE BIG ❓ **Evaluate** Why is it important that scientists' conclusions are based on evidence?

....

....

⬛ **Stop!** I need help with ....

⏸ **Wait!** I have a question about ....

▶ **Go!** Now I know ....

How does a banana slice change over time?

As you carry out this investigation, practice the inquiry skills you have learned.

Follow a Procedure

☐ **1.** Place a whole banana slice in a cup.

☐ **2.** Use a spoon to cut another banana slice into 4 pieces. Place the pieces in a second cup.

☐ **3.** Put another banana slice into a third cup. Mash this slice with a spoon.

Materials

3 banana slices

3 plastic cups

plastic spoon

 Be careful! **Wash your hands when finished.**

Inquiry Skill
Scientists begin by asking a question. Then they make careful observations and record data accurately. They use their data to help make **inferences.**

5.NS.3 Plan and carry out investigations as a class, in small groups or independently, often over a period of several class lessons.
5.NS.8 Identify simple patterns in data and propose explanations to account for the patterns.

4. Observe the slices when you place them in the cup and each hour for 3 hours.
Record your observations in the chart.

Time	Observations		
	Whole Slice	**Cut-Up Slice**	**Mashed Slice**
When placed in cup			
After 1 hour			
After 2 hours			
After 3 hours			

Changes to Banana Slices over Time

Analyze and Conclude

5. Communicate Examine your data. Identify a simple pattern you **observed.**

....

....

6. Make an **inference** to explain about the pattern you identified.

....

....

7. UNLOCK THE BIG ? How can investigating cut bananas help scientists learn about other fruits?

....

....

....

Interpret Graphs

In science, graphs are often used to analyze, interpret, and display data. By looking at a graph, a scientist can visualize any trends, or patterns, that might be present. Scientists are able to support the conclusions they draw from data by using graphs.

Example

The students at Oakview School want to find out what things are most popular to collect among boys and girls. They asked 50 boys and 50 girls to choose their favorite collectible. Look at the double-bar graph.

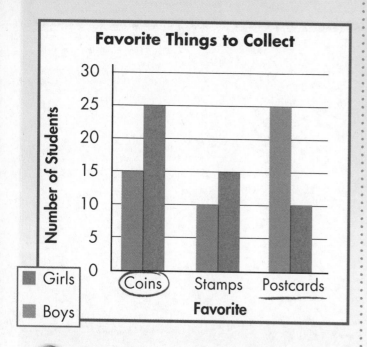

Favorite Things to Collect

1 **Circle** the most popular collectible among girls.

2 **Underline** The most popular collectible among boys.

Practice

Parents at Oakview School want to buy books for the library. They asked 30 fifth-graders to come into the library to choose their favorite type of book to read: science fiction, biography, or nonfiction. Look at the bar graph.

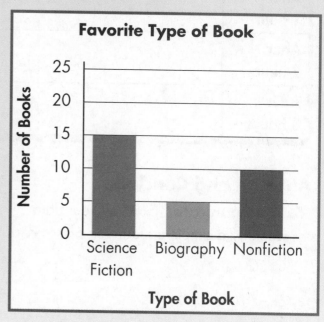

Favorite Type of Book

3 **Circle** the most popular type of book.

4 **Analyze** The parents decide to buy more biography books because they think those are better for the students. Is this decision based on fact or opinion? Explain.

....

....

....

34

Vocabulary Smart Cards

hypothesis
observation
experiment
variable
control group
procedures
data
precision
accuracy
inference
evidence

Play a Game!

Cut out the Vocabulary Smart Cards.

Work with a partner. Choose a card.

Say one word you can think of that is related to that vocabulary word in some way. It might be an example.

Have your partner guess the word. How many clues did it take to guess the correct word?

variable

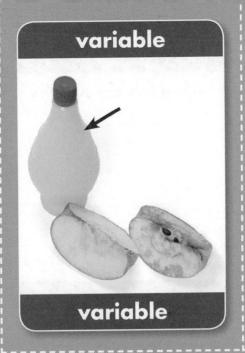

variable

hypothesis

If... then... because...

hipótesis

control group

grupo de control

observation

observación

procedures

procedimientos

experiment

experimento

statement of what you think will happen during an investigation

Write three related words.

....

....

....

enunciado de lo que crees que ocurrirá en una investigación

---

something that can change in a test

Write a sentence using this term.

....

....

....

algo que puede cambiar durante una prueba

---

something you find out about objects, events, or living things using your senses

Write a sentence using this term.

....

....

algo que descubres con tus sentidos sobre los objetos, sucesos o seres vivos

---

a standard against which change is measured

Write a sentence using this term.

....

....

....

estándar que se usa para medir un cambio

---

the use of scientific methods to test a hypothesis

Write three related words.

....

....

....

uso de métodos científicos para poner a prueba una hipótesis

---

step-by-step instructions for completing a task

Give an example of a procedure you have followed.

....

....

....

instrucciones paso por paso para realizar una tarea

Interactive Vocabulary

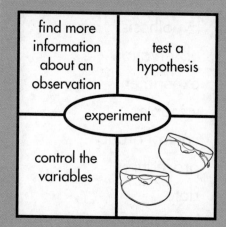

Make a Word Square!

Choose a vocabulary word and write it in the center of the square. Fill in the squares with related ideas, such as a definition, a characteristic, an example, or something that is not an example.

inference

The dog is barking because it sees a rabbit.

inferencia

data

datos

evidence

evidencia

precision

precisión

accuracy

exactitud

Card 1

information from which a conclusion can be drawn or a prediction can be made

Write the singular form of this word.

....

....

....

información de la cual se puede sacar una conclusión o hacer una predicción

Card 2

a conclusion based on observations

Use any form of this word in a sentence.

....

....

....

....

conclusión basada en observaciones

Card 3

Card 4

the ability to consistently repeat a measurement

Name the adjective form of this word.

....

....

capacidad de repetir una medición de manera consistente

Card 5

observations that make you believe something is true

Write a sentence using this word.

....

....

....

observaciones que te hacen creer que algo es cierto

Card 6

Card 7

ability to make a measurement that is as close to the actual value as possible

Name the adjective form of this word.

....

....

capacidad de hacer una medición que se aproxime como sea posible al valor verdadero

Card 8

Card 9

Chapter 1

Study Guide

REVIEW THE BIG **?** What is science?

Indiana

Lesson 1

What do scientists do?

- Scientists define a problem and try to find answers.
- Scientists make hypotheses and observations.
- Scientists draw conclusions based on their investigations.

Lesson 2

How do scientists investigate?

- Scientists use many different types of scientific investigations.
- Scientists use models, surveys, and sampling to gather data.
- Scientific methods are organized steps for doing an investigation.

Lesson 3

How do scientists collect and interpret data?

- Scientists collect data with tools.
- Scientists organize data using tables and graphs.
- Scientists interpret and draw conclusions from the data they collect.

Lesson 4

How do scientists support their conclusions?

- Scientists use facts, not opinions, when drawing conclusions.
- Scientific investigations should be based on evidence.
- Other scientists must be able to replicate scientific investigations.

myscienceonline.com | my science COACH

Lesson 1   5.NS.1, 5.NS.9

What do scientists do?

1. **Vocabulary** What is observation?
   A. something that helps you measure
   B. something that has been made for the first time
   C. using the senses to gather information
   D. new ideas or new understandings

2. **Demonstrate** Why do scientists make hypotheses before beginning scientific investigations?

Lesson 2   5.NS.1, 5.NS.2, 5.NS.3, 5.NS.4

How do scientists investigate?

Do the math!

3. The Wright brothers' airplane, *Flyer,* had a wingspan of 12 m. You build a model with a wingspan of 10 cm. How many times larger is *Flyer* than your model?

4. **Communicate** Explain why a control group is important in an experiment.

Lesson 3   5.NS.5, 5.NS.8

How do scientists collect and interpret data?

5. **Analyze** Suppose you are doing a presentation for your class about the daily growth of a bean plant over the course of a month. Would you use a chart, a table, or a graph to help explain your results to your class? Explain your answer.

6. **Text Features** Use the following paragraph to answer the question.

   In order for scientists to be able to predict tornadoes more successfully, they need to collect large amounts of **data.** Data are information from which a conclusion can be drawn.

   Why is the word *data* highlighted in yellow?

Lesson 4 5.NS.6, 5.NS.7

How do scientists support their conclusions?

7. Identify How do scientists use evidence in their investigations?

....

....

....

....

....

....

....

8. Write About It Why is it important that scientists communicate?

....

....

....

9. Identify You watch your neighbors as they leave their apartment building. They have suitcases with them. They all get into the car and drive away. You think they are going on vacation. Is your thought a fact or an inference? Explain.

....

....

....

10. APPLY THE BIG ? **What is science?**

••••••••••••••••••••••••••••••••••••

Explain why scientists will do exactly the same experiments that other scientists have done.

....

....

....

....

....

....

....

....

....

....

....

....

....

41

Multiple Choice

1 _____ are observations from which a conclusion can be drawn.

    A. Predictions
    B. Inventions
    C. Data
    D. Discoveries

5.NS.8

Constructed Response

2 Scientists make measurements when performing experiments. Write three ways you can make sure your measurements give meaningful information.

....

....

....

....

....

....

....

....

....

5.NS.4, 5.NS.5, 5.NS.7

Extended Response

3 You are testing to see if music helps plants grow better. You divide the plants into four groups.

Plant Groups	
Group	Music Type
A	jazz
B	classical
C	rock
D	none

What is group D called?

....

What are you varying in your experiment?

....

....

Suppose the plants that were in the group exposed to jazz music grew more leaves than the plants in the group exposed to rock music. What conclusion might you draw? How could you defend the conclusion?

....

....

....

....

5.NS.2, 5.NS.8

5.NS.1, 5.NS.3

Research Scientist

one of the instruments on the Dawn spacecraft

Have you ever wondered what it would be like to be a professional scientist? Research scientists ask questions and design experiments. They rarely work alone. Research scientists often work with groups at universities or for the government. Research scientists often have advanced degrees such as master's degrees or doctoral degrees.

Dr. Carol Raymond is a research scientist working for NASA at its Jet Propulsion Laboratory. In 2003, Dr. Raymond led a team of scientists to find out if earthquakes can be predicted from space. Her project made a plan to launch satellites into space. These satellites will monitor Earth for signs that an earthquake might occur.

A research scientist works on several projects throughout his or her career. Currently, Dr. Raymond is the Deputy Principal Investigator, a type of research scientist, for the Dawn Discovery mission. This mission will study two large asteroids that were young planets when our solar system was first formed.

What kinds of questions do you think Dr. Raymond and her team members are trying to answer with their Dawn Discovery mission?

What can robots do?

Design and Function

Investigate It!   How can you make and redesign a model of a robotic arm?

Robots are designed to do many different tasks. This robot assists shoppers in finding and carrying their groceries. Other robots help people who cannot walk get in and out of their wheelchairs.

Predict   What do you think robots will be used for in the future?

....

....

THE BIG ?   How does technology affect our lives?

How can you design a strong glue?

☐ **1.** List 3 properties of a strong glue.

....

☐ **2. Observe** the properties of each mixture. **Record.**

Mixture	Properties
Cornstarch and water	
Flour and water	
Gelatin and water	

Materials

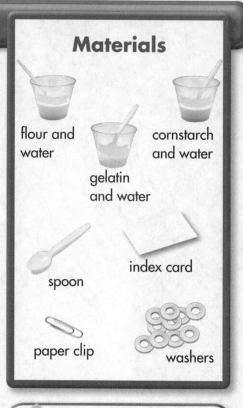

flour and water

cornstarch and water

gelatin and water

spoon

index card

paper clip

washers

☐ **3. Design** a glue that will hold the most weight by combining up to 2 spoonfuls of each mixture.

☐ **4. Test** your glue. Spread it at the bottom of an index card. Pull out the large end of a paper clip to make a hook. Press the small end into the glue. Let the glue dry overnight.

Inquiry Skill

Recording your observations on a chart can help you make **inferences.**

☐ **5.** Hold the card. Hang washers on the hook until the paper clip pulls off the card. Record your results.

Mixture	Spoonfuls	Number of Washers Held
Cornstarch and water		
Flour and water		
Gelatin and water		

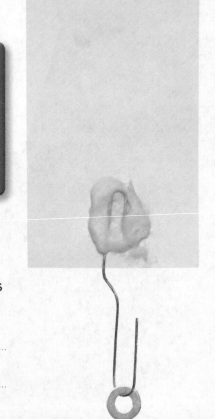

Explain Your Results

6. **UNLOCK THE BIG ?** Compare you results with other groups.

Infer Did different quantities of starting materials result in glue with different properties? Explain.

....

....

5.DP.6 Create the solution through a prototype. **5.DP.7** Test and evaluate how well the solution meets the goal.

⊙ Main Idea and Details

- Learning to find **main ideas** and **details** can help you understand and remember what you read.
- Details can help you to infer the main idea of the article.

Technology and Our Homes

Technology can be found throughout our homes and is used in many ways. Technology makes it easier to do many things in the home. Thermostats can maintain or change the temperature inside the home. Dishwashers get dishes and eating utensils clean. We use technology for entertainment purposes too. Televisions, video games, and MP3 players are all technology. The way people keep and store food has been improved by technology. Refrigerators and freezers offer a healthy way of keeping food fresh for longer periods of time. Even plastic containers offer airtight storage to keep food fresher.

Practice It!

Use the graphic organizer below to list the main idea and details from the article above.

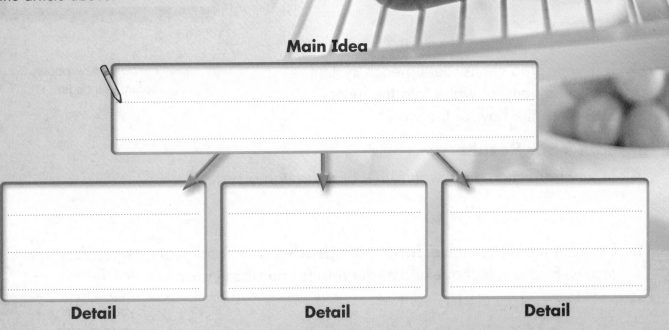

Main Idea

Detail   **Detail**   **Detail**

What is technology?

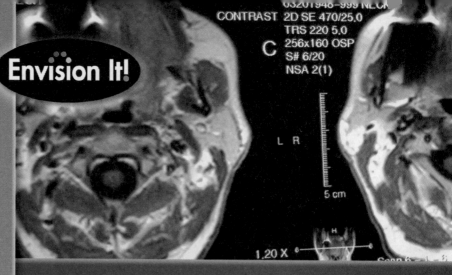

5.DP.1 Identify a need or problem to be solved.
5.4.2 Investigate the purpose of prototypes and models when designing a solution to a problem and how limitations in cost and design features might affect their construction.

Envision It!

Tell how you think this kind of image can help doctors.

Inquiry Explore It!

Which transport system works best?

☑ **1.** Examine *Possible Water Transport Systems.*

☑ **2. Predict** which systems will always work, which will never work, and which will trap some water.

☑ **3.** Test your predictions. Set up each system. Pour a half cup of water into the funnel. **Observe** the flow of the water.

Explain Your Results

4. In what direction does water flow best through a system?

5. Examine the different **designs,** your **predictions,** and your results. Find a rule that explains the results you **observed.**

Materials

newspaper   plastic tube

empty cup and cup with water

funnel

Possible Water Transport Systems

Put down newspaper before you begin.

Repeat each test. This will help make your results more reliable.

myscienceonLine.com | **Explore It!** Animation

5.DP.4 Select a solution to the need or problem. 5.NS.6 Test predictions with multiple trials. 5.NS.9 Compare the results of an investigation with the prediction.

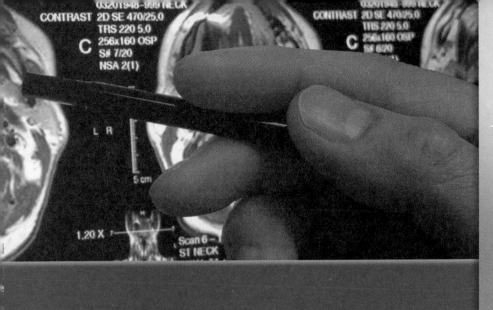

I will know how technology solves problems and provides solutions.

Words to Know

technology
microchip

Problems and Solutions

People constantly gain knowledge and make new discoveries. This knowledge and these discoveries often result in technology that makes tasks easier, faster, or more efficient. **Technology** is the knowledge, processes, and products that solve problems and make work easier. Many years ago, illnesses were treated with few medicines. Over time, people began to learn the causes of some illnesses. This allowed people to develop better ways of treating and preventing disease.

Technology has improved people's lives, but it has also caused problems. Medical products and other technologies help people stay healthy. However, new medicines may cause unanticipated side effects.

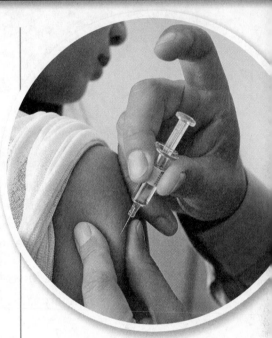

Vaccines were discovered by Edward Jenner in 1796.

1. **Main Idea and Details** Use the graphic organizer below to list two details and the main idea found in the last paragraph of the text.

2. **Apply** What problem did this technology in the picture above solve?

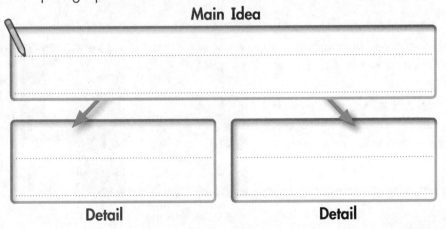

Main Idea

Detail   **Detail**

Tools in Medicine

Technology has contributed to the scientific knowledge of medicine. Since the late 1800s there have been many advances in medical technology.

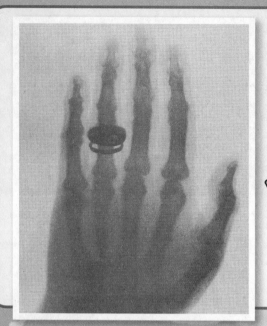

Then *William Röntgen took this X ray image of his wife's hand in 1895. It is one of the first X-ray images used in medicine. X rays allowed doctors and scientists to see things inside a living thing. An X ray is a wave with very high energy. It can go though materials light rays cannot. The harmful effects of exposure to large amounts of X-ray radiation were not known until later.*

3. **Infer** What features can you recognize? What are the dark oval areas?

....

....

....

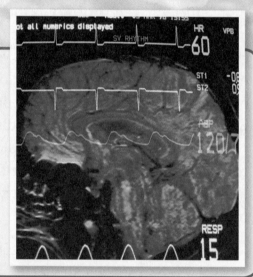

Now *Magnetic resonance imaging (MRI) produces images of the body. The procedure uses magnetic fields and radio wave pulses. Scanned information is fed into a computer. The result is a highly-detailed image. MRI technology does not use harmful radiation.*

4. **Analyze** What are two advantages of MRI over other imaging technologies?

....

....

Now *X rays are still very useful and widely used in medicine. Care is taken to keep exposure to radiation as low as possible for both the patient and the technician.*

Now *CT (computed tomography) scans, or CAT scans, are made with a series of X rays. The X-ray images are cross section "slices" of the body. The information is fed into a computer. The process produces an image that can be viewed in three dimensions.*

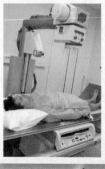
X-ray machine

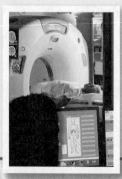
CT scanner

THE BIG ? I Will Know...

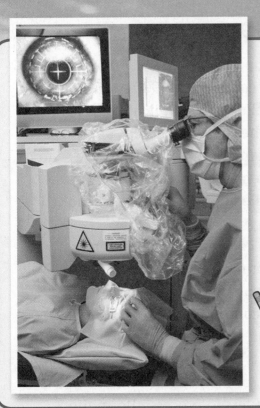

Then *This antique scalpel has a wooden handle. Wood cannot be sterilized to remove germs. The idea that germs cause disease was not widely accepted in this country until the 1890s.*

Now *Surgeons still use scalpels, but they are made of steel and plastic. These scalpels can be sterilized easily to remove germs. However, today there is another option. Lasers produce light waves that are concentrated on a tiny spot. Laser scalpels are able to cut through skin and other soft tissue.*

antique scalpel

5. **CHALLENGE** Weaker lasers are found in everyday life. Give an example where a laser might be used.

....

....

Then *Doctors used stitches, also called sutures, to hold wounds closed until they healed. Some sutures are made with a material that dissolves into the body and does not need to be removed.*

Now *Researchers are developing a glue to hold wounds together. The idea for glue came from animals called mussels that live in the ocean and can bond, or stick, to things underwater. Sutures are still preferred for some procedures, but one day doctors may be able to use glue during surgery.*

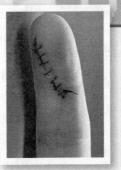

stitches

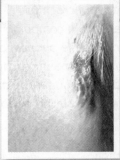
glue

6. **Predict** Do you think surgical glue or sutures are better at keeping water out of wounds?

....

....

At-Home Lab

Design Solutions
Cut out pictures from magazines of three different technologies that help people. Write a short paragraph about who would use each technology.

UNIVAC (Universal Automatic Computer) was built in the United States in 1951. It was the first electronic computer. UNIVAC took up a space of 943 cubic feet.

Today, microchips are used in computers, cars, mobile phones, and video games. Some microchips are the width of a fingernail and others as wide a strand of hair.

7. Infer How did the invention of the microchip change computers?

Computer Technology

Early Computers

Computer technology began in the 1930s and 1940s. These early computers replaced mechanical parts with electrical parts, but used the same basic steps as today's computers—input, processing, output, and feedback—to solve mathematical problems. Early computers were so large that most of them filled entire rooms and weighed thousands of pounds.

The large size and high cost of early computers made them impractical for most people. Computer manufacturers became aware of the need for smaller, faster, and less expensive computers. One of the most important developments in computer technology was the microchip. A **microchip** is a small piece of a computer that contains microscopic, or tiny, circuits. Microchips make it possible for computers to process information very quickly. They also made the cost of a computer much lower because it became less expensive to manufacture computers.

World Wide Web

In the 1980s, computer technology was used to solve another problem. A British computer scientist wanted to make it easier for physicists to communicate with each other. The result was the World Wide Web. The World Wide Web is a computer-based network of information sources. It was first developed for use by the European Organization for Nuclear Research. The first version of the Web was completed in 1990. Today, a person using a computer can search through the Web to find information about practically anything.

8. Explain How has the World Wide Web improved communication and research?

Computers Today

Before computer technology, people spent months doing work that one of today's computers does in seconds. A computer only takes a few moments to process tasks such as calculating workers' salaries or figuring out how to steer a rocket. However, some tasks take even computers a long time to complete. Powerful supercomputers or computer networks often help out with very complex tasks.

The invention of the computer has led to many other technologies. Computers can be used with many tools and devices. Several kinds of microscopes, telescopes, thermometers, and cameras use computers. They help people find and record accurate information or results. Computer and other technologies can be found in schools. Students can easily find information for research using the Internet. DVD players and interactive whiteboards help present information in new ways.

9. ⊙ **Main Idea and Details**
Underline the main idea in the second paragraph.

 **Got it?**

🕒 5.DP.1, 5.4.2

10. **UNLOCK THE BIG ?** **Identify** What are three additional technologies that you can benefit from?

....

....

11. **Analyze** Name a technology that has changed quickly. Name a technology that has changed more slowly.

....

....

■ **Stop!** I need help with ....

❙❙ **Wait!** I have a question about ....

▶ **Go!** Now I know ....

Lesson 2

How does technology mimic living things?

5.4.1 Investigate technologies that mimic human or animal musculoskeletal systems to meet a need.

How can this device help someone speak?

my planet Diary *for* Indiana

Did You Know?

Robotics is the study, design, construction, and use of robots. New Lutheran Hospital in Fort Wayne, Indiana is using robotics to help save lives. The Sensei X Robotic Catheter System looks like a thin, flexible tube. The design allows it to go into areas of the heart that are hard for doctors to reach. A video camera connects to the robot. This allows doctors to see inside a patient's body. The video camera also helps doctors control the robot's movement.

What is the need for robotics in the medical field?

....

....

....

During surgery, the doctor uses a joystick to control movements of the Sensei X.

Hi there. What are you doing?

Send

I will know how some technologies can mimic the muscular and skeletal systems.

Word to Know

prosthetic limb

Technology and the Human Body

The human body is an amazing structure. Engineers sometimes use scientific knowledge of how the body works to develop technologies. Some of the technologies help people whose bodies do not function as they should. Some technologies do tasks that are too dangerous for people.

Technologies that have moving parts can be like the human body. A robot is one of these technologies. Robots can have a body structure and movable joints, which are similar to the human skeletal and muscular systems. Robotic technologies use an electrical energy source to help them move. The human body uses energy from food to help it move. Robots have a sensor system and a computer to control movements. In the human body, the brain and nervous system help to control movement.

1. **Explain** How do you think this robot is like you?

....

....

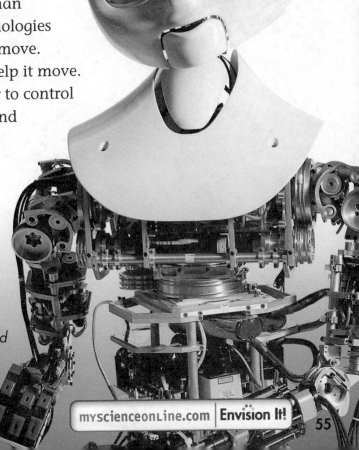

Nexi is a social robot developed by engineers at Massachusetts Institute of Technology.

Even though these prosthetic legs look different than real legs, they allow this man the ability to run.

2. Compare How are this runner's prosthetic legs similar to the legs of the other runners?

_____

_____

myscienceonline.com | **THE BIG ?** | **I Will Know...**

Prosthetic Limbs

Robotic technology that mimics movements of the human body is also used to make a prosthetic limb move. A **prosthetic limb** is an artificial arm, hand, leg, or foot that replaces a missing one. Modern prosthetic limbs can be controlled by electrical signals from the brain.

In the past prosthetic hands had few fingers and could not do many things. Today, they have a thumb and four fingers that are controlled individually. These prosthetic hands can turn a key, pick up small objects, and hold a glass.

Currently prosthetic legs and feet allow their users to walk and even run. As technology advances, prosthetic legs and feet work more like real legs and feet. The latest prosthetic limbs also look more like real limbs.

3. **Summarize** How do prosthetic limbs help people?

....

....

Each finger on this prosthetic hand can be moved separately. This woman can do many everyday things that she could not do without a prosthetic hand.

At-Home Lab

Technology Walk
Walk around your neighborhood with an adult. Observe any ways in which technology mimics living things. Record these observations in your science notebook.

Animals and Technology

Some technologies mimic the muscular and skeletal systems of animals. These systems help animals to move in different ways. The wings and tails of birds help the birds fly. Fish have muscular and skeletal systems that help them swim.

Airplanes have parts that mimic the wings and tails of birds. Like the wings and tails of birds, airplane wings and tails can be adjusted to control how the airplane moves. Some robots can also fly. The robotic bat flaps its wings and flies like a bat. It can search collapsed buildings and other areas people cannot get to. Some robots used to explore the ocean have parts that mimic the muscular and skeletal systems of fish.

Scientists use robotic animals to study the behavior of real animals. A robotic squirrel makes noise and moves its tail like a real squirrel. It can be placed in an area where real squirrels live. A real squirrel may wiggle its tail and make noises at the robotic squirrel. Scientists can use this information to learn how squirrels communicate with one another.

Robotic bats have movements similar to a real bat. They can access places too small or dangerous for people to access.

Robotic squirrels can help scientists study the behavior of real squirrels. This robotic squirrel can make sounds and wiggle its tail like a real squirrel.

4. **Predict** Why do scientists use robotic squirrels to help study real squirrels?

....

....

....

Nanobots

How can you build a robot that is only a few billionths of a meter long? Scientists hope to be able to build these tiny robots using nanotechnology. Scientists have found ways that they can move one atom at a time. They hope to be able to use this technology to build tiny robots, or nanobots, that can perform all kinds of tasks.

One idea is to use nanobots inside the human body. Nanobots may be able to deliver medications better than current methods. Scientists are also researching how to make a nanobot that can remove cholesterol from the walls of arteries.

5. **Generate** How do you think nanobots might be useful?

....

....

This illustration shows how a nanobot might attack viruses in a blood vessel.

Got it?

5.4.1

6. **UNLOCK THE BIG ?** How does one kind of technology mimic human muscular and skeletal systems?

....

....

7. **Hypothesize** Why do you think engineers build robots that mimic human or animal systems?

....

....

⬜ **Stop!** I need help with ....

⏸ **Wait!** I have a question about ....

▶ **Go!** Now I know ....

What is the design process?

5.4.2 Investigate the purpose of prototypes and models when designing a solution to a problem and how limitations in cost and design features might affect their construction. 5.DP.8 Evaluate and test the design using measurement. (Also 5.DP.1, 5.DP.3)

Envision It!

Explain how you think people design new technologies.

Inquiry Explore It!

How can the design of a model arm help you learn about how your arm works?

☑ **1. Make a model** of an arm as shown.

☑ **2.** Pull on Yarn A. **Observe.** Pull on Yarn B. Observe.

☑ **3.** Bend the arm pieces together. What happens to the yarn?

Materials

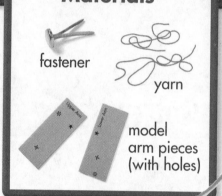

fastener

yarn

model arm pieces (with holes)

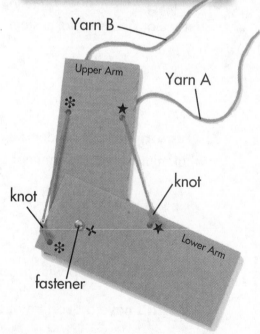

Explain Your Results

4. Communicate   In your model, what do the yarn, the cardboard, and the fastener represent?

5. Draw a Conclusion   How can people use models to help them learn about the human body?

myscienceonLine.com | **Explore It!** Animation

5.4.3 Design a solution to a problem in the context of musculoskeletal body systems. Using suitable tools, techniques and materials, draw or build a prototype or model of a proposed design. (Also 5.4.1, 5.DP.3, 5.NS.7)

Words to Know

design process
prototype

Design Process

Technology helps to solve many of the problems we have. We use technology in our homes, schools, and offices. There are technologies for constructing buildings, communicating with others, transporting people and products, and so much more.

Who makes all this technology? People all over the world develop technologies. You may be surprised to know that even students your age develop new technologies. An engineer is a person who designs new technologies. People work in many different fields to apply scientific knowledge to everyday life. People use the design process to develop new technologies. The **design process** is a set of steps for developing products and processes that solve problems.

1. **Circle** what a person who designs technology is called.

2. **Predict** Why is it important to use the design process when developing new technologies?

....

....

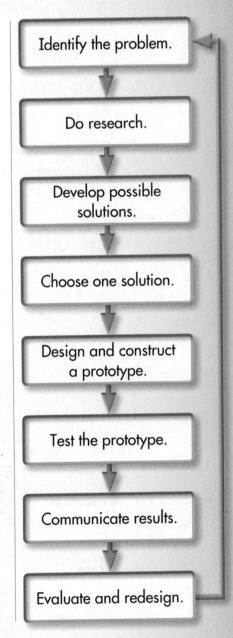

Identify the problem.

Do research.

Develop possible solutions.

Choose one solution.

Design and construct a prototype.

Test the prototype.

Communicate results.

Evaluate and redesign.

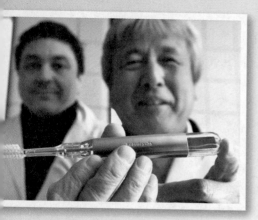

Dr. Kunio Komiyama is an engineer in the field of dentistry. He designed a new kind of toothbrush.

3. Apply What kind of product would you make to help solve a problem? Who would your product help?

....

....

....

....

....

4. Identify Underline the source you would use to find out what other scientists are working on.

Steps of the Design Process

While some engineers may use different steps or use them in a different order, they all have an end goal of finding a solution to a problem.

Identify the problem.

The first step in the design process is to identify a need or problem. All technology comes from the need for a solution to a problem. It is important in this step to determine who would be helped by the solution. For example, a toothbrush that cleans teeth with less effort could potentially help everyone reduce cavities and gum problems.

Do research.

Research is another important step in the design process. In order to make or improve on existing technology, scientists need to know what technology already exists. Scientific journals, magazines, the Internet, informational books, and encyclopedias can be helpful as you study ways to solve a design problem. Sometimes the best way to find the information you need is to interview an expert.

Engineers designing a new toothbrush might research how the shape of the handle affects how people brush their teeth. Engineers should also know how different bristle materials affect teeth.

Develop possible solutions.

Using what they learned in their research, scientists and engineers think of ways to improve an existing technology. Each possible solution should be carefully planned. Charts and diagrams can be used to communicate the design solution to others.

5. **Interpret** Look at the drawing below. What information can you find in the drawing?

....

....

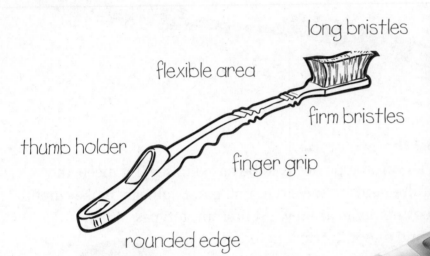

long bristles

flexible area

firm bristles

thumb holder

finger grip

rounded edge

This toothbrush uses advanced technology. It works very well, but it costs more than other toothbrushes.

Choose one solution.

It is important to choose wisely the one solution you will build. Making many solutions may take too much time. The cost of making the solution can also affect your decision. For example, if the toothbrush works very well, but is very expensive, people may not buy it.

6. **Identify** Circle two things that may affect which design solution you choose to build.

7. Explain Why do engineers build prototypes of their design solutions?

_____
_____
_____
_____
_____

8. Infer What do you think this toothbrush is made of? Why do you think the engineers used those materials?

_____
_____
_____
_____
_____
_____

9. Interpret What do you think is one important thing that must be done when making a test to evaluate a prototype?

_____
_____
_____
_____
_____
_____

Design and construct a prototype.

The next step is to build a version of the solution, called a **prototype.** It is used to test the solution. It is important to identify the kinds of materials you use to build your prototype. The properties of the materials you use affect the function of your prototype. You will need a strong, flexible material for parts that bend. If you do not want the part to bend you should use a rigid material. You will also need to identify the tools you use to build your prototype.

toothbrush prototype

Test the prototype.

The prototype needs to be tested to see if it meets the requirements to solve the problem. Engineers make careful measurements as they test their prototypes. When testing a toothbrush, engineers might measure how much plaque is left on the teeth after brushing for one minute. These measurements help the engineers evaluate how well the prototype works.

Testing a toothbrush is important to make sure it works for everyone that will be using it.

64

Communicate results.

Throughout the design process it is important to document your work. Document means to record what you learn. Documentation helps you communicate with others. If you are working in a company, you will need to communicate your process and design to managers, salespeople, and many others. Often others will need to repeat your tests to verify the results. They will need to know your test procedures and the specifics of your design. The people who you share your design with may be able to offer advice on how to improve your idea.

Your design solution can be communicated in many ways. Labeled diagrams can show the size and shape of the parts of your product. Graphic organizers can be used to show how parts are put together. You will also need a list of materials and tools used to make each part. Tables, charts, and graphs can help you communicate the results of your tests.

Evaluate and redesign.

Using the results of your tests and feedback from others, you can evaluate how well your design solved the problem. This information can help you redesign your product to make it work better. You may need to make minor adjustments or choose a completely new solution.

10. Infer Why do you think an engineer might redesign a prototype?

....

....

11. Predict What might happen if you fail to document your design?

....

....

....

....

12. Evaluate Look at the redesigned prototype below. It has improvements such as a better handle. Work with a partner. Tell why you think the handle is a better design.

....

....

....

....

....

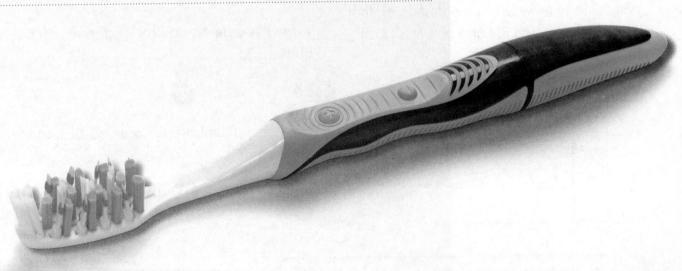

Designing Robotic Arms

Engineers use the design process to develop robotic arms. Robotic arms are designed and built to mimic the movement of human arms.

The first robotic arm used in a factory was developed by George Devol. The robotic arm picked up and stacked metal parts that were too hot for workers to handle. George Devol and his partner, Joseph Engelberger, called the robotic arm, the *Unimate*.

The *Unimate* had a "shoulder" but no "elbow." Devol and Engelberger continued to redesign the robotic arm. They developed a new robotic arm with an "elbow" that allowed it to perform more tasks. Today's robotic arms can move in many different directions.

PUMA, an industrial programmable robot, was introduced in 1980. It had all the characteristics of a human arm.

13. Compare How do you think the picture on the right might be better than the PUMA robotic arm?

Do the math!

Ordered Pairs

The computer that controls robot movement uses a coordinate grid system. An ordered pair is used to identify a point on a coordinate grid. The x-coordinate, or the first number, tells how many units to move to the right. The y-coordinate, or second number, tells how many units to move up. The ordered pair that identifies Point D on the grid below is (2, 5).

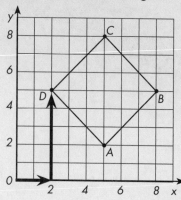

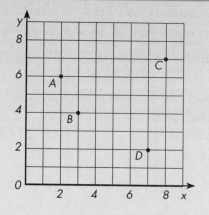

Write the ordered pair for each point on the above grid.

1 A _____   **2** B _____

Name the point for each ordered pair on the above grid.

3 (7, 2) _____   **4** (8, 7) _____

myscienceonline.com | Got *it*? 60-Second Video

14. Identify Label the parts of the robotic arm that are like the parts of a human arm.

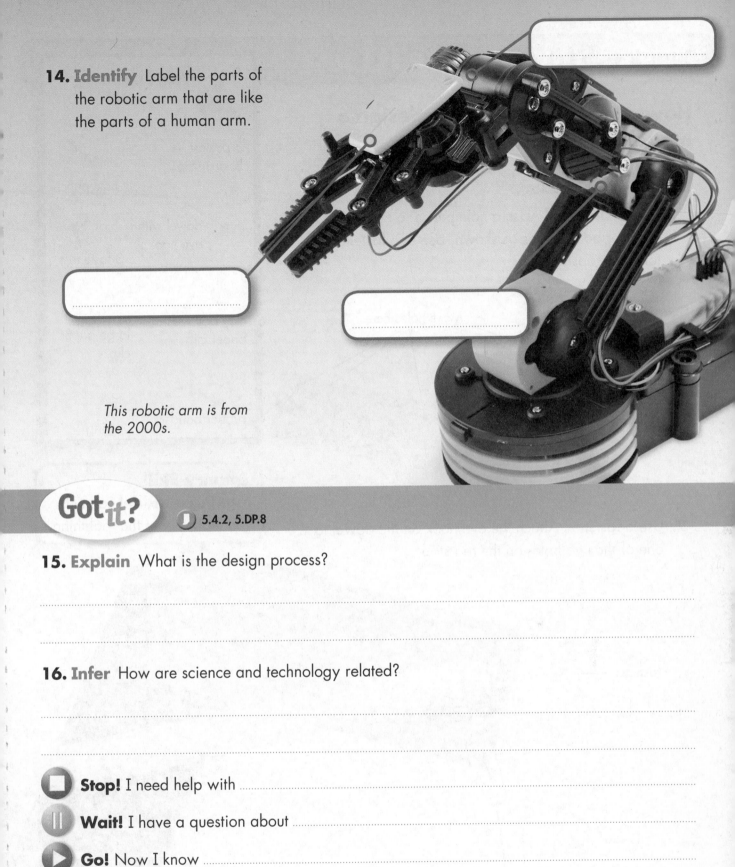

This robotic arm is from the 2000s.

15. Explain What is the design process?

....

....

16. Infer How are science and technology related?

....

....

■ **Stop!** I need help with ....

❚❚ **Wait!** I have a question about ....

▶ **Go!** Now I know ....

How can you make and redesign a model of a robotic arm?

Follow a Procedure

☑ **1. Make a Model** Use a hole punch to make holes in 3 poster board strips as shown. Use two fasteners to join the strips together.

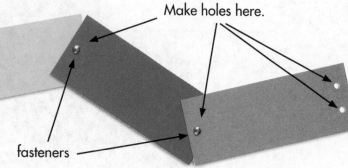

Make holes here.

fasteners

Materials

3 poster board strips

metric ruler

hole punch

dowel with eye hook

3 fasteners

clay ball with paper clip

large paper clip

rubber band

string

☑ **2.** Use a fastener. Attach the eye hook on the dowel to one of the two holes on the red strip.

Inquiry Skill
Making a model can help you learn about the real thing.

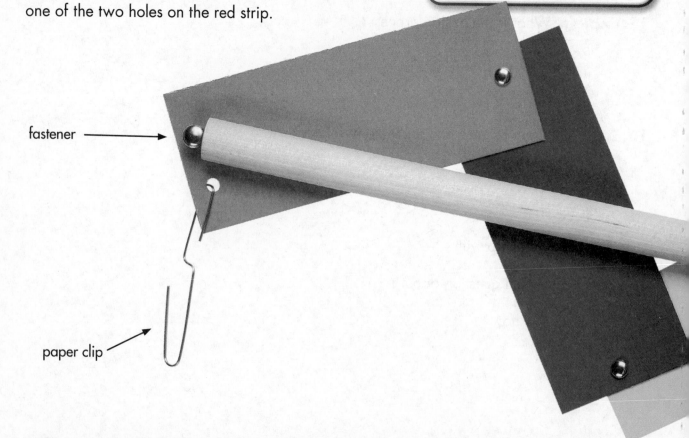

fastener

paper clip

5.4.3 Design a solution to a problem in the context of musculoskeletal body systems. Using suitable tools, techniques and materials, draw or build a prototype or model of a proposed design. **5.DP.6** Create the solution through a prototype. **5.DP.9** Present evidence using mathematical representations (graphs, data tables). **5.DP.11** Communicate how to improve the solution.

3. Bend a large paper clip into an S shape.
Put the top of the S through the other hole in the red strip.

4. Use the robotic arm. Try to pick up the objects listed in the chart.
Record the number of tries you need. Use up to 5 tries for each object.

5. Redesign your model of a robotic arm. Repeat Step 4.

Objects Chart		
Objects	Number of Tries	
Clay ball with paper clip		
Paper clip		
Rubber band		
String		

Analyze and Conclude

6. Communicate What **design** change did you make to your **model**?

....

....

7. UNLOCK THE BIG ? Describe two ways in which the model is not like a
real robotic arm.

....

....

....

Move this end of the poster board back and forth.

Hold the dowel with one hand so it does not move.

Denim Insulation

5.DP.1, 5.DP.4, 5.DP.7

Are you wearing your favorite pair of jeans right now? When they wear out, they could serve another purpose. The surprise is that they might end up in someone's attic or walls—as insulation.

More than half the energy used in your home goes toward keeping it cool in summer and warm in winter. A good way to save money and use less energy is to insulate. One of the newest technologies is a process that turns denim cloth into fiber insulation.

Denim scraps and old denim jeans are processed into fibers. The fibers are treated with borate, which makes the product fire retardant and resistant to mold. About 500 pairs of jeans are needed to make the insulation for an average home. The insulation itself is 100 percent recyclable. Jeans are no longer just blue. They are also "green"!

APPLY THE BIG ? What steps did scientists use to determine the insulating properties of denim?

....

....

Vocabulary Smart Cards

technology
microchip
prosthetic limb
design process
prototype

Play a Game!

Cut out the Vocabulary Smart Cards.

Work with a partner. One person puts the cards picture-side up. The other person puts the cards picture-side down.

Take turns matching each word with its definition.

design process

proceso de diseño

technology

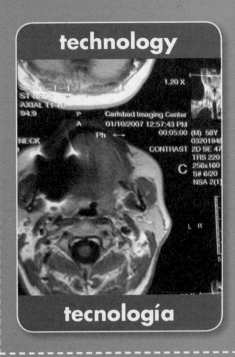

tecnología

prototype

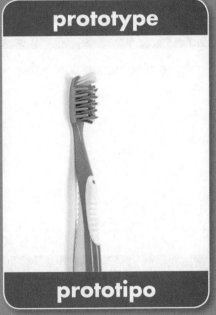

prototipo

microchip

microchip

prosthetic limb

prótesis

the knowledge, processes, and products that solve problems and make work easier

Name three technologies that begin with the same letter of the alphabet.

....

....

conocimiento, procesos y productos que se usan para resolver problemas y facilitar el trabajo

---

a set of steps for developing products and processes that solve problems

Write a definition for the noun form of the first word in this term.

....

....

serie de pasos para desarrollar productos y procesos que resuelven problemas

---

a small piece of a computer that contains microscopic circuits

Write a sentence using this word.

pequeña pieza de computadora que contiene circuitos microscópicos

---

a version of a solution to a problem

Write a sentence using this word.

....

....

....

versión de la solución de un problema

---

an artificial arm, hand, leg, or foot that replaces a missing one

Write a sentence using this word.

....

....

....

brazo, mano, pierna o pie artificial que reemplaza el miembro o la parte que falta

---

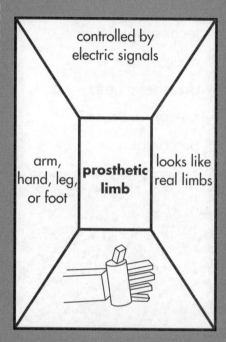

controlled by electric signals

arm, hand, leg, or foot — **prosthetic limb** — looks like real limbs

Make a Word Frame!

Choose a vocabulary word and write it in the center of the frame. Write or draw details about the vocabulary word in the spaces around it.

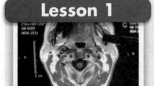

Lesson 1

What is technology?

- Technology is the knowledge, processes, and products that solve problems and make work easier.
- Medical technologies help us live longer and healthier lives.

Lesson 2

How does technology mimic living things?

- Many people use prosthetic limbs to help them do everyday tasks.
- Some technologies mimic the way animals move.

Lesson 3

What is the design process?

- The design process is a set of steps for developing products and processes that solve problems.
- Engineers build and test prototypes of their designs.

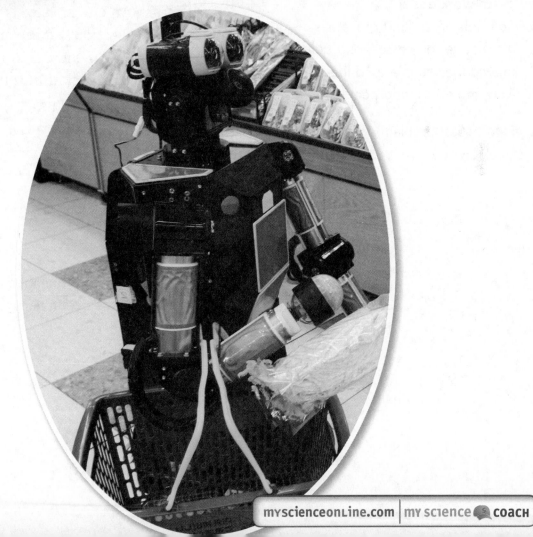

Chapter Review

How does technology affect our lives?

Lesson 1 🕐 5.DP.1, 5.4.2

What is technology?

1. **Write About It** Describe a technology you use every day and the problem it solves.

....

....

....

....

2. **Vocabulary** Technology is the
_____ that solve problems and make work easier.
A. materials, skills, and processes
B. knowledge, processes, and skills
C. knowledge, people, and ideas
D. skills, materials, and people

3. **Explain** What problem does an X-ray machine solve?

....

....

....

....

Lesson 2 🕐 5.4.1

How does technology mimic living things?

4. **Give an Example** What is one technology that mimics the human muscular and skeletal systems?

....

....

5. **⊙ Main Idea and Details** Use the following paragraph to answer the question below.

> Robotic arms can have different end effectors. An end effector is the attachment that is put on the end of the robotic arm. An end effector may be a claw that can pick things up and place them. Other end effectors include a welding tool and a drill.

What is the main idea of this paragraph?

....

....

6. **Infer** What kind of animal might a robot that explores the ocean mimic?

....

....

....

Lesson 3   🄳 5.DP.8, 5.4.2

What is the design process?

7. Suppose a robot arm can put a toy together five times as fast as a person. If a person can make 56 toys in 8 hours, how many toys can the robot make in the same amount of time?

8. Apply How would an engineer use the design process to build a car that uses less gas?

9. Vocabulary The design process is a set of steps for _____.

  A. developing a product or process

  B. doing an experiment

  C. drawing a diagram

  D. researching a product or process

10. APPLY THE BIG ？   **What is science?**

Tell how a technology has affected human life.

Extended Response

1 Many students like to eat a snack while reading a book. Deanna wants to develop a product that will help students keep their book crumb-free while reading. Deanna has described what she did for the first four steps of the design process. Complete the last four steps of the design process. Describe what Deanna must do next.

Identify the problem.
The problem is crumbs getting into a book while reading and eating a snack.

Do Research.
I looked in magazines, informational books, and the Internet to see if a product to keep crumbs out of a book exists.

Develop a possible solution.
I drew 2 different diagrams of possible design solutions. I labeled the different parts of the possible solutions.

Choose one solution.
Since it didn't have many parts or pieces to put together, I chose Solution 2.

Design and construct a prototype.

....

Test the prototype.

....

Communicate Results.

....

Evaluate and redesign.

....

5.4.2

mYscienceonLine.com | ISTEP+ Practice

BigWorld My World

Infrared Technology

5.NS.1

Do you remember the last time you got your temperature taken at the doctor's office? Perhaps the doctor used a thermometer that uses infrared technology.

The word *infrared* describes a type of light energy that people cannot see. Infrared energy is often thought of as light energy from a heat source. You cannot see infrared energy, but you can use tools to measure it.

NASA developed technology that uses a special tool to measure the infrared energy that comes from Earth and outer space. These tools are on satellites that orbit Earth and on probes that travel through space. Infrared technology is useful because infrared radiation can pass through areas of dust and gas. The information can give scientists clues about clouds on Earth as well as clues about the formation of planets and stars.

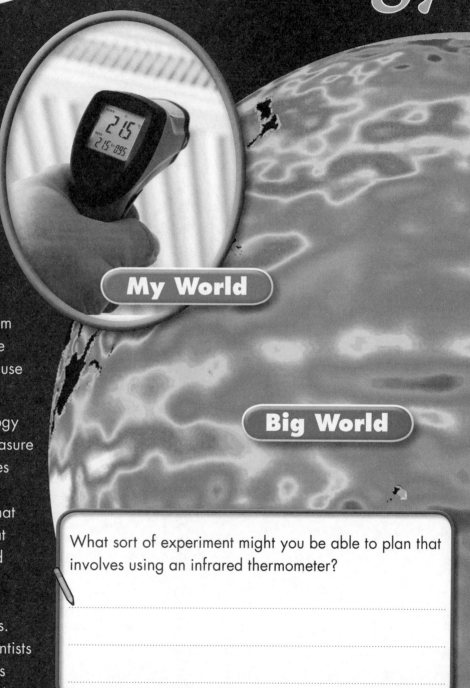

My World

Big World

What sort of experiment might you be able to plan that involves using an infrared thermometer?

....

....

....

How much weight can a model arm support?

An arm must be able to raise and lower objects of different weights. The arm also needs to support the weight it picks up. You must make a model arm that will be able to pick up different weights. The model arm will be used to pick up a cup holding 25 gram cubes. You will repeat the test by adding 25 gram cubes to the cup each time. Your testing is over when your arm bends the wrong way.

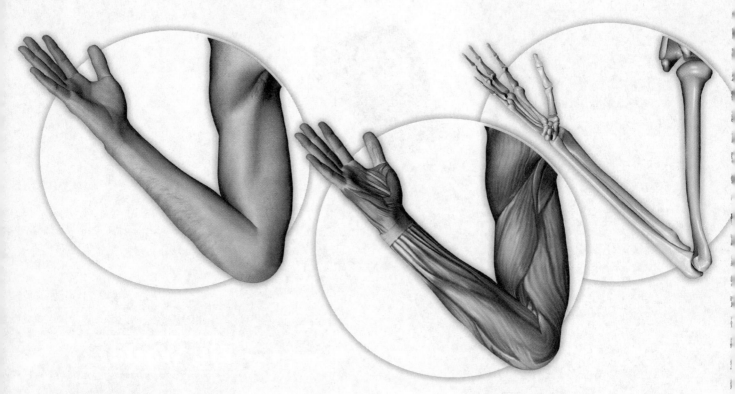

Identify the Problem.

☐ **1.** Identify the task your **model** arm will perform.

....

....

....

....

....

Possible Materials

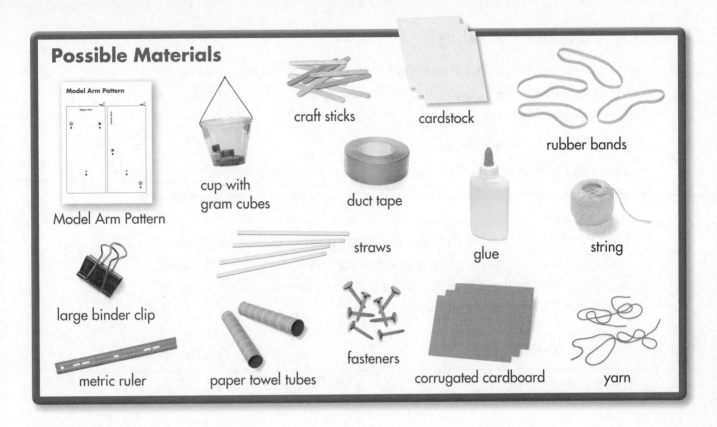

Model Arm Pattern

cup with gram cubes

craft sticks

cardstock

duct tape

glue

rubber bands

string

large binder clip

straws

metric ruler

paper towel tubes

fasteners

corrugated cardboard

yarn

Do Research

☐ **2.** Consider the tasks you have identified. Research design solutions others have created to perform those tasks. Brainstorm ideas with others. List three solutions others have used or suggested.

5.4.1 Investigate technologies that mimic human or animal musculoskeletal systems in order to meet a need. **5.4.2** Investigate the purpose of prototypes and models when designing a solution to a problem and how limitations in cost and design features might affect their construction. **5.4.3** Design a solution to a problem in the context of musculoskeletal body systems. Using suitable tools, techniques and materials, draw or build a prototype or model of a proposed design. **5.DP.1** Identify a need or problem to be solved. **5.DP.2** Brainstorm potential solutions. **5.DP.3** Document the design throughout the entire design process. **5.DP.4** Select a solution to the need or problem. **5.DP.5** Select the most appropriate materials to develop a solution that will meet the need. **5.DP.6** Create the solution through a prototype. **5.DP.7** Test and evaluate how well the solution meets the goal. **5.DP.8** Evaluate and test the design using measurement. **5.DP.9** Present evidence using mathematical representations (graphs, data tables). **5.DP.10** Communicate the solution including evidence using mathematical representations (graphs, data tables), drawings or prototypes. **5.DP.11** Communicate how to improve the solution.

Develop Possible Solutions.

3. Consider the problems your model arm **design** needs to overcome and the solutions you researched. Using this information, design two possible arms that will perform the task.

When you **test** your prototype:

- mount the arm to the back of the chair using a binder clip.
- attach the cup to your model arm. Consider where a real arm would hold weights.
- weights will be added to the cup. For the first trial you will test your prototype with 25 grams. The arm should be level at the end of the lift.
- Add 25 grams to the cup. Repeat the test. Your testing is over when your model arm bends the wrong way.

Design A	Design B

Choose One Solution.

4. Choose one **design** to build and test. Tell which design you chose. Explain why you chose that design.

Design and Construct a Prototype.

☑ **5.** Draw the **design** you will use to make a prototype.

☑ **6.** List the materials you used in your prototype.

....

....

....

Test the Prototype

☑ **7.** Start with 25 grams in the cup. **Record** if the arm passes or fails. A pass is when the arm lifts the cup. A fail is when the arm bends the wrong way.

☑ **8.** Add 25 grams to the cup. Repeat your **test.** Continue testing by adding 25 grams to the cup. Keep repeating your test until the arm fails.

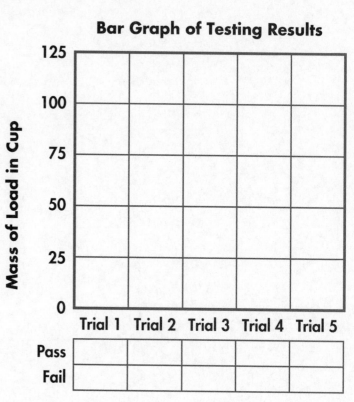

Testing Results

Trial	Load (grams)	Pass or Fail
1	25	
2	50	
3	75	
4	100	
5	125	

Bar Graph of Testing Results

Communicate Results

☑ **9.** Which parts of your design worked well in your prototype? Use your test results and your observations to support your conclusions.

....

....

☑ **10.** Which parts of your design could be improved?

....

....

....

....

Evaluate and Redesign

☑ **11.** Evaluate what did and did not work in your prototype.
Use what you learned from testing to redesign your prototype.

Write or draw your design changes.

_____

_____

_____

_____

_____

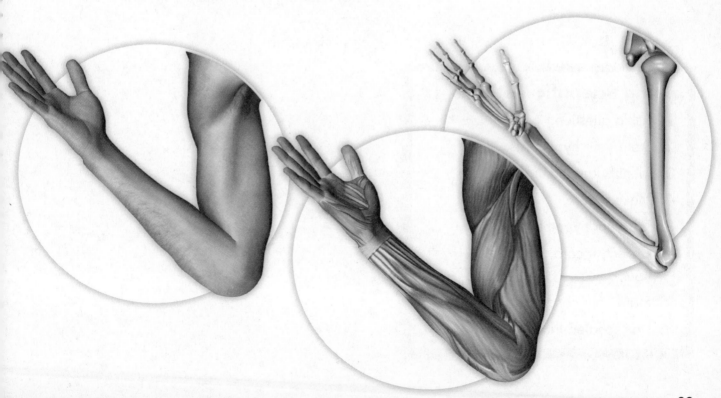

Make a Graph

Test a rubber ball, a table-tennis ball, and a marble to see which bounces the highest. Remember to identify and control all the variables. Measure the height of each bounce. Make a graph of your results. Share your results with your class.

🌑 5.NS.2

Write a Story

Think of a technology that might be invented in the future. Write a story about how using the technology will affect the lives of people. Describe what the technology will be and what it will do.

🌑 5.4.1

Make a Model

Make a model of an animal. Design a way to make the legs, wings, or fins of your model move like the animal you chose. Test how your model works. Redesign your model to make it work better.

🌑 5.4.3, 5.DP.6, 5.DP.11

Using Scientific Methods

1. Ask a question.
2. State your hypothesis.
3. Identify and control variables.
4. Make a plan.
5. Test your hypothesis.
6. Collect, record, and interpret your data.
7. State your conclusion.
8. Do repeated trials.

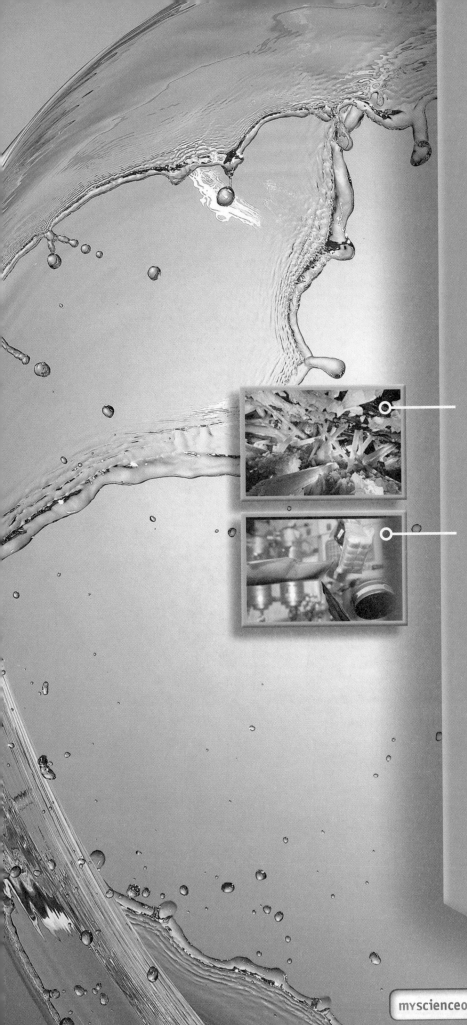

Physical Science

What makes up these GIANT crystals?

Properties of Matter

Try It! How are weight and volume affected when objects are combined?

Lesson 1 What makes up matter?

Lesson 2 What are solids, liquids, and gases?
5.NS.3, 5.NS.7

Lesson 3 What are mixtures and solutions?

Investigate It! What are some ways to separate a mixture?

You see small crystals every day, such as sugar or salt. But have you ever seen crystals like these? These giant crystals are in a cave in the Chihuahuan Desert.

Explain This cave was once filled with water that had minerals dissolved in it. How do you think the crystals formed?

....

....

THE BIG ? What are the properties of matter?

How are weight and volume affected when objects are combined?

Materials

beads

graduated cylinder

plastic cup

plastic spoon

spring scale with bag

sand

☐ **1.** With the bag attached hold up the spring scale. Set the scale to zero. Now the spring scale will only show the weight of what is in the bag.

☐ **2.** Fill a graduated cylinder with 25 mL of beads. **Record** the volume on the chart.

☐ **3.** Put the beads in the bag and weigh them. Record. Pour the beads into a cup.

☐ **4.** Repeat Steps 2 and 3 with sand.

Pour the sand into the cup with the beads.

☐ **5.** Mix the beads and sand with a spoon. Repeat

Steps 2 and 3 with the mixture of beads and sand.

Inquiry Skill
When you interpret data, you can make an **inference.**

Measurements of Matter

Objects	Volume (mL)	Weight (g)
Beads		
Sand		
Beads and sand		

Explain Your Results

6. Interpret Data Did the total volume or weight change after mixing? Explain.

....

....

7. **Infer** What did you learn about volume?

....

....

5.1.1 Describe and measure the volume and weight of a sample of a given material. **5.1.3** Demonstrate that regardless of how parts of an object are assembled, the weight of the whole object is identical to the sum of the weight of the parts, but the volume can differ from the sum of the volumes. **5.NS.8** Identify simple patterns in data and propose explanations to account for the patterns. (Also **5.NS.5, 5.NS.7, 5.DP.9**)

Compare and Contrast

- You **compare** when you tell how things are alike.
- You **contrast** when you tell how things are different.

Copper and Malachite

Copper is a very useful metal. It has a reddish color. It can be formed into sheets and wires without breaking. Malachite is a green mineral. It breaks if you try to change its shape. Malachite and copper are solid and durable. They are often used for decoration.

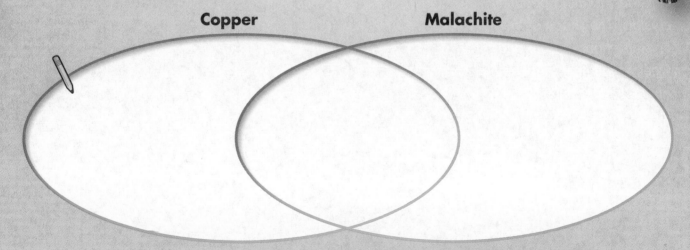

This jewelry box is carved from malachite. The legs are made from copper.

Practice It!

Complete the graphic organizer below to compare and contrast copper and malachite.

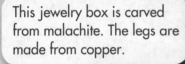

Copper   Malachite

What makes up matter?

Stand back and look at this picture from a distance. Tell what colors you see.

MY PLANET DIARY

FunFact

Have you ever noticed how nice it smells when you walk into some buildings? There is a type of air freshener that comes in solid lumps, about the size of a soap bar. These scented lumps do not melt at room temperature, but microscopic particles of them become loose and are released into the air, where we can enjoy their fragrance. If you keep these particles in a closed container, they will slowly collect on the sides, forming beautiful crystals. The shape of the crystals changes from one week to the next, depending on the temperature of the room.

Describe what you think would happen over time to this air freshener if you left the container open.

....

....

....

....

Now look at the dots closely. **Tell** what colors you see.

UNLOCK THE BIG ?

I will know that all things are made of very small particles called atoms and molecules, which cannot be seen without magnifying instruments.

Words to Know

atom   compound
atomic theory   molecule

Matter

Like ice, water, and air, you are made of matter. All living and nonliving things are made of matter. Matter is anything that has mass and takes up space. Matter includes the food we eat, our homes, our furniture, the sun, the moon, and this book.

A large sand sculpture is made of matter. It takes up a lot of space. It has a large mass. But if you look at it closely, you will see that it is made of tiny sand grains. A sand grain is also made of matter. It is gritty and tan colored, like the sculpture. But unlike the sculpture, a sand grain has a small mass and it does not take up a lot of space. All matter is made of tiny parts.

1. ◎ **Compare and Contrast** Use the graphic organizer below to describe how a sand sculpture and a grain of sand are alike and different.

Sand Sculpture   Grain of Sand

These sand grains are small particles. They are easy to see under a microscope. They are made of even smaller particles, too small to see with a regular microscope.

myscienceonLine.com | **Envision It!**   91

Elements

You can probably think of many kinds of food, many different medicines, or several types of fabric. Have you ever wondered how many different kinds of matter exist?

The world around you is made of thousands of materials, but all these materials are made of the same basic kinds of matter, called elements. Elements are the ingredients that make up all the other substances. Elements cannot be broken down into other substances with ordinary physical or chemical processes.

There are over 100 elements. Each element has specific characteristics. Each element will react in its own way with other elements.

Metals

Most elements are metals. Metals are good conductors of electricity and heat. They can be shaped into sheets or wires that can bend without breaking. Most metals, such as iron, are solids and have a gray color. Smooth metal surfaces can reflect light, which makes them appear shiny.

Aluminum *is light and strong. It is used to make ladders, airplane parts, and other items that need to be strong without being heavy.*

3. Identify What metal properties can you see in this ladder?

....

....

....

Calcium *is important for strong bones. You get calcium from food, but pure calcium is a metal! The calcium in food is combined with other elements. Dairy products can be good sources of calcium.*

2. List Write one food that is probably rich in calcium.

....

Mercury *is a liquid metal. It has many uses. For example, it can be used in thermometers and in energy-saving light bulbs. Mercury is toxic and must be handled with care.*

Nonmetals and Semimetals

Elements that do not conduct heat or electricity very well are called nonmetals. Some nonmetals are gases. One example is the oxygen you breathe. Other nonmetals, such as carbon, are solid.

Semimetals are elements that are sometimes like metals and sometimes like nonmetals. For example, they may conduct electricity, but only when light is shining on them. One of the most useful semimetals is silicon.

Silicon can be obtained from sand. The rod on the right is made of purified silicon. It will be used to make chips for electronic devices such as pocket calculators and computers.

4. Give an Example What other electronic devices might have silicon chips inside?

....

....

....

Sulfur is a solid nonmetal. It can be found in nature as a mineral. Sulfur is brittle and burns easily. Sulfur compounds are used to make matches.

5. Interpret What would happen if you tried to break down a sample of sulfur?

....

....

Neon belongs to a group of elements called the noble gases. These gases usually do not combine with other elements. Neon is used in neon signs.

Atoms

The smallest part of an element that still has the properties of the element is called an **atom.** Atoms are too small to be seen with a regular microscope, but special instruments can show how atoms are arranged.

The atoms of each element are different from the atoms of other elements. However, the atoms of all elements have something in common. They are made of the same three types of particles—protons, neutrons, and electrons.

The number of protons determines what element an atom will be. For example, an atom of carbon always has six protons. No other element has atoms with six protons. Carbon atoms usually have six neutrons and six electrons as well, but some atoms of carbon may have different numbers of electrons and neutrons. As long as an atom has exactly six protons, it will be an atom of carbon.

Since all substances are made of elements and all elements are made of atoms, all the matter around you is made of atoms. The idea that everything is made of small particles is known as the **atomic theory.**

Gold *is a pure element. All gold is made of the same type of atoms. Every atom of gold has exactly 79 protons.*

6. **List** What types of particles make up a carbon atom?

7. CHALLENGE **Draw** what you think a carbon atom might look like. Use the gold atom below as a model.

This image shows how atoms in a solid are tightly packed.

Protons and neutrons cluster at the center of the atom. This cluster is called the nucleus. Electrons move around the nucleus.

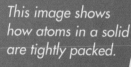

myscienceonline.com | THE BIG ? | I Will Know...

Atomic Arrangement

Atoms are often connected to other atoms in specific ways. The way atoms are connected affects the properties of an element. For example, when carbon atoms are connected as flat sheets, the carbon is soft and black. This form of carbon is called graphite. If the same carbon atoms are connected as pyramids, they form diamonds. Unlike graphite, diamonds are transparent and very hard. However, diamonds and graphite are both made of carbon atoms.

8. ⦿ **Compare and Contrast** Tell how a diamond and a piece of graphite are alike and different.

....

....

....

....

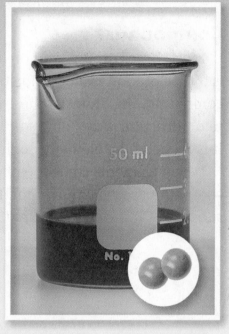

Bromine is an orange-red liquid. It evaporates easily. Its atoms are connected in pairs.

9. **Infer** In the picture above, do you think there are more atoms of bromine in liquid or gas form?

....

Diamonds are used to make jewels. The model below shows how carbon atoms are connected in a diamond.

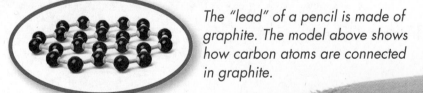

The "lead" of a pencil is made of graphite. The model above shows how carbon atoms are connected in graphite.

Lightning Lab

Letters and Atoms
There are more than 100 kinds of atoms. Most arrangements are not possible, but there still are millions of ways to combine atoms. Write the letters *A, B, C, D,* and cut them out. How many ways can you put them in order? (Examples: *DBCA, CADB*)

Compounds

Most things around you are compounds. A **compound** is a type of matter made of two or more elements. In a compound, the atoms of these elements are joined together in a particular way. Table salt is an example of a compound. It is made of the elements sodium and chlorine.

When elements come together to form a compound, the compound is not simply a mixture of elements. It is a new substance. It is different from its ingredients.

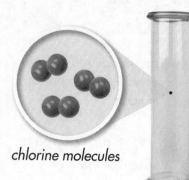

chlorine molecules

Chlorine *is a poisonous gas. It is greenish-yellow. Chlorine reacts strongly with sodium.*

Table salt *is white and solid. It is not poisonous. Chlorine and sodium combine to form ordinary table salt.*

sodium chloride

sodium atoms

Sodium *is a soft metal. It can be cut with a knife. It reacts strongly with chlorine.*

10. Contrast List two ways in which salt is different from chlorine.

....

....

....

myscienceonline.com | Got it? | 60-Second Video

The smallest particle of a compound that still has the properties of that compound is called a **molecule.** For example, the smallest particle of water is a water molecule. A water molecule only has three atoms, but other molecules, like those of sugar, may have many atoms.

Changing the number, kind, or position of the atoms in a molecule would result in a molecule of a different substance. For example, a water molecule always has one atom of oxygen and two atoms of hydrogen. Adding an extra oxygen atom would turn a water molecule into a molecule of a different substance.

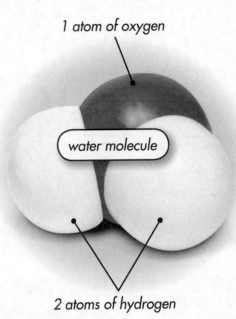

1 atom of oxygen

water molecule

2 atoms of hydrogen

11. Calculate Suppose you count all the hydrogen atoms in a group of water molecules. There are 8 hydrogen atoms in total. How many water molecules are in the group?

....

....

Got it?

12. Explain What makes up matter? Use the definition of atomic theory to answer.

....

13. **UNLOCK THE BIG ?** A scientist is combining two gray elements. He thinks he will get a gray compound. Use what you learned in this lesson to explain why this prediction may not be correct.

....

....

⬜ **Stop!** I need help with ....

⏸ **Wait!** I have a question about ....

▶ **Go!** Now I know ....

Lesson 2

What are solids, liquids, and gases?

Envision It!

5.NS.3 Plan and carry out investigations as a class, in small groups or independently, often over a period of several class lessons. (Also 5.NS.7)

Where are some solids, liquids, and gases in the picture? **Tell** how you know.

Inquiry **Explore It!**

How can water change state?

☑ **1.** Stick a straw halfway inside a bag. Seal the bag up to the straw.

☑ **2.** Slowly exhale through the straw. Remove the straw and seal the bag shut.

☑ **3.** Lay the bag on dark paper under bright light. Use a hand lens to **observe.**

Explain Your Results

4. Communicate What did you **observe**? Explain.

....

....

....

....

Materials

plastic bag

straw

hand lens

dark paper

Be careful! Do not use a straw that someone else has used.

myscienceonLine.com | **Explore It!** Animation

5.NS.4 Perform investigations using appropriate tools and technology that will extend the senses.

I will know some basic properties of solids, liquids, and gases.

Words to Know

solid   gas
liquid

States of Matter

Water has three forms. Water is a solid when it is frozen as ice. Water is a liquid in the oceans. In the air, water can be a gas. Solid, liquid, and gas are the most familiar states of matter, or phases.

The phase of water, or of any material, is due to the motion and arrangement of its particles—its molecules or its atoms. The particles are always moving.

Most materials around you are solids, liquids, or gases. For example, cooking oil is a liquid. Butter is a solid when it is cold, but butter can turn into a liquid if it gets hot.

1. **Compare and Contrast** Look at the picture. How are the solid butter and liquid oil alike and different?

Oil   Butter

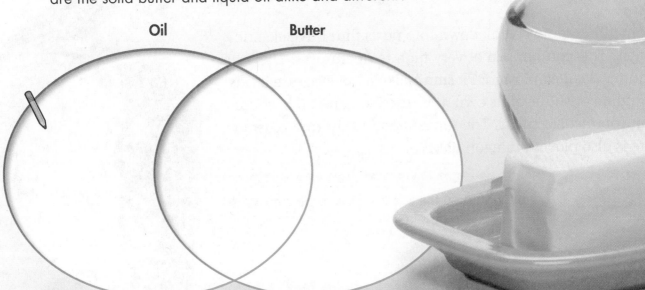

Solids

A **solid** is a substance that has a definite shape and volume. Volume is the amount of space an object takes up. The particles of a solid are very close together. For the most part they stay in the same place. They do not slide easily past each other. However, they vibrate in place.

Liquids

A **liquid** is a substance that has a definite volume but no definite shape. The particles of a liquid can move by gliding past each other. A liquid can take the shape of its container. Forces hold liquid particles together, so a liquid keeps a definite volume.

Gases

A **gas** is a substance without a definite volume or shape. The particles of a gas are far apart compared to the particles of solids and liquids. A gas can be squeezed into a smaller volume. Gas particles only affect one another when they collide as they move. If a gas is placed in an empty container, its particles will spread out evenly. The gas will fill all the space and take the shape of that container.

Plasmas

Sometimes atoms break down into parts that have electric charges. This can happen at very high temperatures. This state of matter is called plasma. Plasma is like a gas because it has no volume or shape of its own. It is also like a metal because it can conduct electricity. The sun is made of gas and plasma. There is also plasma in neon lights.

2. [CHALLENGE] Describe what you think is inside of a plasma TV.

....

....

....

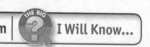

myscienceonline.com | THE BIG ? | I Will Know...

Freezing and Melting

As liquids get colder, their particles slow down. At some point they stop gliding past each other and can only vibrate in place. The liquid becomes a solid. The temperature at which a material changes between solid and liquid states has two names. It is called the freezing point when a liquid turns into a solid. It is called the melting point when a solid turns into a liquid. Therefore, the melting point and the freezing point are the same temperature. This temperature is often just referred to as the melting point.

Each material has its own melting point. Therefore, the melting point can be used to help identify a material.

Some materials are more useful in their solid state than in their liquid state. For example, lead is a metal that is dense. Solid lead is used to weigh down or sink fishing hooks.

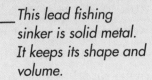

This lead fishing sinker is solid metal. It keeps its shape and volume.

The melting point of lead is 327°C. At this temperature, solid lead becomes liquid and can be poured into molds to give it any shape we want.

3. **Compare** What is the difference between the melting point and freezing point of a substance?

....

....

4. **[CHALLENGE]** Why might you want to consider the melting point of a substance before choosing materials for frying pans or engine parts?

....

....

....

....

5. **Recognize** Water has a melting point of 0°C. What is its freezing point?

....

Lightning Lab

Wandering Ice
Place an ice cube on a dish and set it in a place where it will not be disturbed. Observe how long it takes for the ice cube to melt. Observe how long it takes for the water to evaporate.

Evaporation

Evaporation takes place when particles leave a liquid and become a gas. Particles evaporate from a liquid when they are at the surface of the liquid and are moving upward with enough speed. This is how rain puddles and the water in wet clothes evaporate.

If the temperature of a liquid is high enough, particles will change to a gas not only at the surface, but also throughout the liquid. As gas particles move quickly upward through a liquid, bubbles of gas form under the surface of the liquid. The boiling point of a liquid is the temperature at which this occurs.

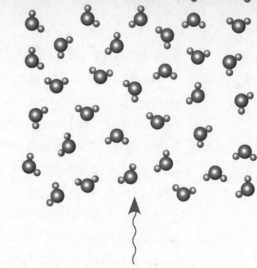

Molecules of water evaporate from the clothes as they dry. In water vapor, the molecules of water are far apart.

6. **Explain** How can clothes dry without heating them to the boiling point of water?

....

....

....

Do the math!

Ranges

The chart shows the temperatures at which 5 different substances change form.

Boiling Points (°C)	
Liquid	**Boiling Point**
Water	100°C
Acetic acid (found in vinegar)	118°C
Chlorine	−34°C
Propane	−42°C
Iodine	185°C

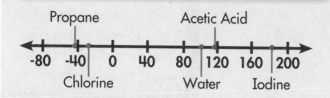

1 Which liquid has the highest boiling point?
  A. Water   C. Acetic acid
  B. Iodine   D. Propane

2 In which temperature range is the greatest gap between boiling points?
  F. 185°C to 100°C
  G. −34°C to −42°C
  H. 118°C to −42°C
  I. 100°C to −34°C

3 [CHALLENGE] Choose a common substance, such as ammonia or rubbing alcohol. Research its boiling point, and add this information to the chart. Plot the new data point on the number line.

myscienceonline.com | Got it? | 60-Second Video

Condensation

Condensation occurs when a gas turns into a liquid. This process often occurs when gas particles touch a cold surface and the temperature of the gas drops. Clouds in the sky and dew on the ground form through condensation of water vapor.

As air temperature decreases, the molecules of water vapor come together and condense, forming the liquid water droplets we call dew.

7. Describe What is one thing needed for condensation to occur?

....

....

8. Infer The dew on the spider's web formed before sunrise. What might this tell you about the air temperature before sunrise?

....

....

....

Got it?

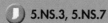 5.NS.3, 5.NS.7

9. Interpret A substance fills a 1-liter bottle. A scientist transfers the substance to a 2-liter bottle. The substance increases in volume and fills the new space. What is the state of matter of this substance?

....

10. UNLOCK THE BIG ? Why can you use the melting point to help identify a material?

....

....

⬛ **Stop!** I need help with ....

⏸ **Wait!** I have a question about ....

▶ **Go!** Now I know ....

Lesson 3

What are mixtures and solutions?

Once per year, the Chicago River in Illinois is dyed green. What are the parts of the mixture shown in the picture?

Inquiry Explore It!

How can a mixture be separated?

☑ **1.** Place the paper clips and fasteners in a cup. Move the magnet around in the cup slowly. Lift out the magnet. **Observe.**

☑ **2.** Fill the cup with water. Observe.

Explain Your Results

3. Infer What property made it possible to separate the mixture with a magnet?

....

....

4. What property made it possible to use water to separate the mixture?

....

....

Materials

5 brass fasteners

5 metal paper clips

5 plastic paper clips

magnet

water

plastic cup

---

myscienceonline.com | **Explore It!** Animation

5.NS.3 Plan and carry out investigations as a class, in small groups or independently, often over a period of several class lessons. **5.NS.8** Identify simple patterns in data and propose explanations to account for the patterns.

I will know properties of solutions and that mixtures can be separated based on properties of their parts.

Words to Know
....

mixture
solution

Mixtures

In a **mixture**, different substances are placed together but each material in the mixture keeps its own properties. If vegetables are cut and put together to make a mixture, different vegetables do not change their flavors or colors. Most foods that you eat are mixtures of different materials.

Different parts of a mixture can be separated from the rest of the mixture. Suppose your favorite breakfast is a mixture of cereal and raisins. You could easily separate out the raisins with a spoon to eat them first. The parts of a mixture may be combined in different amounts. The bowl of cereal you eat today could have more raisins than the one you ate yesterday.

The bowl of fruit is a mixture. It contains several different parts.

1. **Suggest** What mixture is your favorite to eat? List the parts.

....

....

....

2. **Support** Why is the bowl of beads to the right not a mixture?

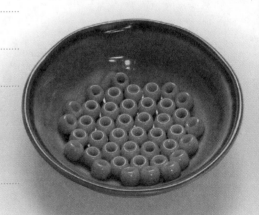

....

....

At-Home Lab

Mixed-Up Foods

Find two different mixtures you eat at home. What are the parts of the mixtures? Tell whether you would ever eat any of the parts separately.

Separating Mixtures

You can use the physical properties of a substance to separate it from a mixture. The materials in a simple mixture can be separated because they have different physical properties. For example, a magnet can separate iron filings from sand. This separation happens because iron has the property of being attracted by magnets. Sand does not have that property. A screen filter can be used to separate a mixture of pebbles and sand. The smaller particles go through the screen but the pebbles do not. Sometimes you can sort the parts of a mixture by hand.

3. **Classify** Complete the chart below. **Draw** a mixture in the first row. **Write** how to separate the erasers and screws and the items in the new mixture.

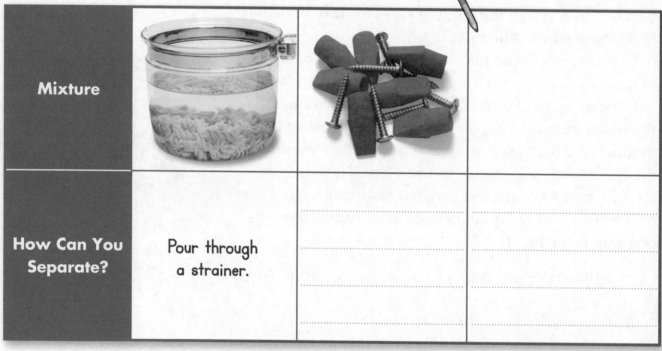

Mixture			
How Can You Separate?	Pour through a strainer.		

4. [CHALLENGE] Suppose you had a mixture of sand and small, hollow beads. How might you separate the mixture?

myscienceonline.com | I Will Know...

5. Categorize Look at the mixture above. In the boxes provided below, **draw** four parts of the mixture or **write** their names.

6. Infer A compound forms when two or more elements combine to form a new substance with new properties. How is a compound different from a mixture?

Solutions

A mixture in which substances are spread out evenly and will not settle is called a **solution.** In a solution, the substance that is dissolved is called the *solute*. The substance in which the solute is being dissolved is called the *solvent*. In a solution of sugar and water, the solute is sugar and the solvent is water. Water is sometimes called a "universal solvent" because it can dissolve many substances.

Solutions of a Solid in a Liquid

When a solid dissolves, individual particles separate from the solid and spread evenly throughout the liquid. You can make solids dissolve in a liquid faster by stirring or heating the solution. Grinding a solid into smaller pieces will also help it dissolve faster.

These crystals dissolve easily in water.

7. **Draw** what you think the mixture of purple solid and water will look like after stirring.

Other Solutions

Not all solutions are made by dissolving a solid in a liquid. Two liquids can make a solution. For example, vegetable oils used in cooking might be a solution of soybean and sunflower oils. A gas can also dissolve in a liquid. For example, water can contain dissolved oxygen and carbon dioxide gases.

8. **Infer** Why do you think it is important for sea organisms that some gases dissolve in water?

....

....

....

This toy has a colorless liquid floating on a blue-colored liquid. The colorless liquid and the plastic figures will not dissolve in the blue liquid. They are insoluble *in it.*

Solubility

Many materials can make solutions with water. You can dissolve more of some materials than others in the same amount of water. Some materials will not dissolve in water at all. This describes a material's solubility in water. Different substances can have different solubility in other solvents.

9. CHALLENGE The plastic figures in the picture are insoluble in the blue liquid. What else can you tell about their solubility?

....

....

....

Got it?

10. **Describe** Gelatin dessert is made by chilling a mixture of gelatin mix and water. What do you think would happen if you used too much or too little gelatin mix?

....

....

11. **UNLOCK THE BIG ?** Write one way you can use properties of matter to separate mixtures.

....

....

⬜ **Stop!** I need help with ....

⏸ **Wait!** I have a question about ....

▶ **Go!** Now I know ....

What are some ways to separate a mixture?

Follow a Procedure

☑ **1.** Label the 4 cups A, B, C, and D.
In Cup A place 1 spoonful of salt, 2 spoonfuls of sand, 3 marbles, and 100 mL of water.

☑ **2.** Carefully make 4 holes in the bottom of Cup B by pushing a pencil through the bottom of the cup from the inside.

☑ **3.** Hold Cup B over Cup C. All at once, pour the mixture from Cup A into Cup B. Move Cup B around to clean the marbles. **Record** the part of the mixture that was removed by straining.

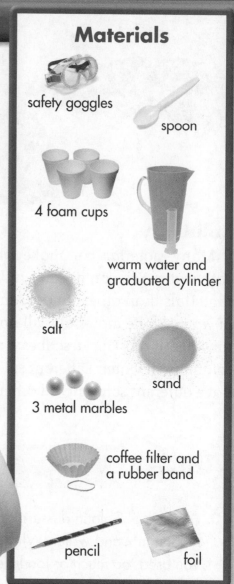

Materials

safety goggles

spoon

4 foam cups

warm water and graduated cylinder

salt

sand

3 metal marbles

coffee filter and a rubber band

pencil

foil

Be careful!

Wear safety goggles.
Do not taste the water.
Be careful with sharp objects.

Inquiry Skill
Scientists record data on charts and use the data to help make **inferences.**

5.NS.3 Plan and carry out investigations as a class, in small groups or independently, often over a period of several class lessons. 5.NS.7 Keep accurate records in a notebook during investigations and communicate findings to others using graphs, charts, maps and models through oral and written reports. (Also **5.NS.8**)

Results of Separation		
Separating Method	Part Removed	Part Not Removed
Straining		
Filtering		
Evaporation		

4. Put a coffee filter in Cup D. Slowly pour the mixture from Cup C into Cup D. Record the part of the mixture that was removed by filtering.

5. Remove the filter. Use the spoon to drip 2 drops of the liquid onto the foil. Let the liquid evaporate. Record the results.

Use a rubber band to fasten the filter to the cup.

Analyze and Conclude

6. Communicate Name a property you used to separate parts of the mixture.

....

....

7. **UNLOCK THE BIG ?** **Infer** Describe another mixture. How could the properties of matter help you separate it into its parts?

....

....

....

....

John Dalton

John Dalton (1766–1844) was an English chemist and physicist. His family was poor, and Dalton started working at a very young age. He taught, did farm work, and helped his brother run a school.

Later in life, Dalton became a scientist. He had many scientific interests. For example, he kept detailed notes on the weather for many years, and he studied the pressure of gases. He even studied his own body. Dalton suffered from a type of color blindness, and he became the first person to describe this medical condition.

Dalton is best remembered for his work on the atomic theory. The Greeks had proposed this theory more than 2,000 years ago, but Dalton added more details. He thought that there was one type of atom for each element, and that atoms could only be rearranged, but not created or destroyed.

The word *daltonism* is still used to refer to a type of color blindness. There is a crater on the Moon named after Dalton.

Dalton made up graphical symbols for each element, but today we use letters. For example, the symbol for sulfur is S.

What do you think are some advantages and disadvantages of using letters instead of graphical symbols to represent chemical elements?

Vocabulary Smart Cards

atom
atomic theory
compound
molecule
solid
liquid
gas
mixture
solution

Play a Game!

Cut out the Vocabulary Smart Cards.

Work with a partner.

Player 1 chooses a Vocabulary Smart Card.

Say as many words as you can think of that describe that vocabulary word to Player 2.

Player 2 guesses the word.

molecule

molécula

atom
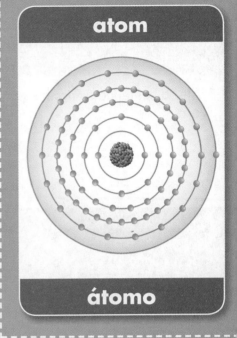
átomo

solid

sólido

atomic theory

teoría atómica

liquid

líquido

compound

compuesto

the smallest part of an element that still has the properties of the element

Write a sentence using this word.

....

....

la partícula más pequeña de un elemento, que todavía tiene las propiedades de ese elemento

the smallest particle of a compound that still has the properties of that compound

Draw an example of this word.

la partícula más pequeña de un compuesto, que todavía tiene las propiedades de ese compuesto

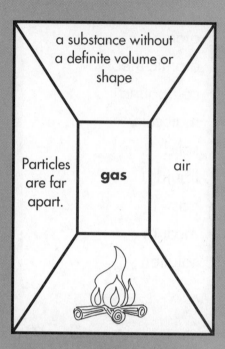

a substance without a definite volume or shape

Particles are far apart.

gas

air

Make a Word Frame!

Choose a vocabulary word and write it in the center of the frame. Write or draw details about the vocabulary word in the spaces around it.

the idea that everything is made of small particles

Write a sentence using this term.

....

....

....

la idea de que la materia está formada por partículas pequeñas

a substance that has a definite shape and volume

What are two other meanings of this word?

....

....

....

sustancia que tiene una forma y un volumen definidos

a type of matter made of two or more elements

Write a different meaning of this word.

....

....

....

tipo de materia formada por dos o más elementos

a substance that has a definite volume but no definite shape

Draw an example.

sustancia que tiene un volumen definido pero no una forma definida

gas

gas

mixture

mezcla

solution

solución

a substance without a definite volume or shape

Write an example of this word.

....

....

sustancia que no tiene ni volumen ni forma definidos

---

different materials placed together but each material keeps its own properties

Write three other forms of this word.

....

....

unión de materiales diferentes durante la cual cada material mantiene sus propiedades

---

a mixture in which substances are spread out evenly and will not settle

What is a different meaning of this word?

....

....

mezcla en la cual una sustancia se dispersa de manera uniforme en otra sustancia y no se asienta

Study Guide

REVIEW THE BIG ?

What are the properties of matter?

Indiana

Lesson 1

What makes up matter?

- Matter is made of atoms. Atoms may combine to form molecules.
- Elements are basic kinds of matter. Each element has different atoms.
- Compounds are made up of two or more elements.

Lesson 2

What are solids, liquids, and gases?

- States of matter include solid, liquid, gas, and plasma.
- Changes in state are caused by changes in the motion of particles.

Lesson 3

What are mixtures and solutions?

- A mixture is made up of two or more materials.
- The parts of a mixture can be separated.
- A solution is a type of mixture. Parts do not settle out of a solution.

Chapter Review

REVIEW
THE BIG
?

What are the properties of matter?

Lesson 1

What makes up matter?

1. **Summarize** Your classmate has a magnifying glass, and he is looking for atoms. What would you tell him?

2. **Predict** A scientist finds that a sample of matter contains three types of atoms. The sample can be any of the following, except:
   A. a compound
   B. a molecule
   C. an element

3. **Infer** The chart below shows the number of protons and neutrons in three different atoms. Which two atoms are atoms of the same element, and why?

Atom	Protons	Neutrons
A	1	1
B	2	1
C	2	2

Lesson 2

What are solids, liquids, and gases?

4. ◉ **Compare and Contrast** Write two ways in which water and ice are different and two ways in which they are the same.

5. **Infer** A substance has a melting point of 104°C. Its freezing point will be
   A. 104°C.
   B. lower than 104°C.
   C. higher than 104°C.

6. **Main Idea and Details** <u>Underline</u> the main idea and (circle) the details in the following paragraph.

At room temperature, iron is a solid and oxygen is a gas. However, molten iron is useful because it can be shaped easily. Liquid oxygen takes up less room than oxygen gas. Iron becomes liquid if it is heated to 1,538°C. Oxygen becomes liquid if it is cooled to –183°C. Temperature allows us to choose the most useful state of matter of a substance for a particular job.

Lesson 3

What are mixtures and solutions?

7. Explain Sulfur burns easily. Iron is attracted by magnets. The mineral below is made of sulfur and iron, but it does not burn and it is not attracted by magnets. Is it a mixture? Why or why not?

8. Write About It A cough drop is placed in a jug of water. A few days later, the cough drop seems to have disappeared. Use the words solubility, solute, and solvent to describe what you think happened.

9. APPLY THE BIG **?** **What are the properties of matter?**

Think about the materials used to make a car. Some materials are glass, steel, cloth, and plastic. Choose three materials. For each one, describe one property that makes it useful. For example, windshield glass should be clear so that people can see through it.

Multiple Choice

1 Which of the following elements is NOT a metal?

- A. mercury
- B. sulfur
- C. iron
- D. calcium

Constructed Response

2 A client buys four cans of paint for her living room. To match her color choice, a machine at the paint store blends three cans of blue paint with one can of white paint. Later, the client comes back to buy four more cans of the same color, and the store offers to blend two cans of blue with two cans of white. Why won't this work?

Extended Response

3 The chart shown below lists four elements that are part of the same group. They are arranged from smallest to largest number of protons. Scientists can use the number of protons to predict the properties of elements within a group. Their predictions must be confirmed by experiments.

Melting Points of Some Elements

Element	Protons	Melting Point
Sodium	11	98°C
Potassium	19	63°C
Rubidium	37	39°C
Cesium	55	

Look at the melting points listed in the chart. What pattern do you observe?

Based on the pattern you observed, make an approximate prediction of the melting point of cesium.

5.NS.8

Electron Microscopes

My World

The Braille alphabet is made of raised dots that readers can feel with their fingers.

Big World

An electron microscope produced this image of healthy skin.

Atoms are so small that light is useless when we try to see them. Fortunately, there are other ways to observe how atoms are arranged.

Have you ever had to reach under a car seat to find a pen that was dropped? When you hold an object in the dark, you can tell its shape, its size, and its texture even if you can't see it. The sense of touch is so good at feeling shapes that people with little or no vision can use it to read with their fingers.

Electron microscopes are also capable of producing images of small objects without using any light at all. They can even make images of atoms. The microscope bombards the atoms with electrically charged particles and then records how the atoms scatter the particles. Computer programs then use the data to produce a picture that people can see on a screen or on paper.

Suppose you are looking into a deep well but cannot see the bottom. What can you learn by dropping a small pebble into the well?

121

How does FOOD taste in space?

Physical and Chemical Changes

Try It! What happens to water during freezing?

Lesson 1 How do you measure matter?
5.1.1, 5.1.2

Lesson 2 How do physical changes affect properties?
5.1.3, 5.1.4, 5.NS.1

Lesson 3 How do chemical changes affect properties?

Investigate It! What can happen if different amounts of water are added to cornstarch?

On Earth, food is often sold by weight. The weight of food is also printed on labels. In space, however, food floats around. It appears to have no weight at all.

 Explain How do you think the nutritional value of the food is affected in space? How is its flavor or shape affected?

....

....

....

THE BIG ? What are the properties of matter?

What happens to water during freezing?

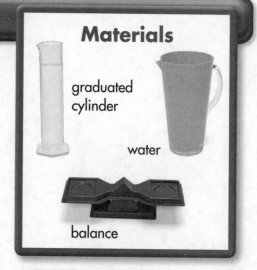

Materials

graduated cylinder

water

balance

☑ **1.** Put 40 mL of water in a graduated cylinder.

☑ **2.** **Measure** the mass of the water and cylinder. **Record** on the chart.

☑ **3.** Freeze the water. Record the volume of the ice.

☑ **4.** Measure the mass of the ice and cylinder. Record.

Measurements of Water

	Volume (mL)	Mass (g)
Before freezing	40	
After freezing		

Inquiry Skill
You can **measure** mass in grams and volume in milliliters.

Explain Your Results

5. **UNLOCK THE BIG ?** **Communicate** How did freezing affect the volume and mass of the water?

....

6. **Infer** How did freezing affect the amount of matter? Explain.

....

....

....

7. **Predict** How might dissolving salt in water affect the mass of the salt and water?

....

With your teacher's permission, make and carry out a plan to find out.

5.1.1 Describe and measure the volume and weight of a sample of a given material. **5.1.4** Determine if matter has been added or lost by comparing weights when melting, freezing, or dissolving a sample of a substance. **5.NS.1** Make predictions and formulate testable questions. **5.NS.4** Perform investigations using appropriate tools and technology that will extend the senses. (Also **5.DP.9, 5.NS.8**)

◉ Cause and Effect

- A **cause** is why something happens. An **effect** is what happens.

- When you read, sometimes clue words such as *because* and *since* indicate a relationship of cause and effect.

Let's Read Science!

Expansion Under Heat

Many materials expand when the temperature rises. On a hot day, a steel beam will be a little longer than it is on a cold day. Since this expansion is very small, you may not notice it. But people who design railroads must take it into account because an expanding beam will push against other beams next to it. The force of the push is so great that it can bend beams out of shape. This would create a hazard for trains. When beams are laid down, engineers leave small gaps between them. This allows the beams to expand without pushing against each other.

Practice It!

Use the graphic organizer below to list one cause and one effect found in the example paragraph.

rail gap

Cause	Effect

Lesson 1

How do you measure matter?

5.1.1 Describe and measure the volume and weight of a sample of a given material.
5.1.2 Describe the difference between weight and mass, with the understanding that weight is dependent on gravity and mass is the amount of matter in a given substance/material.

Envision It!

Tell how many of these balloons you think could be filled with gas from the canister.

Inquiry Explore It!

How can dividing clay affect weight?

Materials

spring scale with plastic bag

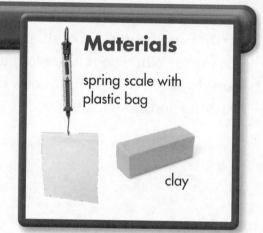

clay

☑ **1.** With the bag attached, hold up the spring scale. Set the scale to zero. Now the spring scale will show only the weight of what is in the bag.

☑ **2.** Place the clay in the bag. Use the spring scale to **measure** the weight. **Record.**

☑ **3.** Remove the clay. Divide the clay into two pieces. Repeat Step 2 for each piece.

Piece A   Piece B

Explain Your Results

4. Interpret Data Compare the total weight of the clay before and after dividing it.

5. Draw a Conclusion How did dividing the clay affect the amount of matter? Explain.

myscienceonline.com | **Explore It!** Animation

5.1.3 Demonstrate that regardless of how parts of an object are assembled, the weight of the whole object is identical to the sum of the weight of the parts, but the volume can differ from the sum of the volumes.
5.NS.5 Use measurement skills and apply appropriate units when collecting data. (Also **5.NS.4**)

I will know how to measure
and describe weight,
volume, and mass. I will
know that the weight of a
whole object is equal to the
weight of all of its parts.

Words to Know

volume   weight

mass

Volume

You can add a few items of clothing to a laundry basket that looks full, but at some point, there will be no more space. This is because all objects take up a certain amount of space. The amount of space an object takes up is its **volume.** Anything that is made of matter has a volume. Even the air we breathe is made of matter, and for this reason we have to make more room in our chests when we take in more air. Volume is a property of matter, and it can be measured.

Volume of Liquids

Liquids are made of matter. Therefore, they have volume. An easy way to measure the volume of a liquid is by using a graduated cylinder like the one shown to the right. Graduated cylinders are marked with volume units such as the milliliter (mL) or the liter (L). One liter is equal to 1,000 milliliters. The volume of liquid in a graduated cylinder can be read directly on the side of the cylinder.

1. **Analyze** A liter of sea water weighs more than a liter of fresh water. Which sample takes up more volume?

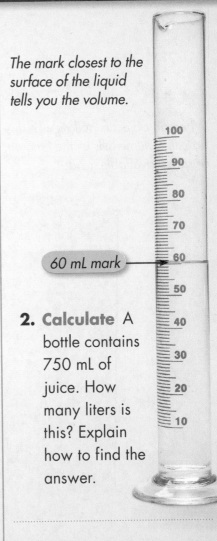

The mark closest to the surface of the liquid tells you the volume.

60 mL mark

2. **Calculate** A bottle contains 750 mL of juice. How many liters is this? Explain how to find the answer.

3. Measure The length and width of this clear box both measure 7 cm. Use a ruler to measure the height of the box, and use the three measurements to find its volume.

Volume of Solids

Solids are also made of matter and therefore they also have volume. Remember that solids have a definite shape. If a solid has a regular geometric shape, you may be able to find the volume of the solid by using a formula. There are formulas to determine the volume of cones, cylinders, spheres, pyramids, and many other familiar shapes. For example, the volume (V) of a rectangular box can be found by using the formula

$$V = L \times W \times H.$$

This formula tells you to multiply the length (L) times the width (W) times the height (H) of the box. If a box measures 10 cm long, 3 cm wide, and 4 cm high, then L = 10 cm, W = 3 cm, and H = 4 cm. You can find the volume V as follows:

$$V = 10 \text{ cm} \times 3 \text{ cm} \times 4 \text{ cm}$$
$$V = 120 \text{ cubic centimeters (cm}^3).$$

When an object is hollow, like this box, its volume tells us the amount of space available inside.

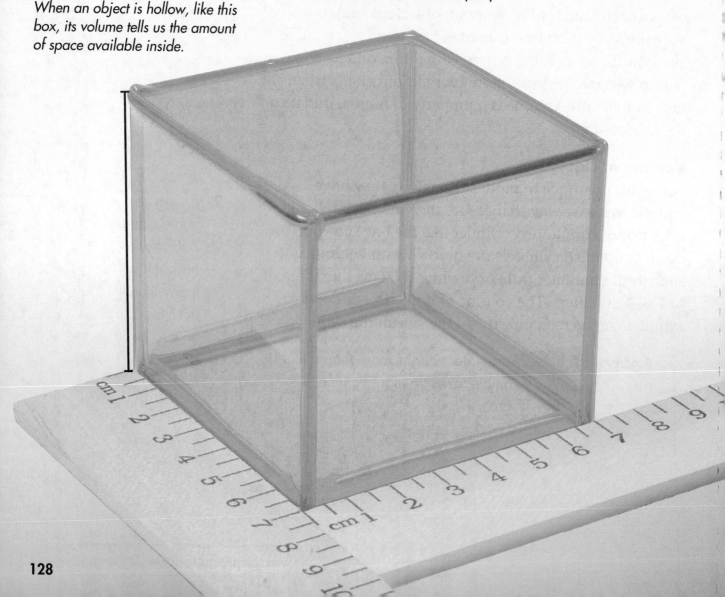

Sometimes we need to find the volume of solids that do not have a regular shape. One way to do it is to put the solid in a graduated cylinder that has liquid in it. Since the solid has volume, it will take up some space and push some liquid aside. The liquid is forced to go up. As a result, the level of the liquid will rise. It will look as if more liquid had been added. You may have seen this happen in a glass of water when you put ice cubes in it.

The apparent change in the volume of the liquid will be equal to the volume of the solid. For example, if you drop a marble in the liquid and the level rises by 2 mL, this means that the marble has a volume of 2 mL.

Volume of Gases

Gases are made of matter. Therefore, they have volume. In fact, a small amount of gas can fill a large volume. We often don't realize that gases are made of matter. You can measure the volume of a gas with a graduated cylinder held upside-down, as shown in the picture below, on the right. At first, the cylinder is filled with water. When air is blown into the cylinder, bubbles rise and push some water down. The volume of the water that was pushed down is equal to the volume of the gas that was blown in.

Lightning Lab

A Drop in Volume

Work over a sink. Fill two identical cups to the top with water. Find two objects that sink. Place one object in each cup. Remove the objects with a spoon without spilling more water. Compare the drop in the water level. Tell which object has the greater volume.

4. ◎ **Cause and Effect** Circle one cause and **underline** one effect in this section.

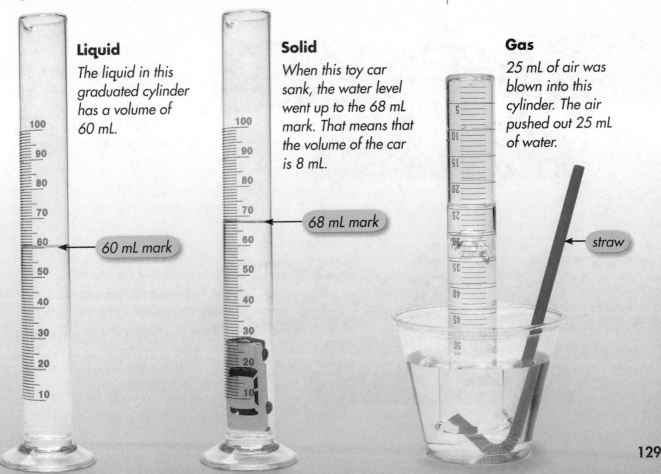

Liquid
The liquid in this graduated cylinder has a volume of 60 mL.

60 mL mark

Solid
When this toy car sank, the water level went up to the 68 mL mark. That means that the volume of the car is 8 mL.

68 mL mark

Gas
25 mL of air was blown into this cylinder. The air pushed out 25 mL of water.

straw

Mass

The amount of matter in a solid, liquid, or gas is called its **mass.** The mass of an object makes the object resist a push or a pull. It takes a bigger push or pull to change the motion of an object if it has a large mass.

The mass of a small object can be measured in units called grams (g). The gram is a small unit: a $1 bill has a mass of approximately 1 g. For objects with more mass, the kilogram (kg) can be used. One kilogram equals 1,000 g.

To measure mass, you can use a pan balance. The pan balance helps you to compare a mass that you know with a mass that you do not know. First, you place the unknown mass on one pan of the balance. Then, on the opposite pan, you place masses that you know. You keep adding known masses until the pans are level. At that point, the masses on the left and right pans are equal. Since you know the total mass on one side, you can figure out the mass on the other side. For example, a plastic box was placed on the left pan of the balance shown in the top picture below. On the right pan, gram cubes were added until the arms of the balance were level. The total mass of all the cubes equals the mass of the box.

5. CHALLENGE Look at the picture at the bottom of the page. Count the cubes. What is the mass of the water inside the container? How can you tell?

....

....

....

....

....

....

....

....

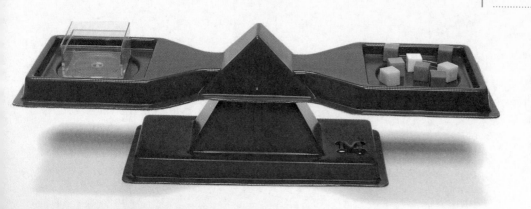

It takes 8 cubes to balance the empty plastic box on the left pan. Each cube has a mass of 1 g. Therefore, we know that the box also has a mass of 8 g.

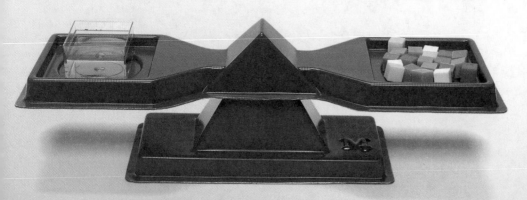

Now the box has some water. More cubes are needed to balance the additional mass. The mass of all these cubes balances the total mass of the box and the water.

Weight

Earth is constantly pulling all objects down. This downward pull is a force. The force of Earth's pull on an object is called **weight.** One way to get an idea of the weight of an object is to lift the object. An object that feels heavy has a lot of weight.

Weight can be measured in units called newtons (N). The newton is not a very large unit. An apple weighs approximately one newton.

To measure weight, you may use a spring scale like the one shown on the right. The heavier an object is, the more the spring in the scale stretches. You can read the weight directly on the scale.

Earth pulls with more force on objects that have a large mass. Therefore, objects that feel heavy usually have more matter than objects that feel light. However, you must be careful when you measure weight because heavy objects can appear to be light in some situations. For example, heavy objects feel lighter when you are underwater. They do not actually weigh less, because Earth does not stop pulling down on them. But water exerts an upward push that helps you with the lifting.

6. **Measure** Since weight is a force, it can stretch a spring. Look at the pictures to the right. Measure the amount of stretch caused in the spring by three chain links and by six chain links. Describe the pattern.

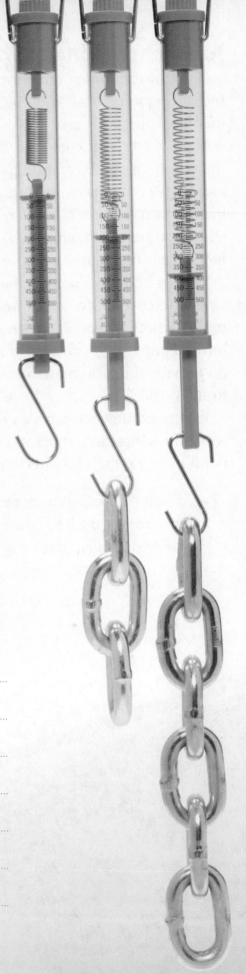

Amount of Matter

The true amount of matter in an object is its mass. Measuring mass gives you the correct amount of matter an object has.

However, it is often more convenient to measure the weight of an object than its mass. For this reason, we often use weight instead of mass to measure an amount of matter. For example, when you step on a bathroom scale, you are in fact measuring your weight.

Weight and mass are not the same thing. One difference is that your mass is the same no matter where you go. It does not depend on the force of gravity. By contrast, your weight depends on gravity and it decreases as you move away from Earth.

Another difference between weight and mass is that weight has direction: it points down. Mass does not point in any particular direction.

7. **Calculate** The person standing on the scale below has a mass of 81.8 kg. The scale reads 180 pounds. How many pounds does a mass of 1 kg weigh?

The man above is carrying a load that has a large volume. However, he does not seem to find it too heavy.

A bathroom scale may measure your weight in pounds. The pound is not a metric system unit. Metric units are used for science all over the world, but other units, like the cup or the degree Fahrenheit, are still used for other purposes.

myscienceonline.com | Got it? | 60-Second Video

Weight depends both on the mass of an object and on its distance from Earth. Since most of us spend all our lives close to the surface of our planet, we normally don't weigh things far away from Earth. Therefore, to us, the weight of an object depends only on its mass. Weight can give us a good idea of the amount of matter in an object.

Volume also gives us some idea of the amount of matter in an object. Mountains are large and have a large amount of matter. A grain of rice is small and has a small amount of matter. But volume is not always the best way to measure an amount of matter. A large volume does not always guarantee a large amount of matter. For example, a small mass of air can fill a large volume, and a small volume of gold can have a large mass.

8. Infer Look at the man carrying a load on the previous page. What can you infer about the amount of matter he is carrying?

Got it?

🔵 5.1.1, 5.1.2

8. Describe What is the difference between weight and mass?

9. UNLOCK THE BIG ? What is an advantage of measuring the mass of an object instead of its weight?

⬜ **Stop!** I need help with

⏸ **Wait!** I have a question about

▶ **Go!** Now I know

How do physical changes affect properties?

5.1.3 Demonstrate that regardless of how parts of an object are assembled, the weight of the whole object is identical to the sum of the weight of the parts, but the volume can differ from the sum of the volumes. 5.1.4 Determine if matter has been added or lost by comparing weights when melting, freezing, or dissolving a sample of a substance. (Also 5.NS.1)

1

The pictures above show a possible series of steps in the process of preparing to eat an orange. **Label** the steps.

my planet diary

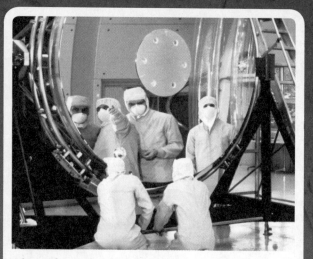

The safe cooling of this giant mirror required patience and care. What precautions can a baker take to prevent the shattering of a glass dish that has just been taken out of the oven?

FunFact

The mirrors of large telescopes can crack easily if they cool down or heat up too fast. To make one of these mirrors, glass is first melted in a furnace. Then, to cool down safely, the mirror needs to stay in the furnace for a very long time. In fact, very large mirrors must stay in the furnace for months! The furnace is kept hot, and its temperature is lowered only little by little.

You can see this effect at home. Have you noticed how an ice cube cracks when you put it in water at room temperature? This happens because the outside of the ice cube warms up as soon as it touches the water, but the inside is still cold. The different rate of warming causes parts of the cube to pull away from each other, causing cracks to form.

2 [_____]   3 [_____]

UNLOCK THE BIG ?

I will know whether matter is added or lost during physical changes.

Words to Know
physical change
melting
freezing

Physical Changes

Matter changes all the time. Some changes are physical changes. A **physical change** is a change in some properties of matter without forming a different kind of matter.

There are many kinds of physical changes. When you cut a piece of paper into smaller pieces, you do not produce a new material. You still have paper. The paper has undergone a physical change. Some of its properties have changed, but the properties that make it paper are still there. For example, the pieces are smaller than the whole sheet and have a different shape, but they can burn or absorb water. They also keep their color.

Breaking glass and stretching a rubber band are also physical changes. After breaking glass or stretching a rubber band, you still have glass or rubber.

1. **Give an Example** Cutting, stretching, and breaking are three examples of physical change. Write three more examples.

....

....

....

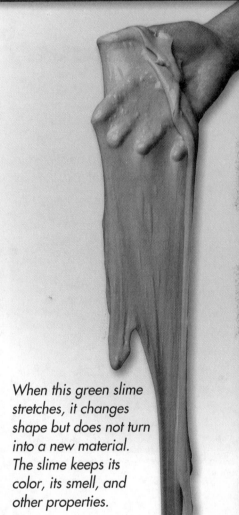

When this green slime stretches, it changes shape but does not turn into a new material. The slime keeps its color, its smell, and other properties.

Temperature and Physical Change

Physical changes may happen more easily or less easily depending on the temperature. For example, butter becomes easier to spread as it gets warm, and rubber becomes less elastic as it gets cold. A wet towel may take longer to dry in the shade than in the sunlight, and sugar is easier to dissolve in hot water than in cold water.

Some physical changes cannot even happen unless the temperature is right. For example, the wax in a candle does not melt unless its temperature rises above a certain point. We know that this is a physical change because the melted wax of a candle still is wax. It hasn't turned into a new substance. It has just become liquid for a while. It becomes solid again as soon as it cools off.

2. **Infer** What physical change do you think is happening to the scented oil below? How does the candle help?

....

....

....

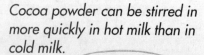

Cocoa powder can be stirred in more quickly in hot milk than in cold milk.

Parts and Whole

Suppose you take the loose plastic blocks in the picture and weigh them one by one. Then, you add their weights to find the total weight. After that, you put the blocks together to form a toy house like the one in the picture. Finally, you weigh the toy house as a whole.

How much do you think the assembled toy house will weigh? It looks different from the loose blocks. It has a different shape. Maybe it seems stronger and more compact. Do you think it will have the same weight as the loose blocks?

The weight of the house is in fact the same as the weight of the loose blocks. It is the same because the house is made of the same blocks. No new blocks were added and no blocks were left over.

In the same way, physical changes happen without any particles being created or destroyed. Physical changes can make an object look different, but the parts of the object are simply rearranged. Matter is not added or taken away. Therefore, the weight is the same before and after a physical change.

3. **Infer** Suppose the toy has a weight of 23 N. You take it apart and attempt to weigh all of the pieces separately. The weights total 19 N. What can you infer about your measurement?

....

....

....

....

Effects of Melting

The change of a solid into a liquid is called **melting.** When a solid melts, its shape changes. If it is inside a container, it collapses and collects at the bottom, like the crayons shown at the right. The new shape matches the shape of the container.

The particles of a solid are very close together and stay in place. When the solid turns into a liquid, the particles are free to move around. However, they still stay very close together. For this reason, the volume of a solid does not change much when the solid becomes a liquid.

Suppose you fill a bucket with ice and pile a few additional cubes on top. You might think there is so much ice that, if you let it melt, the bucket will overflow with water. Instead the melted ice does not fill the bucket all the way. The volume of the ice decreases a little bit when the ice becomes water.

Ice does not lose particles just because it melts. It still has the same number of water molecules after it becomes a liquid. Therefore, its mass and weight stay the same after melting.

4. **Predict** Look at the crayons to the right. What can you say about their weight and volume before and after melting? Which statement can be confirmed by a measurement from the picture?

....

....

....

....

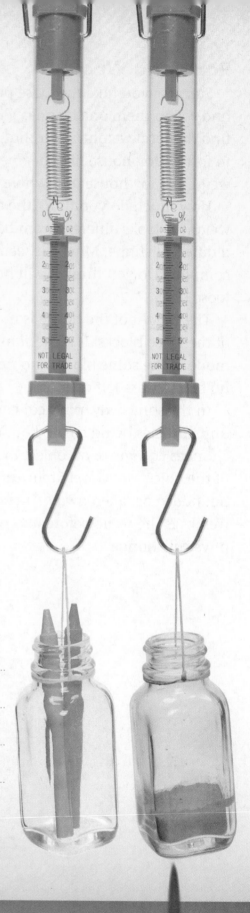

myscienceonline.com | **?** THE BIG | **I Will Know...**

Effects of Freezing

The change of a liquid into a solid is called **freezing.** Most liquids shrink when they freeze. As their particles slow down and take fixed positions, the particles become more closely packed.

A few liquids, such as water, expand when they freeze. In fact, the expansion of freezing water can push out with enough force to burst steel pipes! In many places that have very cold winters, homes can suffer expensive damage when water pipes break and water leaks out. The pipes break because water freezes inside and pushes out as it expands.

5. ◉ **Cause and Effect** (Circle) one cause in the text above. **Underline** one effect.

6. **Explain** As it freezes, the water in the bottle below pushes out hard enough to stretch the bottle. Explain what happens to the mass and volume of the water as the water becomes ice.

....

....

....

....

....

....

Effects of Dissolving

When you mix two different types of matter, the properties of the two substances that are mixed affect the properties of the mixture.

Some properties of the substances are blended in the mixture. For example, the mixture on the right was made by mixing a red liquid and a blue liquid. Therefore, it has a color that is a blend of blue and red.

In contrast, other properties of the two liquids are added when the liquids are mixed. For example, to find the mass of the purple mixture you can add the masses of the red liquid and the blue liquid. Notice that the total mass is the same before and after mixing.

Finally, some properties may change in unexpected ways. Before mixing, the red and blue liquids fill the bottle. After mixing, the total volume is reduced, even though no liquid has been spilled!

7. Infer How could you determine whether matter was lost as the volume of the liquid decreased?

....

....

....

....

....

8. ⊙ **Cause and Effect**
(Circle) one cause and **underline** one effect in the second paragraph of this section.

As the volume of the liquid decreases during mixing, the level of the liquid drops.

unmixed liquid

mixed liquid

The mass stays the same.

The Correct Blend

The mixture on the facing page would be much redder if one bottle of blue liquid had been mixed with seven bottles of red liquid.

When you mix different types of matter, the properties of the mixture do not depend only on the properties of the ingredients. They also depend on the quantity of each ingredient. For example, a can of lemonade concentrate will tell you how much water to add in order to get the right flavor. If you add too little water, the flavor will be too strong. If you add too much, there will be little flavor.

9. **Identify** Look at the picture at the right. Aside from flavor, what other properties of the juice can be adjusted by adding water?

....

....

Got it?   🕐 5.1.3

10. **Explain** Two boxes of breakfast cereal weigh the same, but one seems to have less cereal. A label on each box says that the box was filled by weight, not by volume. Which box do you think has more cereal? Explain.

....

....

11. **UNLOCK THE BIG ?** An origami artist makes a bird figure by folding a square piece of green paper. **Circle** the properties that were NOT changed by this physical change.

   weight   color   shape

⬜ **Stop!** I need help with ....

⏸ **Wait!** I have a question about ....

▶ **Go!** Now I know ....

How do chemical changes affect properties?

Put an ✗ by each material on the car that can rust.

Inquiry Explore It!

How can temperature affect a change?

☑ 1. **Measure** 100 mL of cold water. Pour into a cup. Put 100 mL of warm water into the other cup. Place a thermometer in each cup.

☑ 2. **Record** the temperatures after 1 minute.
cold water _____ °C   warm water _____ °C

☑ 3. Add 2 fizzy antacid tablets to each cup. **Observe.**

Explain Your Results

4. **Communicate** one property that changed. Explain how you know it changed.

....

....

....

5. **Interpret Data** How did temperature affect how long the reaction lasted?

....

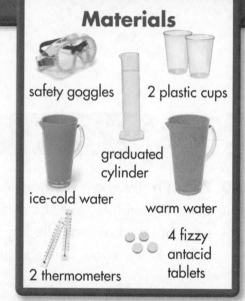

Materials

safety goggles   2 plastic cups

graduated cylinder

ice-cold water   warm water

2 thermometers   4 fizzy antacid tablets

Be careful! Wear safety goggles. Do not taste.

 5.NS.5 Use measurement skills and apply appropriate units when collecting data. (Also **5.NS.4**)

mYscienceonLine.com | **Explore It!** Animation

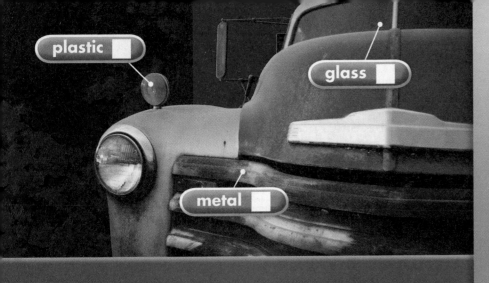

plastic

glass

metal

UNLOCK THE BIG ?

I will know that the amounts of starting materials affects the properties of the products.

Words to Know

chemical change
Law of Conservation
of Mass

Chemical Changes

Remember that physical changes do not form new substances. To form a new substance, a chemical change has to happen. In a **chemical change,** one or more types of matter change into other types of matter with different properties. When a chemical change occurs, atoms rearrange to form new kinds of matter.

It is not always easy to tell if a substance has changed chemically. Evidence of a chemical change may include heat and light, a change in color, a new smell, gas bubbles, or the formation of a solid.

The rusting of iron is a familiar chemical change. When you leave an iron object outside, it slowly becomes rusty. Rust is red and brittle. It is a new substance.

Chemical changes happen all the time around us. The process of photosynthesis, in which plants use water and carbon dioxide to make a new substance—sugar— is a chemical change. Old newspapers also go through a chemical change as they turn yellow with age.

1. **Compare** Silver items can get a dark coating called tarnish over time. How is tarnish like rust?

....

....

These two solutions have no color. When we mix them, a bright yellow substance forms. This suggests that a chemical change has happened.

Effects on Volume and Weight

When you boil an egg, chemical changes take place inside. For example, the egg white starts out runny and clear, but after a few minutes of boiling it becomes hard, white, and opaque. The process of ripening is another common example of chemical change. For example, when a tomato ripens, new substances are formed inside. These substances change the color and the flavor of the tomato.

A raw egg and a green tomato do not shrink or grow as they become a cooked egg and a ripe tomato. They keep their original volume. The chemical changes that transform them have little or no effect on their volume.

In those chemical changes, the particles that make up the egg or the tomato are simply rearranged to form new substances. The new substances that are formed are made from the matter of the substances that were already there. No matter is added or taken away. Therefore, the weight is not affected either.

2. ◉ **Cause and Effect** Use the graphic organizer below to list one cause and its effect from the text above.

Ripening tomatoes release some matter in gas form. The amount of matter lost in this way is very small.

Raw eggs and hard-boiled eggs have very different properties.

Cause

Effect

Some chemical changes do cause a large change in volume. For example, some chemical changes in liquids or solids produce gases. When these chemical changes produce gases, the total volume of the products can be much larger than the volume of the original materials. This happens because solids and liquids occupy a small volume compared to gases.

You probably know that most breads are spongy. Why are they? Bread dough is mixed with a microorganism called yeast. The yeast is alive when mixed into the dough, and it immediately starts chemical reactions that release tiny bubbles of gas. As the bubbles grow, the dough gets bigger and bigger. It can grow to twice its original volume! These little bubbles make the dough spongy. When the dough is baked, the bubbles grow even more.

This machine breaks down liquid water into hydrogen and oxygen, which are gases. As bubbles of gas are released, they fill the volume at the top of the tubes.

3. **Infer** When water is broken down into oxygen and hydrogen, these gases can fill a volume 1,000 times larger than the volume of the water. Explain why or why not matter has been gained in the reaction.

....

....

....

Conservation of Mass

Have you ever seen the ashes left after a log burns? When wood burns, much of the wood seems to disappear. The ash weighs much less than the wood. It also takes up less space. It seems as if burning destroyed some of the matter that was in the log at the beginning.

Chemical changes rearrange matter into new forms, but the amount of matter actually stays the same. Chemical changes often give the impression that matter has been created or destroyed. However, the **Law of Conservation of Mass** states that, in a chemical change, matter cannot be created or destroyed; matter only changes from one form to another.

In the case of burning wood, the ash weighs less than the log because a large part of the matter in the log has become smoke and gas. The original mass of the log has not been destroyed—it has only changed form.

4. **Compare** How are a glowing glow stick and a burning log alike?

....

....

....

5. **Apply** As a candle burns, it becomes shorter and shorter. Does it disappear? Explain.

....

....

....

When wood burns, it combines with oxygen. The products of this change are ash, smoke, soot, and hot gas.

The chemicals inside a glow stick are sealed in. All their matter is still inside the glow stick after the chemical changes are over.

Measuring the weight or the mass of gases and smoke is tricky. For many centuries people did not even realize that smoke and gas have mass. The Law of Conservation of Mass can be confirmed by observing chemical changes in sealed containers that do not allow matter to get in or out. If you place a piece of wood inside a closed container with enough air to let it burn completely, you will find that the total weight of the container and its contents is the same before and after burning. Mass is conserved even if the volume of the products of a chemical change is very different from the volume of the original substances.

6. **Explain** As the fuel in a car tank is used up, the mass of the fuel decreases. What do you think happens to this mass?

7. **Infer** This milk is spoiled after being left out of the refrigerator. It has separated into two parts. What can you infer about the total weight of these two parts?

At-Home Lab

Where does the mass go?
Wear goggles. Put a few milliliters of vinegar in a bottle. Add a spoonful of baking soda. Quickly cover the opening of the bottle with the mouth of a balloon. Observe the change. What happens to the balloon? What does this tell you about the amount of matter in the bottle?

Same Components, Different Products

We use the letters *s*, *o*, and *n* to write the words *son* and *soon*, but the word *soon* has one more *o*. A difference of a single letter can result in two words with very different meanings. In a similar way, the products of chemical reactions can be very different depending on the number and arrangement of their particles.

For example, the two minerals shown on this page have different colors. They also melt at different temperatures. However, they turn out to be made of the same components: the elements arsenic and sulfur. If their components are the same, why are the minerals different? One reason is that a sample of orpiment contains more sulfur than an equal quantity of realgar.

8. **Observe** List three differences in physical properties between realgar and orpiment.

....

....

People used to crush orpiment into a fine powder to make yellow paint.

Realgar has been used to make red paint and fireworks.

When propane gas burns in a stove, it combines with oxygen. This chemical change produces carbon monoxide and carbon dioxide, two gases made of oxygen atoms and carbon atoms. Like orpiment and realgar, these two gases are made of the same type of atoms but have different properties. Carbon monoxide is more toxic than carbon dioxide. If a fire gets enough oxygen, there tends to be more carbon dioxide and less carbon monoxide. The amount of oxygen available affects the products of the fire and sometimes the color of the flame.

9. **Suggest** How can you reduce the amount of carbon monoxide produced in a fireplace?

....

....

....

....

Got it?

10. **Summarize** What does the Law of Conservation of Mass say?

....

....

11. **UNLOCK THE BIG ?** What properties might change during a chemical reaction?

....

....

⬜ **Stop!** I need help with ....

⏸ **Wait!** I have a question about ....

▶ **Go!** Now I know ....

Investigate It!

What can happen if different amounts of water are added to cornstarch?

Follow a Procedure

☑ **1.** Add 50 mL of water to Cup A.

☑ **2.** Stir slowly. **Observe** the mixture.
Record your observation on the chart.
Stir quickly. Observe. Record. Repeat several
times to make sure your results are consistent.

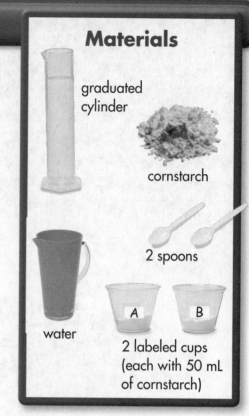

Materials

graduated cylinder

cornstarch

2 spoons

water

2 labeled cups
(each with 50 mL
of cornstarch)

Inquiry Skill Scientists
make careful observations
and record data accurately.
They use their data to help
make **inferences.**

Mixture Observation Chart

	Amount of Water (mL)	Observation of Properties	
		Slow stir	Quick stir
Cup A	50		
Cup B	25		

3. Add 25 mL of water to Cup B. Repeat Step 2, but first **predict** what you will observe. Discuss your prediction with other students. Then repeat Step 2.

Analyze and Conclude

4. Compare the **prediction** you made in Step 3 with results of your **investigation.**

5. UNLOCK THE BIG **?** **Infer** You started with different quantities of water in Cup A and Cup B. Did different quantities of starting material result in a mixture with different properties? Explain.

Sidewalks & Playgrounds

Concrete is everywhere in our world. Highways, skyscrapers, sidewalks, and skate parks are often made of concrete. Ancient Romans used materials similar to concrete to build structures. Some of those structures are still standing today.

Concrete is made of many different materials. The main ingredient is cement—a human-made material. Cement is a fine powder that includes several different minerals. To make concrete, cement is mixed with sand, gravel, crushed rock, and water. Once concrete is set, or hardened, it is very strong and long-lasting.

What makes concrete so strong? One of the materials that makes it so strong is water. Surprised? When workers pour concrete it is very wet, but days later it is dry. The water does not just evaporate—it changes chemically! The water and cement react to form a gel. As the water and cement continue to react, they harden into concrete.

APPLY
THE BIG
?

How does mixing water and cement change their properties?

Vocabulary Smart Cards

- volume
- mass
- weight
- physical change
- melting
- freezing
- chemical change
- Law of Conservation of Mass

Play a Game!

Cut out the Vocabulary Smart Cards.

Work with a partner.

Player 1 chooses a Vocabulary Smart Card.

Say as many words as you can think of that describe that vocabulary word to Player 2.

Player 2 guesses the word.

physical change
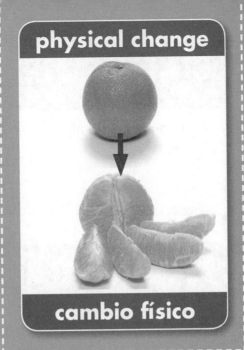
cambio físico

volume
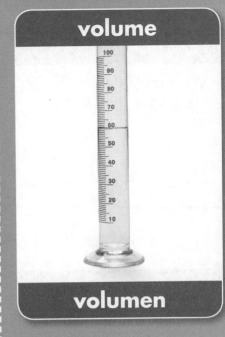
volumen

melting
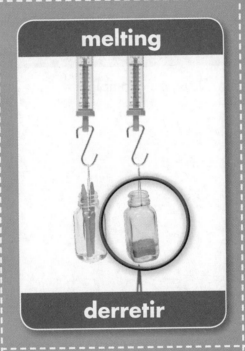
derretir

mass

masa

freezing

congelación

weight
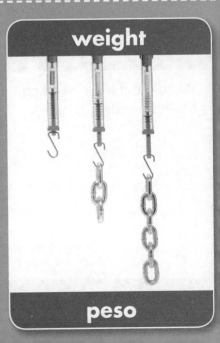
peso

the amount of space an object takes up

What is a different meaning of this word?

....

....

....

cantidad de espacio que un objeto ocupa

a change in some properties of matter without forming a different kind of matter

Write an example of this term.

....

....

cambio en algunas de las propiedades de la materia sin que se forme un nuevo tipo de materia

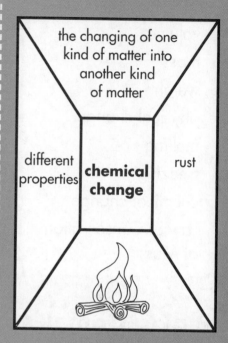

the changing of one kind of matter into another kind of matter

different properties

chemical change

rust

the amount of matter in a solid, liquid, or gas

Write a sentence using this word.

....

....

....

cantidad de materia que tiene un sólido, líquido o gas

the change of a solid into a liquid

Draw an example

cambio de sólido a líquido

Make a Word Frame!

Choose a vocabulary word and write it in the center of the frame. Write or draw details about the vocabulary word in the spaces around it.

the force of Earth's pull on an object

Write a different meaning for this word.

....

....

....

....

fuerza con que la Tierra atrae un objeto

the change of a liquid into a solid

Write a sentence using this word.

....

....

....

....

cambio de líquido a sólido

chemical change

cambio químico

Law of Conservation of Mass

Ley de la Conservación de la Masa

a change of one or more types of matter into other types of matter with different properties

Write an example of this term.

....

....

cambio de uno o más tipos de materia a otros tipos de materia con propiedades diferentes

a rule stating that in a chemical change, mass is not created or destroyed; it only changes from one form to another

Write an example of this term.

....

regla que dice que en un cambio químico la masa no se crea ni se destruye; solamente pasa de una forma a otra

Lesson 1

How do you measure matter?

- Volume is the amount of space that an object takes up.
- Mass is the true amount of matter in an object.
- Weight is a force but it can give an idea of the mass of an object.

Lesson 2

How do physical changes affect properties?

- Physical changes do not change substances into new substances.
- Weight is not affected by mixing, freezing, or melting.
- Volume can be affected by mixing, freezing, and melting.

Lesson 3

How do chemical changes affect properties?

- In a chemical change, one or more new substances form.
- Two chemicals in different amounts can form different substances.
- Mass is not created or destroyed in chemical changes.

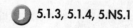
Lesson 1   5.1.1, 5.1.2

How do you measure matter?

1. **Describe** What is one tool you could use to measure the mass of a marble?

2. **Write about It** Describe the difference between weight and mass.

3. **Vocabulary** _____ is the amount of space an object takes up.
   A. Weight
   B. Volume
   C. Mass
   D. Balance

Lesson 2   5.1.3, 5.1.4, 5.NS.1

How do physical changes affect properties?

4. **Classify** List five examples of physical changes.

5. **Infer** Someone leaves a chocolate bar on a park table in the sun. After one hour, the heat has melted the bar. **Circle** the properties that have changed.

   temperature   color   shape   flavor

6. **Calculate** A miner found three gold nuggets and melted them together to form a single large nugget. This large nugget weighed 5.5 N. If two of the original nuggets weighed 1.0 N and 2.3 N, what was the weight of the third nugget?
   A. 1.3 N
   B. 2.0 N
   C. 2.2 N
   D. 5.1 N

Lesson 3

How do chemical changes affect properties?

7. ⊙ **Cause and Effect** (Circle) one cause in the text below. **Underline** one effect.

> Some fruits ripen faster inside a closed bag. Many fruits release a small amount of gas as they ripen. This gas makes ripening faster. In a closed bag, the gas cannot drift away and the fruit is exposed to the gas more directly. As a result, the fruit ripens faster.

8. **Suggest** At the pharmacy, you can buy hydrogen peroxide to disinfect wounds. Hydrogen peroxide is made of oxygen and hydrogen, just like water. Why doesn't water act as a disinfectant, too?

9. **Determine** Which of the following is not an example of a chemical change?
   A. lighting a match
   B. popping popcorn
   C. slicing an apple
   D. burning a marshmallow

10. **APPLY THE BIG ?** **What are the properties of matter?**

Think about the physical and chemical changes matter can go through. What properties of an object can be affected when the object goes through a physical or chemical change? What properties stay the same? Give examples.

Multiple Choice

1 Suppose you boil an egg. What property is changing?

   A. volume

   B. mass

   C. weight

   D. color

Constructed Response

2 When an object goes through a chemical change, does the amount of matter change? Give an example and explain.

....

....

....

....

....

....

....

....

....

🔵 5.1.4

Extended Response

3 After learning about the universe, Lilly wondered how much she would weigh on other planets. On Earth, Lilly weighs 82 lb. She asked her teacher to help her find out how much she would weigh on Jupiter, Mars, and Saturn. The chart below shows how much she would weigh on those planets.

Lilly's Weight on Other Planets

Planet	Weight (lb)
Jupiter	208.3
Mars	30.9
Saturn	87.2

What two things affect how much Lilly weighs?

....

....

....

Why do you think that Lilly's weight on Saturn is similar to her weight on Earth?

....

....

....

🔵 5.1.2

Aerogels

aerogel

When many people think of oil polluting the environment, they often think on a large scale, such as an oil tanker spilling millions of gallons of oil into the ocean. Small amounts of oil are deposited every day in sewers and streams and pose a threat to the environment.

One way to clean up oil contamination is with a substance called aerogels. Aerogels are strong solids made from gels. The liquid is removed from a gel and replaced with gas, which changes the properties of the substance. Aerogels are nicknamed "frozen smoke" because they are translucent and can take on either a blue or yellow color, depending on the amount of light present.

Aerogels made from silica gel are especially good at cleaning up spilled oil because they have a low density and are very absorbent. Scientists have been testing their ability to clean up oil by mixing silica aerogel beads with water and corn oil. In one investigation, the aerogel absorbed seven times its weight! Because they work so well at removing corn oil from water and are relatively cheap to produce, aerogels may become one of the best methods for removing oil pollution from the environment.

Underline one reason why using silica aerogels may be a good way to clean up oil in the environment.

Materials

ice cubes

3 plastic cups

newspaper

wool cloth

masking tape

clock

Which is the best way to slow the rate at which ice melts?

Ask a question.
Which insulator is better at slowing the rate at which ice melts?

State a hypothesis.

1. Write a **hypothesis** by circling one choice and finishing the sentence.

If cups containing identical ice cubes are wrapped in wool cloth or wrapped in newspaper, or unwrapped, then the ice cube
(a) *wrapped in wool cloth*
(b) *wrapped in newspaper*
(c) *unwrapped*
will take longest to melt because

....

....

Identify and control variables.

2. In this **experiment** you will measure the time it takes for each ice cube to melt. You will change only one **variable.** Everything else must remain the same. What should stay the same? List two examples.

....

....

3. Tell the one change you will make.

....

....

....

5.NS.1 Make predictions and formulate testable questions. **5.NS.2** Design a fair test. **5.NS.7** Keep accurate records in a notebook during investigations and communicate findings to others using graphs, charts, maps and models through oral and written reports. **5.NS.9** Compare the results of an investigation with the prediction. (Also **5.NS.3, 5.NS.5, 5.NS.8**)

Design your test.

☑ **4.** Draw how you will set up your test.

☑ **5.** List your steps in the order you will do them.

Do your test.

☑ **6.** Follow the steps you wrote.

☑ **7. Record** your results in the table.

☑ **8.** Scientists repeat their tests to improve their accuracy. Repeat your test if time allows.

Collect and record your data.

☑ **9.** Fill in the chart.

Work Like a Scientist
Scientists work with other scientists. Communicate with other groups to compare the results of your investigation.

Interpret your data.

☑ **10.** Use your data to make a bar graph.

11. Look at your graph closely. Compare the effectiveness of the insulating materials.

....

....

....

....

....

....

12. Identify the evidence you used to answer the question.

....

....

....

....

....

....

....

....

State your conclusion.

13. Communicate your conclusion. Compare your **hypothesis** with your results. How did your results with others compare?

....

....

....

....

....

....

....

Technology Tools
Your teacher may want you to use a computer (with the right software) or a graphing calculator to help collect, organize, analyze, and present your data. These tools can help you make tables, charts, and graphs.

First look at the trend shown by your bar graph. Then conclude which material was the best insulator.

MATERIALS

- safety goggles
- 2 clear plastic cups
- 2 sheets of paper
- plastic spoon and vinegar
- Compound A and Compound B

Using Scientific Methods

1. Ask a question.
2. State your hypothesis.
3. Identify and control variables.
4. Make a plan.
5. Test your hypothesis.
6. Collect, record, and interpret your data.
7. State your conclusion.
8. Do repeated trials.

Plan an Investigation

Suppose your teacher gives you an unknown substance. How can you identify the substance? Think about what you have learned about chemical changes. Use this information to plan an investigation you could use to identify the unknown substance. Your investigation should include the following:

- A testable question
- Written instructions for identifying an unknown substance
- A list of materials and tools for carrying out the investigation

5.NS.3

Take the Salt Out

Conduct research on ways to make fresh water from seawater. Try removing the salt from salt water by evaporation and condensation or by freezing. Draw a diagram showing your equipment and your method.

5.1.4

Make a Poster

Make a poster to show that the weights of the parts of an object are equal to the weight of the whole object. Your poster should include pictures, labels, and measurements. Share your poster with your class.

5.1.3

Earth Science

Chapter 5

The Solar System

? What objects in space make up the solar system?

What is happening in the SKY?

The Solar System

 Try It! What does a spiral galaxy look like from different angles?

Investigate It! How can spinning affect a planet's shape?

You may have seen the moon when it looks like a crescent, a shape that looks like a circle with a bite taken out of it. This happens when we can only see part of the moon's sunlit side. The sun usually looks like a full circle, but sometimes the sun can look like a crescent, too.

Explain When do you think the sun might look like a crescent?

....

....

THE BIG ? What objects in space make up the solar system?

What does a spiral galaxy look like from different angles?

Materials

25 cups

☑ **1.** Use cups to make this spiral galaxy.

These cups represent a spiral galaxy. The sun is an average star near the edge of the Milky Way, a spiral galaxy.

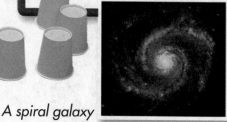

A spiral galaxy

☑ **2. Observe** the cups from directly above. The Milky Way galaxy looks like this from outside the galaxy. Draw a diagram from this angle.

☑ **3.** Kneel to observe the cups at eye level from the edge. The Milky Way galaxy looks like this from Earth, which is near the edge of the galaxy. Draw a diagram from this angle.

Inquiry Skill
You can use a physical **model** to help see things from different angles.

Explain Your Results

4. UNLOCK THE BIG ? Describe the differences in observations from different angles.

....

....

....

5. How is your **model** like a spiral galaxy? How is it different?

....

....

Drawings of Spiral Galaxy Model

Viewed from Above

Viewed from the Edge

 5.2.1 Recognize that our earth is part of the solar system in which the sun, an average star, is the central and largest body. Observe that our solar system includes the sun, moon, seven other planets and their moons, and many other smaller objects, such as asteroids and comets. **5.NS.7** Keep accurate records in a notebook during investigations and communicate findings to others using graphs, charts, maps and models through oral and written reports. (Also **5.NS.3**)

170

Sequence

The order in which events happen is the **sequence** of those events.

The Discovery of a New Planet

William Herschel was an astronomer and a musician who lived in the 1700s. In 1781, Herschel discovered the planet Uranus. Herschel constructed many telescopes over the course of his astronomy career. He used a twenty-foot telescope in 1787 and discovered two moons of Uranus, Titania and Oberon. The most famous of Herschel's telescopes was the forty-foot telescope, which he built in 1789. He used this telescope to see even more details of space objects.

the planet Uranus, as seen from space

Herschel's forty-foot telescope

Practice It!

Use the graphic organizer below to list a sequence of events found in the example paragraph.

First

Next

Finally

Lesson 1

What is the solar system?

5.2.1 Recognize that our earth is part of the solar system in which the sun, an average star, is the central and largest body. Observe that our solar system includes the sun, moon, seven other planets and their moons, and many other smaller objects, such as asteroids and comets.

Envision It!

This object looks different, depending on where you stand.

Inquiry Explore It!

What can you learn from a distance model of the solar system?

☐ **1.** Your teacher will help you select a planet. The chart shows the distance your planet is from the sun in the **model. Measure** and cut adding machine tape to this length. Roll up your tape.

☐ **2.** When all groups are ready go into the hall. Your teacher will be the sun. A student in each group should stand by the sun and hold the free end of the tape. Another student should walk down the hall, unrolling the tape.

Explain Your Results

3. Compare the distances to the planets. Use the **model** to help **make an inference.** Would it be harder to travel to Mars or to Neptune?

....

....

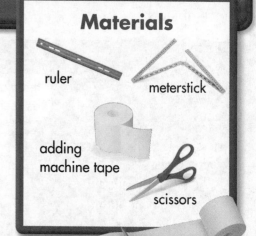

Materials

ruler

meterstick

adding machine tape

scissors

The chart shows distance in cm and m. Select the easier one to use. Select a ruler or a meterstick for your measuring tool.

Planetary Distance Table

Planet		Distance from the Sun in Model: Length of Tape*
Inner Planets	Mercury	30 cm or 0.30 m
	Venus	56 cm or 0.56 m
	Earth	77 cm or 0.77 m
	Mars	120 cm or 1.2 m
Outer Planets	Jupiter	400 cm or 4 m
	Saturn	740 cm or 7.4 m
	Uranus	1500 cm or 15 m
	Neptune	2300 cm or 23 m

*Scale: 1 cm = about 1,940,000 km

5.NS.5 Use measurement skills and apply appropriate units when collecting data. (Also 5.NS.4)

myscienceonline.com | Explore It! Animation

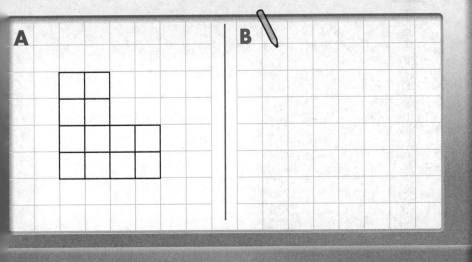

Draw what the object would look like from point B.

I will know what objects in space make up our solar system. I will know that our solar system is part of the Milky Way galaxy.

Words to Know

star   planet

solar system

Lights in the Night Sky

Have you ever been outdoors when the sun sets? At first, you can see no stars. Then, as the sun disappears below the horizon, a few bright stars become visible in the sky. As the sky turns black and your eyes adjust to the darkness, you can see more and more stars forming beautiful patterns.

If you are away from bright city lights and the sky is really dark, you may see what looks like a faint band of light crossing the sky from east to west. This band of light is the Milky Way, our home galaxy. Read on to find out more about galaxies.

The Milky Way is our galaxy.

1. ○ **Sequence** Use the graphic organizer below to show the sequence of events described above.

First

Next

Finally

2. **Suggest** This is what the Milky Way looks like from a mountain. Why do you think it may be hard to see the Milky Way from a big city?

Galaxies

The sun, Earth, and the other planets and moons that together make up the solar system are part of the galaxy known as the Milky Way. A galaxy is a huge system of gas, dust, stars, and other objects that is held together by the force of gravity. There are billions of galaxies in the universe. A few galaxies can be seen without a telescope, but most are so far away that they look like points of light. Using telescopes, astronomers have learned that galaxies come in different shapes and sizes.

Elliptical galaxies are oval. Irregular galaxies have no particular shape. About three-fourths of the galaxies that have been discovered are spiral galaxies. They look like pinwheels. They have bright, bulging middles and thin arms that fan out from the center. The stars in the arms of the galaxy are circling the central bulge of the galaxy. Our Milky Way is a spiral galaxy. However, because we are inside the Milky Way, it does not look like a spiral from our point of view.

3. **Describe** List two types of galaxies and write one characteristic of each.

side view of a spiral galaxy

top view of a spiral galaxy

Our Star

Has it ever occurred to you that the sun has a lot in common with the stars you see at night? The sun is actually a star! A **star** is a huge ball of very hot gas that gives off energy.

The sun is the center of our solar system. The **solar system** is made up of the sun and its planets, along with moons, asteroids, and comets. These objects revolve around the sun in paths called orbits. The sun's gravity holds the objects in their orbits.

The sun has more than 99 percent of the mass in the solar system. The sun is huge compared to Earth. In fact, the sun has more than one million times the volume of Earth. If you think of the sun as a gumball machine, it would take over one million Earth gumballs to fill the sun gumball machine!

The sun is an average-size star, but it gives off large amounts of energy. The temperature inside the center of the sun is very high. The hydrogen particles that make up the sun move very fast. When the particles hit each other, they can combine to form particles of the element helium. This fusion of hydrogen into helium produces most of the sun's energy.

4. **Calculate** Measure the diameter of this dime, in centimeters (cm).

....

Multiply by 100. This would be the diameter of the sun if Earth were the size of the coin:

....

Jupiter

The cloud of dust and gases around a comet reflects sunlight and gives it a fuzzy appearance with a glowing tail.

At-Home Lab

Meteor Shower
Work with an adult. Go online to find information about meteor showers that are visible from where you live. Note the date, the time, and the area of the sky in which they will occur.

Objects in Our Solar System

There are many different objects in the solar system. Some can be seen from Earth without tools. Others require telescopes to be seen.

Planets

A **planet** is a large, round object that revolves around a star and has cleared the region around its orbit. Earth is the third of eight planets revolving around the sun. Some planets have other objects, called moons, orbiting them.

Comets

A comet is a frozen mass of rock, different types of ice, and dust, orbiting the sun. Comets pass through the solar system in very long orbits. As a comet approaches the sun, some of its ice melts into gas, releasing some of its dust. A cloud of dust and gases surrounds and trails behind the comet.

Asteroids

A rocky mass up to several hundred kilometers wide that revolves around the sun is an asteroid. In our solar system, most asteroids orbit in the region between Mars and Jupiter called the Asteroid Belt.

Meteors

A meteor forms when a meteoroid hits Earth's atmosphere. A meteoroid is a small piece of rock that is boulder-sized or smaller. Most are the size of pebbles or grains of sand. When a meteoroid shoots through the air, it heats up quickly. It gets so hot that it glows as a streak of light. Most meteors burn up before they reach Earth's surface. If a meteor does not burn up completely, it may fall to Earth. A meteorite is a meteor that lands on Earth.

5. ◉ **Sequence** What events happen when a meteoroid becomes a meteorite?

....

....

....

....

Meteorites have also fallen on the surfaces of Mars and the moon. Many of the craters on the moon's surface were formed by meteorites. Most meteorites on Earth are quite small. The biggest known meteorite is in Namibia, Africa, and weighs 60 tons.

Meteor Crater, in Arizona, was formed by a meteorite impact.

A

B

6. **Calculate** This crater may be 24 times wider than the meteor that formed it. Measure the diameter of the crater from point A to point B and the diameters of the empty circles. Draw an **X** on the circle that best represents the probable size of the meteor.

Got it?

🔵 5.2.1

7. What is the largest object in the solar system? How much larger is it than Earth?

....

....

8. **UNLOCK THE BIG ?** What objects make up the solar system? What is the sun's position in the solar system?

....

....

⬛ **Stop!** I need help with ....

⏸ **Wait!** I have a question about ....

▶ **Go!** Now I know ....

What is the sun?

5.2.1 Recognize that our earth is part of the solar system in which the sun, an average star, is the central and largest body. Observe that our solar system includes the sun, moon, seven other planets and their moons, and many other smaller objects, such as asteroids and comets.

Envision It!

Discuss whether or not you think the sun has a hard surface like Earth's.

my planet Diary

//// MISCONCEPTION ////

What happens to the stars during the day? You might think they disappear, but they do not. The stars are always in the sky during the day just as they are at night. However, the sun's light is so much brighter than the faint light coming from the stars that the stars cannot be seen. On a dark clear night, without the aid of a telescope, you might see over a thousand stars in the sky.

Do all stars look the same? Explain.

....

....

....

UNLOCK THE BIG ?

I will know the physical characteristics of the sun. I will know why the star Polaris is important.

Words to Know

solar flare
constellation

The Sun as a Star

The sun is the largest object in our solar system. It has more than one million times the volume of Earth. Yet the sun is a medium-sized star. Stars known as giants may be 8 to 100 times as large as the sun. Supergiants are even larger. They may be up to 300 times as large as the sun. Other stars are smaller than the sun.

Scientists are able to calculate the sun's mass. By observing Earth's velocity, its average distance from the sun, and the gravitational constant, scientists have found the sun's mass to be 2 million trillion trillion kilograms.

1. **State** How can scientists determine the mass of the sun?

....

....

2. **Summarize** Compare the size of the sun to the size of other stars. Compare its size to Earth.

....

....

....

....

....

....

....

This is the approximate size of Earth. The distance between Earth and the sun is not to scale.

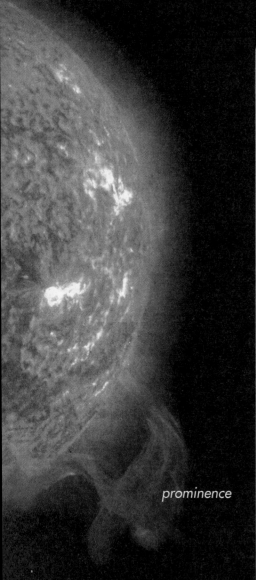

prominence

Characteristics of the Sun

The sun is a fiery ball of hot gases and plasma and has no hard surfaces. It gives off enormous amounts of light and heat. The outer part of the sun is about 5,500°C. The inner core could be as hot as 15,000,000°C.

The Sun's Atmosphere

Like Earth, the sun has an atmosphere. The innermost layer is called the photosphere. It gives off the light energy you see. The thin layer above the photosphere is the chromosphere. The outermost layer is called the corona. The corona extends far into space.

When scientists look at the sun with special equipment, they see dark spots, called sunspots, moving on the face of the sun. Sunspots are part of the photosphere. They may be the size of Earth or larger. They look dark because they are not as hot as the rest of the photosphere. The number of sunspots increases and decreases in cycles of about 11 years.

Solar Eruptions

Two types of eruptions that take place on the sun are prominences and solar flares. A prominence looks like a ribbon of glowing plasma that leaps out of the chromosphere into the corona. Prominences may appear and then disappear in a few days or months.

A **solar flare** is an explosive eruption of waves and particles into space. Solar flares are similar to volcanoes on Earth. A solar flare causes a bright spot in the chromosphere that may last for minutes or hours. Along with extra-bright light, solar flares also give off other forms of energy. This energy is powerful enough to interrupt radio and satellite communication on Earth.

3. **Apply** Why might space agencies not want to send astronauts into space during solar flares?

....

....

4. **Identify** What are the physical characteristics of the sun?

....

....

Solar flares give off more light than other parts of the sun. They emit radio waves, visible light, X rays, plasma, and other radiation.

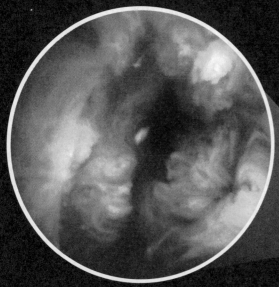

5. **Describe** What is a solar flare similar to on Earth?

6. **Summarize** Fill in the blanks in the captions on this page.

The .... is the outermost layer of the sun's atmosphere.

The sun's surface is the ....

Core

A .... is a dark spot on the sun.

Eruptions of ribbon-like glowing plasma are called ....

7. Explain Why is Polaris called the North Star?

....

....

....

8. Infer How might constellations help scientists study the sky?

....

....

....

....

Constellations

In the past, people looked up at the night sky and "connected the dots" formed by the stars. They saw patterns that reminded them of bears, dogs, and even a sea monster! Today, scientists divide the night sky into eighty-eight constellations. A **constellation** is a group of stars that forms a pattern. Many constellation names are the names of the star patterns that people used long ago.

The star pattern called the Little Dipper contains a star called Polaris. Polaris, or the North Star, is a very hot and very large yellow-white star. It is almost 2,500 times as bright as the sun. It does not look larger than the sun because it is much farther away. Polaris is an important star in navigation. Because it is almost directly above the North Pole, Polaris doesn't seem to move as Earth rotates. If you can find Polaris in the sky, you can tell which direction is north. Early explorers used Polaris as a guide to direct them in their travels. If they located Polaris, then they could determine in which direction they were headed.

At-Home Lab

Light Sky, Dark Sky
Work with an adult. Stand in a brightly lit area at night. Look at the night sky. Then stand in a place that is dark. Look at the sky again. Can you see more or fewer stars than before? Can you see the Milky Way? How did light pollution affect the number of stars you saw?

Little Dipper

Polaris

Big Dipper

myscienceonLine.com | Got it? 60-Second Video

Stars on the Move

Stars are not always in the same place in the sky. They seem to move in predictable ways. Suppose you looked at the sky early one evening and found the Big Dipper. When you looked two hours later, the Big Dipper seemed to have moved toward the west. Actually, the Big Dipper did not move, but you moved. The spinning of Earth makes the stars appear to move from east to west across the sky.

9. **Infer** This time-lapse photo shows how stars seem to move as Earth rotates, or spins. Why are the stars in a circular pattern?

....

....

....

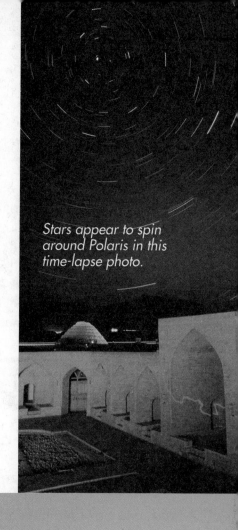

Stars appear to spin around Polaris in this time-lapse photo.

Got it?

🕐 5.2.1

10. **Summarize** If other stars are brighter and larger than the sun, why does the sun appear so large?

....

....

11. **Describe** What is the significance of Polaris, the North Star?

....

....

....

⬜ **Stop!** I need help with ....

⏸ **Wait!** I have a question about ....

▶ **Go!** Now I know ....

Lesson 3

What are the inner planets?

5.2.1 Recognize that our earth is part of the solar system in which the sun, an average star, is the central and largest body. Observe that our solar system includes the sun, moon, seven other planets and their moons, and many other smaller objects, such as asteroids and comets.

Envision It!

What planet do you think this picture shows?

Inquiry Explore It!

How does distance affect orbiting time?

☑ **1.** Make 2 clay balls the size of golf balls.

☑ **2.** Push one ball onto the end of a meterstick. Push the other ball onto the end of a ruler.

☑ **3.** Hold up each stick. Set the empty ends on the floor.

☑ **4.** Let go of both sticks at the same time. **Observe** closely.

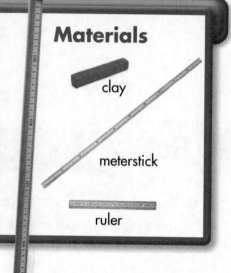

Materials

clay

meterstick

ruler

Explain Your Results

5. Which ball hit the ground first?

....

6. Infer How might a planet's distance from the sun affect the time it takes to make one orbit?

....

....

myscienceonLine.com | **Explore It!** Animation

5.NS.3 Plan and carry out investigations as a class, in small groups or independently, often over a period of several class lessons.

UNLOCK THE BIG ?

I will know the common characteristics of the inner planets and the position of Earth in the solar system.

Words to Know

inner planet
orbit
moon

Planets

The solar system is made of the sun and its planets, along with moons, asteroids, and comets. There are eight known planets that revolve around the sun. The four closest planets to the sun are called **inner planets.** Inner planets have rocky surfaces. Mercury, Venus, Earth, and Mars are the inner planets.

Because all the planets revolve around the sun and the stars that we see in the sky are much further away, we can see the planets change positions relative to the stars from one night to the next.

Even though some planets seem to shine, they do not give off their own light like stars do. A planet shines because light from a nearby star reflects off the planet's surface.

1. **Locate** The illustrations show what the night sky might look like three weeks apart. **Circle** the object in the sky that might be a planet.

November 4

November 25

of gravity. Gravity is the force of attraction between objects. The force of the sun's gravity is large enough to keep planets around the sun. Without this force, the planets would not stay in their orbits.

2. Infer. Planets have years of different lengths because of the lengths of their orbits. Draw an ✗ on the planet with the longest year.

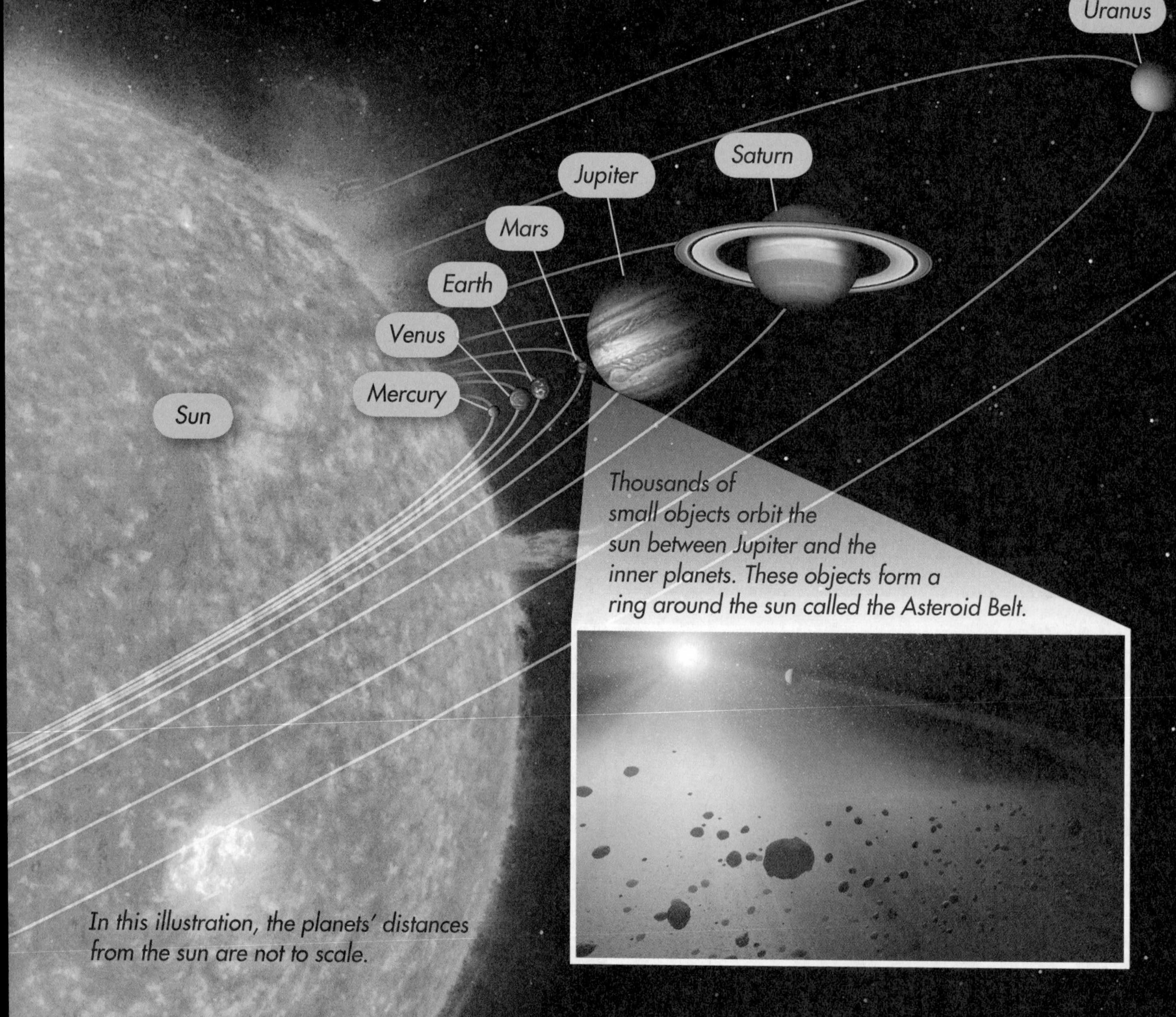

Uranus

Saturn

Jupiter

Mars

Earth

Venus

Mercury

Sun

Thousands of small objects orbit the sun between Jupiter and the inner planets. These objects form a ring around the sun called the Asteroid Belt.

In this illustration, the planets' distances from the sun are not to scale.

Mercury

Mercury is the closest planet to the sun. It is a small planet, slightly bigger than Earth's moon. Mercury is covered with thousands of low spots called craters. Craters are made when meteoroids, or rocks that fall from space, crash into the surface.

The *Mariner 10* was the first spacecraft to visit Mercury. Scientists sent the *Mariner 10* in 1973, and it reached the planet in 1974.

Mercury has almost no atmosphere. Because it is so close to the sun, Mercury is scorching hot during the day. Daytime temperatures are much higher than those in the hottest place on Earth. But with no atmosphere to hold in the heat, Mercury is very cold at night.

Neptune

3. Predict How might Mercury be different if it had a thicker atmosphere?

Without an atmosphere to protect it, Mercury is struck by many objects that leave craters on its surface.

Venus is the second planet from the sun. It is about the same size as Earth, but Venus rotates in the opposite direction. Like Mercury, Venus is very hot and dry. Unlike Mercury, Venus has an atmosphere made of thick, swirling clouds. There are strong winds and lightning.

The clouds of Venus are very hot and toxic. They reflect the sun's light very well. This makes Venus one of the brightest objects in Earth's night sky. The clouds also hide the surface of Venus, but scientists have mapped the surface in spite of the clouds. The image on the right was made using radar data from a space probe. The colors were added by computer for better viewing.

Venus with clouds

This image shows what Venus would look like without clouds.

4. ⊙ **Cause and Effect** What makes Venus so bright?

Do the math!

Weight on Planets

How much does an astronaut weigh? That depends. Weight is the measure of the pull of gravity on an object. Different planets have different amounts of gravitational pull.

When an astronaut wears a complete space suit, he or she might weigh about 480 pounds on Earth! The astronaut would weigh less on Mars. The graph shows how much the astronaut would weigh on different planets.

1. The astronaut's weight on Venus would be about $\frac{9}{10}$ of his or her weight on Earth. What would that weight be on Venus? Fill in the bar graph to show your answer.

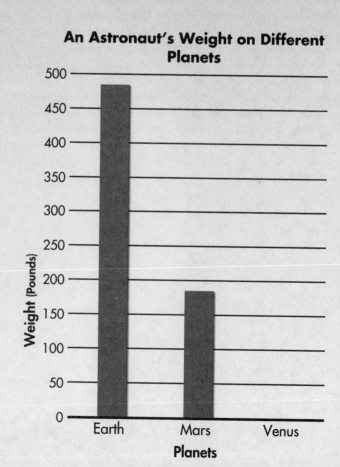

An Astronaut's Weight on Different Planets

Weight (Pounds)

500
450
400
350
300
250
200
150
100
50
0

Earth   Mars   Venus

Planets

Earth, our home, is the third planet from the sun. It is also the solar system's largest rocky planet. Earth is the only planet that has liquid water on its surface. In fact, about $\frac{3}{4}$ of Earth's surface is covered with water.

Earth is wrapped in a layer of gas that extends far out into space. This layer of gas, or atmosphere, makes life possible on Earth. It filters out some of the sun's harmful rays. It also contains nitrogen, oxygen, carbon dioxide, and water vapor. Plants and animals use these gases. Earth is the only planet in the solar system known to support life.

Earth has one large moon, which is about $\frac{1}{4}$ as wide as Earth. A **moon** is a natural object that revolves around a planet. Our moon has almost no atmosphere. It has many craters that formed when meteoroids crashed into its surface. The moon is Earth's natural satellite. A satellite is an object that orbits another object in space. Gravity keeps the moon revolving around Earth, just as it keeps Earth revolving around the sun.

It takes the moon 27 days to revolve around Earth.

Earth spins, or rotates, once every 24 hours.

5. [CHALLENGE] The circles below represent Earth and the moon. Measure the diameter of the large circle, and multiply it by 30. That would be the approximate distance from Earth to the moon at this scale. Draw the two circles in the space provided. Use the distance you found.

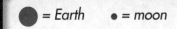 = Earth   • = moon

Mars

Mars is the fourth planet from the sun. The soil that covers most of this rocky planet contains iron oxide. This is a reddish-brown material that makes up rust. This material is why Mars is sometimes called the "Red Planet." Mars has two very small and deeply cratered moons.

The atmosphere of Mars does not have enough oxygen for plants or animals to live. Winds on Mars cause dust storms. These storms are sometimes large enough to cover the whole planet.

Mars has seasons. It also has polar ice caps that grow in the winter and shrink in the summer. Mars has a canyon that is nearly ten times longer than the Grand Canyon in Arizona.

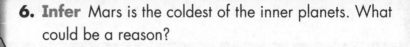

A Martian day is called a sol and lasts just 40 minutes longer than an Earth day. However, the day sky on Mars looks pink instead of blue!

Lightning Lab

Model Planets
Work in small groups. Make models of the inner planets to scale. The diameter of Mercury is 0.4 that of Earth. The diameter of Venus is 0.9 that of Earth. The diameter of Mars is 0.5 that of Earth.

6. Infer Mars is the coldest of the inner planets. What could be a reason?

....

....

myscienceonLine.com | Got it? ⏱ 60-Second Video

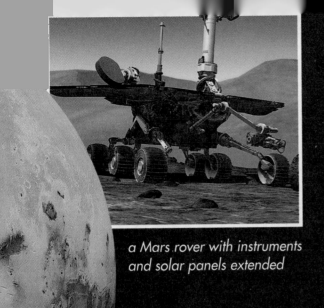

A space probe is a spacecraft that gathers data without a crew. It carries tools for studying different objects in space. Several probes have landed on Mars. The first, *Viking I,* landed on Mars in 1976. In 1997, a robot named *Sojourner* explored part of Mars. In 2004, two robot rovers, *Spirit* and *Opportunity,* landed. These rovers gathered information and sent it back to Earth. Scientists have used the data to learn about the rocks and soil on Mars. The scientists also found evidence that Mars has a lot of frozen water and that it once had an ocean of liquid water.

a Mars rover with instruments and solar panels extended

7. ⊙ **Sequence** Number the space probes in the order in which they landed on Mars.

◯ Viking I   ◯ Spirit and Opportunity   ◯ Sojourner

Got it?

🌙 5.2.1

8. **Compare** What characteristics do Earth and Mars have in common?

....

....

9. **UNLOCK THE BIG ?** Which of the inner planets have moons?

....

▢ **Stop!** I need help with ....

❙❙ **Wait!** I have a question about ....

▶ **Go!** Now I know ....

Lesson 4

What are the outer planets?

5.2.1 Recognize that our earth is part of the solar system in which the sun, an average star, is the central and largest body. Observe that our solar system includes the sun, moon, seven other planets and their moons, and many other smaller objects, such as asteroids and comets.

Envision It!

The surface of Jupiter changes every day. What do you think causes these changes?

Inquiry Explore It!

How are the sizes of the inner and outer planets different?

☑ **1. Measure** the diameter of each paper planet. Use your measurements and the chart to identify and label the planets. Cut out each planet.

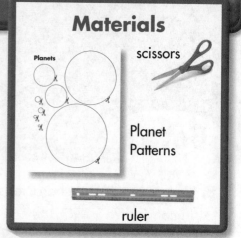

Materials

Planets

scissors

Planet Patterns

ruler

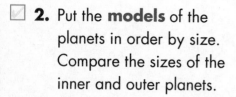

☑ **2.** Put the **models** of the planets in order by size. Compare the sizes of the inner and outer planets.

Explain Your Results

3. After observing your **models,** compare the sizes of the inner and outer planets.

Comparing Planetary Diameters

	Planet	Diameter of Planet (rounded to the nearest 100 km)	Diameter of Model* (mm)
Inner Planets	Mercury	4,900	5
	Venus	12,100	12
	Earth	12,800	13
	Mars	6,800	7
Outer Planets	Jupiter	143,000	143
	Saturn	120,500	121
	Uranus	51,000	51
	Neptune	49,500	50

*1mm=1000 km

myscienceonline.com | Explore It! Animation

5.NS.7 Keep accurate records in a notebook during investigations and communicate findings to others using graphs, charts, maps and models through oral and written reports. (Also **5.NS.3**)

UNLOCK THE BIG ?

I will know that the outer planets consist of Jupiter, Saturn, Uranus, and Neptune, and that they have common characteristics.

Words to Know

outer planet

Gas Giants

There are still four more planets in our solar system beyond Mars—Jupiter, Saturn, Uranus, and Neptune. They are known as the **outer planets.**

The outer planets are much larger than the inner planets. They do not have clearly defined surfaces, like those of the inner planets. We only see the atmospheres of the outer planets. For these reasons these planets are often called gas giants. However, they have liquid inner layers and solid cores.

Each of the outer planets has rings of particles and many moons orbiting it.

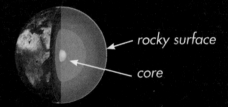

Inner planets have a solid crust.

rocky surface

core

Outer planets do not have a solid crust.

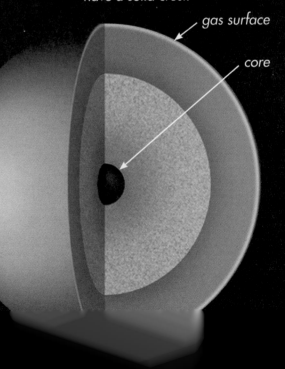

gas surface

core

1. ◎ **Compare and Contrast** Write some similarities and differences between the inner planets and the outer planets.

Jupiter

Jupiter, the fifth planet from the sun, is the largest planet in the solar system. It is a gas giant. Jupiter's atmosphere is mostly hydrogen and helium. The atmosphere of Jupiter shows many bands of color. The planet rotates much faster than Earth. In the time it takes Earth to complete one rotation, Jupiter completes more than two.

Jupiter has many moons. A moon is a natural object that orbits a planet. Some planets, especially the outer planets, have several moons. In 1610, Galileo was the first person to see the four largest moons of Jupiter through his telescope. They are shown to the right.

2. Contrast How are Jupiter and Earth different?

Moons of Jupiter

Ganymede

Io

Europa

Great Red Spot

Callisto

Saturn

The sixth planet from the sun is Saturn. Like Jupiter, Saturn has an atmosphere that contains mostly hydrogen and helium. Saturn is very large, but its density is low.

When Galileo looked at Saturn through his telescope, he saw what looked like a planet with handles! The "handles" were really the brilliant rings that orbit Saturn. The particles making up the rings vary in size from tiny grains to boulders, and they are made of ice, dust, and rock. The inner rings of Saturn revolve faster around the planet than the outer rings.

In 2009 a giant new ring was discovered. The ring is invisible, but its infrared glow was detected by the Spitzer Space Telescope. This ring is tilted relative to the other rings, and rotates in the opposite direction.

3. **CHALLENGE** Two rocks on the rings of Saturn start orbiting at points 1 and 2. After a while, the rock that started at point 1 has moved to point 3. Fill in the number that shows where rock 2 is likely to be, considering its speed.

Lightning Lab

Reading in the Dark
Make a night vision flashlight for reading star charts in the dark. Fold a sheet of red cellophane in half and then into quarters. Use a rubber band or tape to attach it to the end of a flashlight. Test the light. If necessary, add more layers to make the light as red as possible.

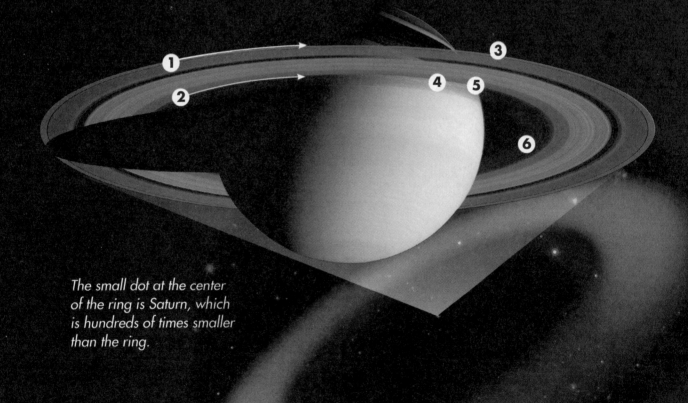

The small dot at the center of the ring is Saturn, which is hundreds of times smaller than the ring.

Uranus

Uranus is the seventh planet from the sun and the most distant planet you can see without a telescope. Uranus has an atmosphere of hydrogen, helium, and methane. The planet is so cold that the methane can condense into a liquid. Tiny drops of this liquid methane form a thin cloud that covers the planet, giving it a fuzzy, blue-green look.

Like the other outer planets, Uranus has rings and many moons. Unlike the rings of Saturn, the rings of Uranus are dark and hard to see with Earth-based telescopes.

Uranus rotates on its side. No one knows why Uranus has this odd tilt. Scientists think a large object may have hit the planet when the solar system was still forming. This bump may have knocked Uranus onto its side.

4. Infer How might Uranus's odd tilt affect its seasons?

....

Neptune

Neptune is too far away to see without a telescope. It is the eighth planet from the sun, and it was discovered in 1846. It takes more than one hundred Earth years for Neptune to orbit the sun. Neptune is the smallest of the outer planets. Even so, if Neptune were hollow, it could hold about 60 Earths.

Neptune's atmosphere is like that of Uranus. Like Uranus, Neptune has a bluish color because of the methane in its atmosphere. Neptune also has storms and bands of clouds like those of Jupiter.

Neptune has at least 13 moons. The largest one is Triton, which may be the coldest object in the solar system.

5. Compare What is similar about the atmospheres of Uranus and Neptune?

....

myscienceonLine.com | Got it? 60-Second Video

Exploring the Giants

Several probes have been sent to explore the outer planets. They were launched from Florida. *Pioneer 10* and *Pioneer 11* were launched in the 1970s, followed by *Voyager 1* and *2*. The *Galileo* probe explored Jupiter in great detail, and the *Cassini* mission has sent back a huge amount of information on Saturn. A smaller probe, named *Huygens*, was launched from *Cassini* and was able to land on Saturn's largest moon, Titan.

6. Write About It What information might you like to have sent to you from a space probe?

....

....

....

Got it?

⬤ 5.2.1

7. Group Think of three terms to describe some characteristics of the inner planets and the outer planets. Use the terms to contrast the inner and outer planets.

....

....

....

8. What are some common characteristics of all planets?

....

....

⬛ **Stop!** I need help with ....

⏸ **Wait!** I have a question about ....

▶ **Go!** Now I know ....

How does Earth move?

Envision It!

> 5.2.2 Observe and use pictures to record how the sun appears to move across the sky in the same general way every day but rises and sets in different places as the seasons change.
>
> 5.2.3 In monthly intervals, observe and draw the length and direction of shadows cast by the sun at several chosen times during the day. Use the recorded data as evidence to explain how shadows are affected by the relative position of the earth and sun. (Also 5.2.1)

The sun is rising in the eastern sky. Describe the path you think the sun will take across the sky during the day.

Inquiry **Explore It!**

How does the sun appear to move?

☑ **1. Observe** the sunrise and sunset for 5 days. Be sure to sit or stand in the same spot each time.

☑ **2.** Use the Sun Chart. Draw pictures to show the sun's position at sunrise. Repeat after 20, 40, and 60 minutes.

☑ **3.** Draw pictures to show the sun's position 60, 40, and 20 minutes before sunset and at sunset.

Materials

Sun Chart

 Be careful! **Do not look directly into the sun!**

Explain Your Results

4. Based on your **observations,** describe the way the sun appears to move each day.

....

....

5. Predict the place the sun will rise and set as the seasons change.

....

....

Go Further *Your teacher may wish to have you test your prediction by repeating this activity in different seasons.*

myscienceonline.com | **Explore It!** Animation

> 5.NS.8 Identify simple patterns in data and propose explanations to account for the patterns. (Also **5.NS.3**)

I will know how Earth rotates and revolves. I will know why the sun, the moon, and stars appear to move across the sky.

Words to Know

axis   revolution
rotation

Earth and the Sun

Think about a time thousands of years ago, before telescopes had been invented and before astronauts had ever traveled into space. If you look at the daytime sky, the sun rises in the east and sets in the west. People naturally thought the sun was moving around Earth.

We now know that the sun is the center of our solar system. Earth and the other planets move around the sun. Earth spins, causing the sun and other objects, such as other stars, to appear to move across the sky.

Before telescopes and space exploration, some people thought Earth was the center of the universe.

1. **Compare and Contrast** Use the graphic organizer below to list what is alike about and different between the way people used to think about Earth and the sun and what we know now.

Then   **Now**

Earth's Rotation

Earth and the other planets of the solar system rotate, or spin, much like a top spins. They each rotate around an imaginary line called an **axis.** The northern end of Earth's axis is the North Pole. The southern end of Earth's axis is the South Pole. One whole spin of an object on its axis is called a **rotation.** One full rotation is what we call a *day*.

Earth rotates around its imaginary axis from west to east. As Earth spins, the sun, moon, stars, and planets only seem to rise in the east and set in the west. When you watch the sun set, remember that it is you who are moving. You are riding on the rotating Earth.

2. Explain Why does the sun appear to move from east to west across the sky?

....

....

3. Fill in the Blank In the illustration below, fill in the missing words in the labels.

Earth completes one

....

in about 24 hours.

Earth's ....
is an imaginary line around
which Earth rotates.

Earth's Revolution

Earth moves in another way too. Earth follows a path called an orbit around the sun. The shape of the orbit is elliptical, which is like a slightly flattened circle. Likewise, the moon moves in an elliptical orbit around Earth. One full orbit of an object around another object is called a **revolution.** Earth's revolution around the sun lasts for just a few hours longer than 365 days. This period may sound familiar to you. It is one year. Also, the moon's revolution around Earth takes 27.3 days, or about a month.

Just as gravity keeps you on Earth, gravity keeps Earth in its orbit around the sun. Because the sun is so massive, its gravity pulls all the planets toward it. This pull keeps the planets from moving in straight lines into space.

Lightning Lab

Day and Night
Shine a flashlight on a globe one meter away. Darken the room. Which parts of the globe have light shining on them? Which are in shadow? Have a partner slowly turn the globe. Explain what you see.

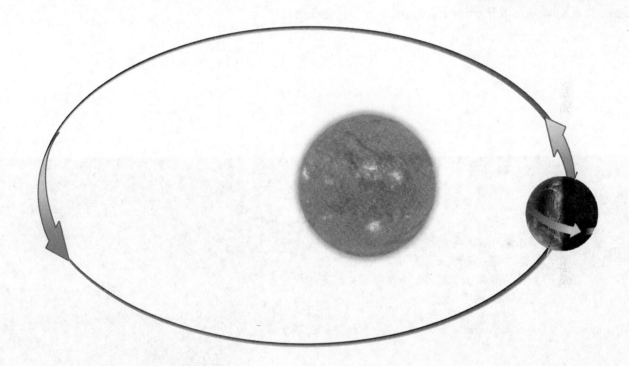

4. **Infer Draw** a representation of the moon's orbit in the diagram above.

5. **Compare and Contrast** How are the orbits of Earth and the moon alike? How are they different?

....

....

Seasons

Earth always tilts the same way during its revolution around the sun. Earth's tilt affects how much sunlight parts of Earth receive. The amount of sunlight an area receives affects its climate and seasons. Seasons change as Earth's axis tilts either toward or away from the sun at different times during its revolution. When the North Pole is tilted away from the sun, sunlight is less concentrated in the Northern Hemisphere. Temperatures drop, and winter sets in. At the same time, the South Pole is tilted toward the sun. The Southern Hemisphere receives concentrated sunlight and has the warm temperatures of summer.

6. [CHALLENGE] In the Northern Hemisphere summer, the northern end of Earth's axis points toward the sun. Describe how you think the axis looks in the spring.

....

....

7. **Calculate** Earth's distance from the sun in January is about 147,000,000 km. In July its distance from the sun is about 152,100,000 km. About how much closer is Earth to the sun in January than in July?

....

....

....

....

....

During the Southern Hemisphere summer, the Sun's rays strike Earth more directly south of the equator. The rays are concentrated, not spread out. Concentrated energy gives this region warm summer weather.

axis

equator

mYscienceonLine.com | Got it? 60-Second Video

The number of daylight hours also changes as the seasons change. On the first day of its summer, a hemisphere has more hours of daylight than at any other time of the year. The least number of daylight hours occurs on the first day of winter. Twice a year the hours of day and night are equal. At this time, Earth's axis points neither toward nor away from the sun.

8. Identify In the diagram, label each part of Earth's orbit with the Northern Hemisphere season that it represents.

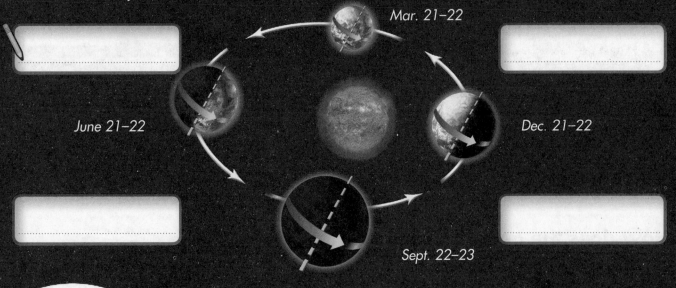

Mar. 21–22

June 21–22

Dec. 21–22

Sept. 22–23

Got it?

5.2.1, 5.2.2

9. Describe What is a rotation? What is a revolution?

....

....

....

10. Explain In what direction do stars, the moon, and the sun seem to move across the sky? Why?

....

....

....

Stop! I need help with ....

Wait! I have a question about ....

Go! Now I know ....

What are the phases of the moon?

5.2.4 Use a calendar to record observations of the shape of the moon and the rising and setting times over the course of a month. Based on the observations, describe patterns in the moon cycle.

Envision It!

Observe the shape of the moon in the sky tonight, and again one night for the next three weeks.

Inquiry Explore It!

How does the appearance of the moon change?

☐ **1. Observe** the moon at the same time each night for 28 days.

☐ **2.** Draw the apparent shape of the moon each night on the Moon Calendar.

☐ **3.** Research the rising and setting times. **Record** these times on the Moon Calendar.

Explain Your Results

4. Draw a Conclusion Think about how the shape of the moon appeared to change. Describe the pattern you observed during the moon cycle. Explain.

....

....

....

....

Materials

Moon Calendar

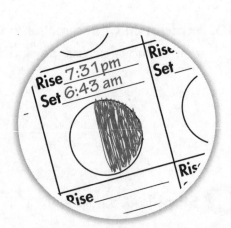

Rise 7:31 pm
Set 6:43 am

myscienceonline.com | **Explore It!** Animation

5.NS.3 Plan and carry out investigations as a class, in small groups or independently, often over a period of several class lessons. (Also 5.NS.8)

Then, color in what you observe. Also write down the time the moon rises in the sky.

UNLOCK THE BIG ?

I will describe the phases of the moon.

Words to Know

eclipse
lunar eclipse
solar eclipse

Sun, Moon, and Earth

The moon is often visible at night. Sometimes you can even see it during the day. From Earth, the moon appears to shine with its own light, just as the sun does. But the moon does not produce its own light. What we call "moonlight" is actually sunlight reflecting off the moon's surface.

It takes about 27.3 days for the moon to complete a trip around Earth. The pull of gravity between the moon and Earth keeps the moon in its orbit. As the moon moves, its inertia keeps it from crashing into Earth.

Like Earth, the moon rotates on an axis. But each time the moon completes a rotation, it also completes one revolution around Earth. This is called synchronous rotation. Because of this synchronous rotation, the same side of the moon always faces Earth. That is the only side you can ever see from Earth.

1. **Analyze** The far side of the moon is often called the "dark side of the moon." Do you think it is always dark on the far side of the moon? Explain.

....

....

....

....

The near side of the moon always faces Earth.

The far side of the moon is never visible from Earth. This photo was taken by a satellite.

Phases of the Moon

The moon's shape in the sky appears to change as you look at it at different times of the month. All the moon's shapes are called the phases of the moon.

As the moon and Earth revolve around the sun, one half of the moon faces the sun and reflects sunlight. However, the side of the moon reflecting sunlight does not always face Earth. How much of that lighted half of the moon faces Earth at any time determines the shape of the moon that we can see.

2. Analyze Study this picture and the calendar below. Circle the description that best matches this phase of the moon.

A Month of Changes

	Sunday	Monday	Tuesday
New moon *Since the moon's dark, unlighted side faces Earth, you cannot see a new moon. The new moon begins a new set of phases.*	3	4	5
First-quarter moon *One half of the lighted half of the moon, or one quarter of the entire moon, is visible.*	10	11	12
Full moon *The entire half of the moon that faces Earth is lighted. You see the moon as a full circle. A full moon appears about a week after the first quarter.*	17	18	19
Last-quarter moon *Gradually, you see less and less of the moon. About a week after the full moon, the moon appears as half of a circle. You see half of the lighted half, or one quarter of the entire moon.*	24	25	26

myscienceonline.com | **THE BIG** **?** | I Will Know...

When the lighted half of the moon directly faces Earth, the moon appears as a full circle of light. It is called a full moon.

We see a full moon only briefly each time the moon revolves around Earth. The rest of the time, only part of the lighted half of the moon faces Earth. Then, you can see only part of the full circle of light. For a short time, you cannot see any of the lighted part of the moon. So, you do not see the moon at all.

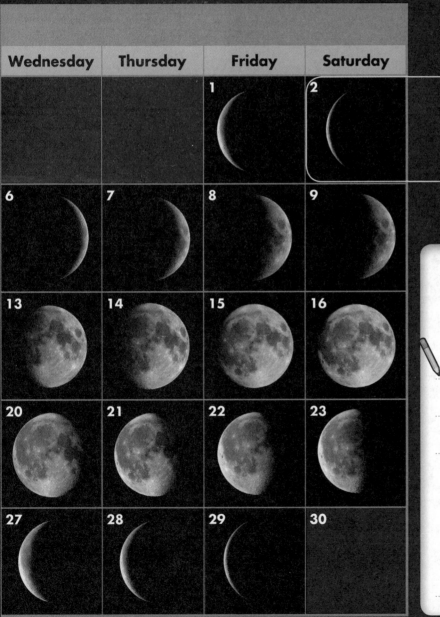

Wednesday	Thursday	Friday	Saturday
		1	2
6	7	8	9
13	14	15	16
20	21	22	23
27	28	29	30

Crescent moon
A sliver of lighted moon appears.

3. **Explain** Does the same side of the moon face the sun at all times? How can you tell?

....

....

....

4. **Infer** During a new moon, what can you infer about the opposite side of the moon?

....

5. Diagram Draw the positions of the sun, moon, and Earth during a lunar eclipse.

Eclipses

An **eclipse** occurs when one object in space passes between the sun and another object and casts its shadow on the other object. Eclipses happen when the moon passes through Earth's shadow and when the moon's shadow falls on part of Earth.

Lunar Eclipses

Reflected sunlight lights up the moon most of the time. However, sometimes the moon and the sun are on exactly opposite sides of Earth. The moon often passes above or below Earth's shadow. A **lunar eclipse** occurs when the moon passes through Earth's shadow.

If only part of the moon is in Earth's shadow during the eclipse, the moon might look as if something took a bite out of it. This is a partial eclipse. If the whole moon is in Earth's shadow, the eclipse is a total lunar eclipse.

Earth's atmosphere keeps the moon visible in a total lunar eclipse. The atmosphere bends and filters sunlight, causing it to shine on the moon and give the moon a reddish color.

A lunar eclipse can last as long as 100 minutes and can happen several times in the same year. Each lunar eclipse is visible from any point on Earth with a clear nighttime view of the moon.

6. Hypothesize If Earth had no atmosphere, what appearance would the moon have from Earth during a total lunar eclipse?

....

....

....

....

Solar Eclipses

When the moon passes between the sun and Earth and casts its shadow on Earth, a **solar eclipse** occurs. From Earth, this looks like something slowly blocking out the sun.

A solar eclipse can be seen only at the places on Earth where the moon casts its shadow. Solar eclipses occur two to five times each year, but each place on Earth experiences one only every few hundred years.

This time-lapse image shows the moon passing between the sun and Earth during a total solar eclipse.

7. **Hypothesize** Why are you more likely to see a lunar eclipse than a solar eclipse?

....

....

Got it?

 5.2.4

8. **Explain** Why does the same side of the moon always face Earth?

....

....

9. **UNLOCK THE BIG ?** Using an almanac or your own observation, record today's date and the phase the moon is in today. Then use a calendar to predict the phase of the moon on the last day of school.

....

....

⬛ **Stop!** I need help with ....

❚❚ **Wait!** I have a question about ....

▶ **Go!** Now I know ....

How can spinning affect a planet's shape?

Follow a Procedure

☐ **1.** Cut 2 strips of construction paper, each 2 cm × 45 cm. Cross them at the center and staple them to make an **X**.

☐ **2.** Bring the 4 ends together and overlap them. Staple them to form a sphere.

Materials

large-size construction paper

scissors   goggles

hole punch   stapler

ruler   pencil

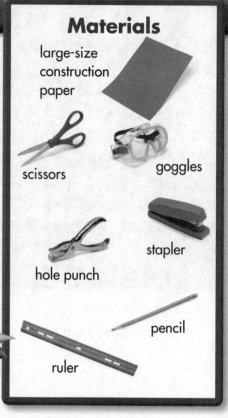

Inquiry Skill Scientists **use a model** when the real object is hard to study.

☐ **3.** Punch a hole through the center of the overlapped ends.

☐ **4.** Push a dull pencil through the hole. Only about 5 cm of the pencil should go in.

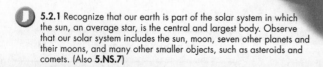

about 5 cm

5.2.1 Recognize that our earth is part of the solar system in which the sun, an average star, is the central and largest body. Observe that our solar system includes the sun, moon, seven other planets and their moons, and many other smaller objects, such as asteroids and comets. (Also **5.NS.7**)

5. Hold the pencil between your palms. Move your hands back and forth to make your **model** spin.

6. What shape do you **observe** when it spins?

....

7. Record your observations.

Effect of Spinning on a Planet's Shape	
Shape When Not Spinning	**Shape When Spinning**
◯	

Analyze and Conclude

8. How did the sphere change shape when you spun it? Make an **inference** about what happened.

....

....

9. UNLOCK THE BIG ？ How is your **model** similar to a spinning planet? How is it different?

....

....

....

....

🔵 5.2.1

Green Bank Telescope

Do you like learning more about the universe? The National Radio Astronomy Observatory in Green Bank, West Virginia, is just the place for young scientists like you to come and explore space.

Green Bank is located in the Allegheny Mountain Range. The telescope there, the Green Bank Telescope, is the world's largest fully movable radio telescope. A radio telescope works by receiving information in the form of radio waves. These waves come from all over the universe. The telescope at Green Bank can be turned so that it can get data from all angles.

APPLY THE BIG ?

How might a trip to the Green Bank Telescope help you know more about the solar system and other objects in space?

....

....

....

....

If you take a trip to Green Bank, you can take a guided tour of the telescope. You can also stop at the science center and view and interact with exhibits about space.

Vocabulary Smart Cards

star
solar system
planet
solar flare
constellation
inner planet
orbit
moon
outer planet
axis
rotation
revolution
eclipse
lunar eclipse
solar eclipse

Play a Game!

Work with a partner. Choose a Vocabulary Smart Card. Do not let your partner see your card.

Play Password. Try to get your partner to say the word or phrase by giving only one-word clues, one at a time. Take turns giving clues and guessing.

213

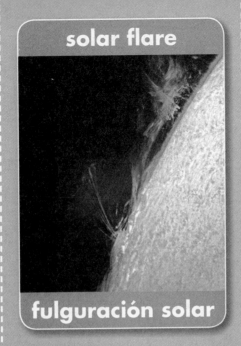

solar flare

fulguración solar

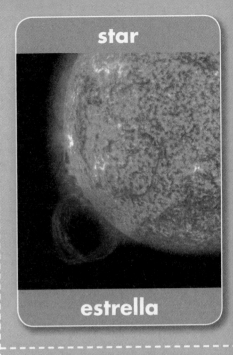

star

estrella

constellation

constelación

solar system

sistema solar

inner planet

planeta interior

planet

planeta

a huge ball of very hot gas that gives off energy

Write a sentence using this term.

....

....

....

bola gigantesca de gas muy caliente que irradia energías

---

an explosive eruption of waves and particles into space

Write one fact about this term.

....

....

....

erupción explosiva de ondas y partículas emitidas hacia el espacio

---

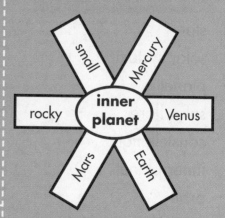

Interactive Vocabulary

Make a Word Wheel!

Choose a vocabulary word and write it in the center of the Word Wheel graphic organizer. Write examples or related words on the wheel spokes.

---

the sun and its planets, along with moons, asteroids, and comets

Write a sentence using this term.

....

....

....

el Sol y sus planetas, junto con las lunas, los asteroides y los cometas

---

a group of stars that forms a pattern

Write one fact about this word.

....

....

....

....

grupo de estrellas que forma una figura

---

a large, round object that revolves around a star and has cleared the region around its orbit

Write two related words.

....

....

cuerpo grande y redondo que orbita una estrella y que ha despejado la zona que rodea su órbita

---

any of the four closest planets to the sun

Write three examples.

....

....

....

cualquiera de los cuatro planetas más cercanos al Sol

214

eclipse	axis	orbit
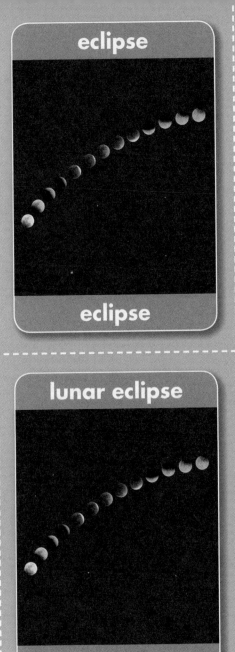		
eclipse	eje	órbita

lunar eclipse	rotation	moon

eclipse lunar	rotación	luna

solar eclipse	revolution	outer planet
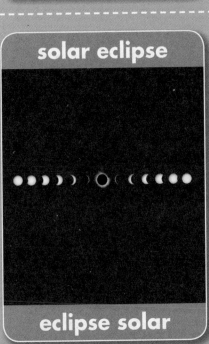		
eclipse solar	traslación	planeta exterior

the path an object takes as it revolves around a star, planet, or moon

Write a sentence using the verb form of this word.

....

....

el camino que sigue un objeto al girar alrededor de una estrella, un planeta o una luna

---

an imaginary line around which an object spins

Draw an example.

línea imaginaria en torno a la cual gira un objeto

---

event in which one object in space gets between the sun and another object

Write another definition for this word, as a verb.

....

....

fenómeno en el que un objeto del espacio se interpone entre el Sol y otro objeto

---

a natural object that revolves around a planet

Draw an example.

satélite natural que orbita un planeta

---

one whole spin of an object on its axis

Write a sentence using this term.

....

....

....

....

una vuelta completa de un objeto en torno a su eje

---

event in which the moon passes through Earth's shadow

Write a sentence using this term.

....

....

....

fenómeno en el que la Luna pasa por la sombra de la Tierra

---

any of the four planets in our solar system beyond Mars

Write a sentence using this term.

....

....

cualquiera de los cuatro planetas de nuestro sistema solar que quedan más allá de Marte

---

one full orbit around an object

Write a sentence using this word.

....

....

....

....

una órbita completa alrededor de un objeto

---

event in which the moon passes between the sun and Earth and casts its shadow on Earth

Write a sentence using this term.

....

....

....

fenómeno en el que la Luna pasa entre el Sol y la Tierra, proyectando su sombra sobre ésta

Study Guide

REVIEW THE BIG ? What objects in space make up the solar system?

Lesson 1

What is the solar system?

- The solar system is made up of the sun and its planets, along with moons, asteroids, and comets.
- The sun is the center of our solar system.

Lesson 2

What is the sun?

- The sun is a medium-sized star.
- A constellation is a group of stars that forms a pattern.
- Stars appear to move across the sky because Earth rotates.

Lesson 3

What are the inner planets?

- Mercury, Venus, Earth, and Mars are the inner planets.
- The inner planets have solid surfaces and are relatively small.
- Objects in the solar system stay in their orbits because of gravity.

Lesson 4

What are the outer planets?

- Jupiter, Saturn, Uranus, and Neptune are the outer planets.
- The outer planets have gaseous surfaces and are relatively large.
- Space probes have been sent to study the outer planets.

Lesson 5

How does Earth move?

- Earth rotates around an imaginary line called an axis.
- Earth revolves around the sun in an elliptical orbit. Earth's tilt and revolution cause seasonal differences in parts of Earth.

Lesson 6

What are the phases of the moon?

- The moon revolves around Earth. The moon is visible from Earth because of sunlight reflecting off the moon's surface.
- The sun, moon, and Earth's positions determine the moon's phases.

Chapter Review

Lesson 1 5.2.1

What is the solar system?

1. **Vocabulary** Explain the difference between meteors, asteroids, and comets.

Lesson 2 5.2.1

What is the sun?

2. **Identify** Which layer of the sun gives off the light energy we see?

Lesson 3 5.2.1

What are the inner planets?

3. **Contrast** What is one way that Mercury and Venus differ from other planets in the solar system?

4. ◉ **Sequence** Read the passage below and then answer the question.

> The solar system is made of the sun and its planets, along with moons, asteroids, and comets. There are eight known planets. The four closest planets are Mercury, Venus, Earth, and Mars.

What is Earth's position in the solar system?

5. **Predict** What would happen to a planet's orbit if the sun disappeared?

Lesson 4 5.2.1

What are the outer planets?

6. Venus orbits the sun at an average distance of 108 million km. Uranus orbits the sun at an average distance of 2.8 billion km. About how many times farther from the sun is Uranus than Venus?

....

....

Lesson 5 5.2.3

How does Earth move?

7. **Explain** The picture below shows how the moon moves in the sky. Why does the

moon appear to move from east to west?

....

Lesson 6 5.2.4

What are the phases of the moon?

8. **Summarize** During which phase does the moon pass between Earth and the sun?
   A. Full moon
   B. New moon
   C. First quarter
   D. Last quarter

9. **ANSWER THE BIG ?** What objects in space make up the solar system?

....

Think about what you have learned about the solar system. Why would it be difficult for humans to travel to visit the planets that you have learned about? Name specific planets and moons in your answer.

....

....

....

....

Multiple Choice Item

1 What kind of movement does this diagram show?

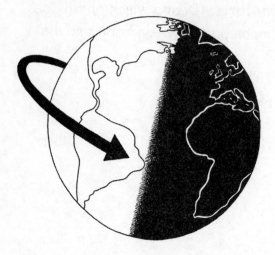

A. Earth' orbit

B. Earth's revolution

C. Earth's rotation

D. Earth's axis

● 5.2.2

Constructed Response Item

2 Alejandra notices that the shape of the moon outside her bedroom window seems to change every night. Why does this happen?

....

....

....

....

● 5.2.4

Extended Response Item

3 The picture below shows a model of the solar system.

List the planets in order from closest to the sun to farthest from the sun.

....

....

Which planets are gas giants? Why are they given this name?

....

....

....

Explain one way the model correctly represents the solar system. Explain one way the model does not correctly represent the solar system.

....

....

....

● 5.2.1

Science in Your Backyard

Changing Shadows

 5.2.1, 5.2.3, 5.NS.2, 5.NS.3, 5.NS.7

The sun appears to move across the sky as Earth rotates on its axis. The shadows cast by sunlight change size and position as Earth moves. Earth's orbit also affects how shadows appear. Try the experiment below to observe how shadows change throughout the day and over longer periods of time!

2:00 P.M.

Work with an adult. Place a plastic straw in a piece of clay. Put the clay and straw in the center of a large sheet of paper or piece of cardboard. Place the paper on a flat area on the ground. On the paper, mark which direction is north.

Observe the straw at three different times during the day. Trace the straw's shadow with a marker. Write the time of day next to each shadow. Repeat this one month later, but use a different marker color. Put the paper in the same exact place on the ground, facing the same exact way.

Compare the shadows from both days. How are they different? What is causing the difference?

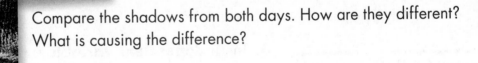

What would happen if Earth did not revolve around the sun, but still rotated on its axis?

221

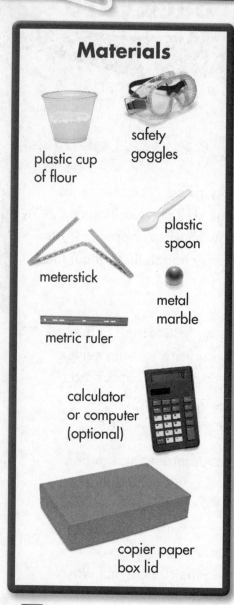

Materials

plastic cup of flour

safety goggles

meterstick

plastic spoon

metal marble

metric ruler

calculator or computer (optional)

copier paper box lid

 Be careful! Wear safety goggles.

Inquiry Skill

When scientists conduct an experiment, they identify the **independent variable,** the **dependent variable,** and the **controlled variables.**

How does the speed of a meteorite affect the crater it makes?

In this **experiment** you will create a model to find out how a meteorite's speed affects the size of the impact crater.

Ask a question.

Will meteorites that move faster make a smaller or larger crater than meteorites that move more slowly?

State a hypothesis.

1. Write a **hypothesis** by circling one choice and finishing the sentence. If a meteorite is moving faster, then it will make a crater with a width that is
a) *larger than*
b) *smaller than*
c) *about the same size as*
a crater made by a slower-moving meteorite because

....

Identify and control variables.

2. The marble is a **model** of a meteorite. The flour is a model of the surface the meteorite hits. **Controlled variables** are things you must keep the same in an experiment if you want a fair test. What will you keep the same?

....

3. The **independent variable** is the variable you change in an experiment. What will you change in this experiment?

....

....

4. The **dependent variable** is the variable you **measure** in an experiment. What will you measure in this experiment?

....

5.2.1 Recognize that our earth is part of the solar system in which the sun, an average star, is the central and largest body. Observe that our solar system includes the sun, moon, seven other planets and their moons, and many other smaller objects, such as asteroids and comets. **5.NS.1** Make predictions and formulate testable questions. **5.NS.2** Design a fair test. **5.NS.6** Test predictions with multiple trials. **5.DP.9** Present evidence using mathematical representations (graphs, data tables). (Also **5.NS.8, 5.NS.9**)

Design your test.

☑ **5.** Draw how you will set up your **model.**

☑ **6.** List your steps in the order you will do them.

Do your test.

☑ **7.** Follow the steps you wrote.

☑ **8.** Select a tool to **measure** the width of the crater in millimeters. **Record** your results in a table.

☑ **9.** Scientists repeat their tests to improve their accuracy. Repeat your test if time allows.

Collect and record your data.

☐ **10.** Fill in the chart.

Interpret your data.

☐ **11.** Use your data to make a bar graph.

Work Like a Scientist
Scientists work with other scientists. They compare their methods and results. Talk with your classmates. Compare your methods and results.

12. Study your chart and graph. What patterns do you see in your data?

13. Infer Describe your results. What can you infer from your results?

State your conclusion.

14. Communicate your conclusion. Compare your **hypothesis** with your results. Share your results with others.

Model a Planet's Orbit

What is the shape of a planet's orbit? Position two pushpins near the center of a piece of cardboard. The pins should be about 5 cm (2 in.) apart. Tie the ends of a piece of string together to form a loop. Place the loop around the pins. Place the point of a pencil against the inside of the loop and stretch the string tight. Move the pencil around inside the loop until it is back at the starting point. What shape does this make? What shape can you draw using only one pin?

5.2.1

Planet Hunting

Research a planet in our solar system. Create a chart explaining this planet's differences from Earth. Include answers to these questions:

• How far away is the planet from the sun?

• How long is its year?

• How long is its day?

• What would a person weighing 85 pounds on Earth weigh on this planet?

5.2.1

Using Scientific Methods

1. Ask a question.
2. State your hypothesis.
3. Identify and control variables.
4. Make a plan.
5. Test your hypothesis.
6. Collect, record, and interpret your data.
7. State your conclusion.
8. Do repeated trials.

Studying Eclipses

If the sky is clear, lunar and solar eclipses can be beautiful to observe. Write a report on how to observe eclipses. Include safety procedures for safely observing a solar eclipse. Research when the next lunar and solar eclipses will be visible in the United States.

5.2.4, 5.NS.4

Life Science

How can a PREDATOR also be PREY?

Ecosystems

The little blue heron, the frog, and the plants all live in the same swamp. Many different living things interact with one another in this ecosystem.

 Predict If the little blue heron left this swamp, what would happen to the frogs there?

....

....

THE BIG ? How do living things interact with their environments?

What happens if an ecosystem changes?

☐ **1.** Place a water plant in the bowl with soil and water. Put the bowl in a warm place with bright light.

☐ **2.** Every other day, add 4 seeds.

☐ **3.** **Observe** and **record** how the **model** of an ecosystem changes.

| Changes in a Model of an Environment ||
Day	Daily Observations
1	
2	
3	
4	
5	
6	
7	
8	
9	
10	
11	
12	
13	

Materials

bowl with soil and water

water plant

birdseed

Be careful! **Wash hands when finished.**

Inquiry Skill
You **interpret data** when you use information in a chart to draw a conclusion.

Explain Your Results

4. **Interpret Data** How did the changes in the **model** of an ecosystem affect the plants that grew?

5.NS.3 Plan and carry out investigations as a class, in small groups or independently, often over a period of several class lessons. (Also **5.3.1, 5.NS.8**)

Main Idea and Details

- The **main idea** is the most important idea in a reading selection.
- Supporting **details** tell more about the main idea.

Wetlands

A wetland is partly covered with water or is flooded at least part of the year. There are many kinds of wetlands, including swamps, marshes, and bogs. A swamp has many trees and bushes. Plants such as water lilies, vines, and cypress trees grow in some swamps. Animals such as alligators, turtles, frogs, and insects may live there too.

Another kind of wetland is a marsh, which is grassy with no trees. Muskrats and wading birds often live in this kind of wetland. Bogs are another kind of wetland. Bogs contain peat, a material formed by decomposing plants that floats on the water. Evergreen trees, shrubs, and moss are some plants that grow in bogs. Moose, deer, and lynx are some animals that live near bogs.

muskrat in wetlands

Practice It!

Complete the graphic organizer below to show the main idea and details in the example paragraph.

Main Idea

Detail   **Detail**   **Detail**

What are the parts of an ecosystem?

5.3.1 Observe and classify common Indiana organisms as producers, consumers, decomposers, predator and prey based on their relationships and interactions with other organisms in their ecosystem. (Also 5.NS.7, 5.NS.8)

Envision It!

Tell how you think the living things in this picture interact with the nonliving things.

MY PLANET DIARY

VOICES FROM History

Can you name an animal that lives in the lowland rainforests of Africa? Chimpanzees! African rainforests provide all the things these animals need to live. These things include water, shelter, fruits, nuts, seeds, and insects to eat. Scientist Jane Goodall made a career of studying chimpanzees in their natural surroundings. She once said, "It can be exhausting climbing high, far and fast, around 3 P.M. you feel very weary because of spending a lot of the day on your stomach, crawling, with vines catching your hair."

Why might Jane Goodall have continued her research despite the hard work it took?

....

....

....

....

....

Jane Goodall began her chimpanzee research in 1960.

mYscienceonLine.com | mY pLaneT DiaRY

I will know some ecosystems in which organisms live and interact.

Words to Know

ecosystem   population
habitat   community

Ecosystems

There are many parts to an ecosystem. An **ecosystem** is all the living and nonliving things in an area and their interactions. Ecosystems can be large, like a desert, or small, like a puddle. What kind of ecosystem are you in right now? Your classroom is an ecosystem. The organisms in an ecosystem live in a habitat. A **habitat** is a place that provides all the things an organism needs to live. These things include food, water, and shelter.

Ecosystems contain biotic and abiotic factors. Biotic factors are all the living organisms in an ecosystem. Abiotic factors are the nonliving parts in an ecosystem. Air, water, soil, temperature, and sunlight are some abiotic factors.

The fish are biotic factors in this ocean habitat. Water is an abiotic factor.

1. ⊙ **Main Idea and Details** Complete the graphic organizer below. **Write** the details about ecosystems.

Main Idea

There are many parts to an ecosystem.

Detail	Detail	Detail
	Ecosystems can be large or small.	

2. Identify Read the description of the ecosystems on these pages. Underline the details in each description that tell how some organisms survive in their environment.

3. Classify What is an example of a population in the picture below of the coral reef?

Types of Ecosystems

There are many different types of ecosystems. The abiotic factors in an ecosystem often determine what kinds of organisms live in it. For example, only organisms that can withstand the extreme heat and dryness of a desert can live there. Organisms living in an ecosystem often have similar traits, or characteristics. These traits help them survive in their ecosystem. Frogs, turtles, and alligators have webbed feet that help them swim in a water ecosystem, such as a swamp.

All types of ecosystems contain populations and communities. A **population** is a group of organisms of one species that live in an area at the same time. A population may be all the oak trees in an area. Different populations in an area make up a **community.** A community may have populations of oak trees, maple trees, and pine trees. Members of a community depend on one another to fill needs, such as food and shelter.

panda butterflyfish

Coral Reef

Organisms that live in a coral reef have traits that help them live in warm, clear, shallow water. For example, some algae carry on photosynthesis. As a result, they grow only in shallow water where sunlight can reach them. The coral reef can support the algae, which produce food for consumers, including the coral animals. A coral reef may have many colorful animals, such as clown fish, anemones, and sponges. A reef is made up mostly of the skeletons of dead coral animals. The coral animals on the top part of the reef are alive.

toucan

Tropical Rain Forest

The traits of organisms that live in a tropical rain forest help them survive in a warm, rainy climate all year long. The shape of the leaves of some plants cause rain drops to fall off the plants quickly. The high amount of moisture in the air allows other plants, such as orchids, to grow on trees, not in soil. Butterflies, tree frogs, monkeys, and parrots are some animals that live in this ecosystem.

Desert

Deserts have little rain, hot days, and cool nights. Some deserts have sand dunes. Some are rocky. Others are covered by a layer of salt. Organisms living in the desert have traits that help them survive the hot, dry conditions. Plants, such as cactuses, can store water in their stems when it rains. To deal with high temperatures, many animals rest during the day. Animals such as coyotes, desert tortoises, lizards, and rattlesnakes live in deserts in the United States.

desert tortoise

Tundra

The traits of organisms that live in a tundra help them survive cold weather with little rain. Thick fur coats cover many of the animals that live there. Most tundras are found in the most northern areas of Earth or high up in mountains. Rodents, rabbits, and caribou feed on small plants and grasses. Weasels, polar bears, and foxes also live in the tundra.

arctic fox

4. Compare How are the traits of organisms living in a desert similar to the traits of organisms living in a tundra?

....

....

Other Types of Ecosystems

In addition to the coral reef, tropical rainforest, tundra, and desert ecosystems you have read about, there are also many more. The United States has a variety of different ecosystems. Four more examples are the taiga, wetland, prairie, and mixed-forest ecosystems.

5. **Identify** Find and color Indiana with a pencil or crayon. Then identify the ecosystem that Indiana is in or near. Describe the ecosystem to a partner.

Taiga
Trees such as fir, spruce, and hemlock are some of the plants that are able to live in the taiga. The taiga has harsh, long, cold winters, and most land has soil that is low in nutrients. Some small animals, such as squirrels, birds, and insects, eat berries and the seeds of trees. Larger animals, such as elk and moose, eat tree bark and young plants. Predators, such as hawks and grizzly bears, eat other animals.

red-tailed hawk

Coastal Wetland
In a wetland, a shallow layer of water covers the surface of the land for some or all of the year. Trees such as the mangrove and some grasses are able to grow in the salty water of a coastal wetland. Some animals that live here may include many types of birds, snakes, and a variety of insects. Coastal wetlands are found along all of the coasts in the United States. Their characteristics may vary depending on where they are found.

6. Describe Draw or write about the type of land, weather, and organisms in an ecosystem near you or one you would like to visit.

raccoon

Mixed Forest

The mixed forests are home to many types of trees and animals. Trees, such as oak, maple, and beech, lose their leaves in the winter. As the leaves decompose, they return nutrients to the soil below. Shrubs and small plants grow in the mixed forest. Songbirds, deer, bears, and raccoons are some common animals. In the cold winter of the mixed forest, many animals hibernate. Many birds migrate to warmer areas for the winter.

Prairie

Prairie ecosystems are found throughout the Midwest and Great Plains. Prairies do not receive enough rain to support many large trees, but they have nutrient-rich soil that is excellent for farming. Every year, millions of tons of wheat, corn, and soybeans are produced in the prairies of the United States. Tall grasses and other small plants cover the land. Some of the largest animals on Earth, including bison, live in prairie ecosystems. Also common are coyotes, prairie dogs, and grasshoppers.

prairie dog

7. ◎ **Compare and Contrast** How are the tropical rainforest and mixed forest ecosystems alike? How are they different?

....

....

....

Balance in Ecosystems

Every organism in an ecosystem has a niche and a habitat. A *niche* is the role that an organism has in an ecosystem. The niche of a northern pygmy owl in the mixed forest is that of a hunter. It eats small animals, such as mice and chipmunks. A habitat is the place where an organism lives. A habitat is made up of the soil, air, and water, as well as the plants of the area. The habitat of northern pygmy owls is the trees and the land on which they live. The trees' habitat is the land.

All the relationships among parts of an ecosystem keep it balanced. For example, in a forest owls eat small animals, such as mice. If the number of mice in the forest decreases, the owls have less food. So, the number of owls will decrease. But with fewer owls hunting, fewer mice will be eaten. As a result, the population of mice will grow. Then, with more mice to hunt, the number of owls will increase again. In this way, the populations of owls and mice balance.

northern pygmy owl
hunting a mouse

8. ⦿ **Main Idea and Details** Read the first paragraph again. **Underline** the main idea. (Circle) the details.

9. CHALLENGE Think of a local ecosystem. Draw an organism you might find there. Label your organism and describe its niche.

mysɔienceonLine.com | Got it? | 60-Second Video

Limiting Factors

The number of organisms that can live in a habitat is called the carrying capacity. Factors that limit the carrying capacity of a habitat are the amount of food, water, space, and shelter. With the right conditions, such as plenty of food, few diseases, and few predators, a population in a habitat will grow larger. But a population may grow only to a certain size and still have all its needs met. Overcrowding may happen if a population grows larger than the carrying capacity. When overcrowding occurs, food supplies can run out. Organisms must move to another area or they will not survive.

10. Predict What may happen to the population of deer if it increases too much?

black-tailed deer

Got it?

🔊 5.3.1, 5.NS.7, 5.NS.8

11. Describe Identify an ecosystem near where you live. Describe the living and nonliving things in that ecosystem.

12. Compare How are the traits of some plants living in a tropical rain forest similar?

⬜ **Stop!** I need help with

⏸ **Wait!** I have a question about

▶ **Go!** Now I know

Lesson 2

How do organisms interact?

5.3.1 Observe and classify common Indiana organisms as producers, consumers, decomposers, predator and prey based on their relationships and interactions with other organisms in their ecosystem. (Also 5.3.2, 5.NS.7)

Envision It!

Tell how these organisms might interact in this ecosystem.

Inquiry Explore It!

What do some molds need to grow?

Be careful! Wear gloves. Wash your hands when finished.

☑ **1.** Rub some mold from a strawberry onto a piece of bread and onto a piece of foil.

☑ **2.** Put the bread in a bag. Put the foil in the other bag. Place 10 drops of water onto the 2 places you rubbed the mold.

☑ **3.** Place the sealed bags in a warm, dark place for 4 days.

☑ **4. Communicate** What did you **observe** in each bag?

....

....

Explain Your Results

5. Draw a Conclusion Why did the mold grow only in one bag?

....

....

Materials

moldy strawberry

plastic cup with water

2 plastic bags

dropper   latex-free gloves (optional)

hand lens

bread slice (without preservatives)

foil square

5.NS.3 Plan and carry out investigations as a class, in small groups or independently, often over a period of several class lessons. 5.NS.4 Perform investigations using appropriate tools and technology that will extend the senses. (Also 5.NS.8)

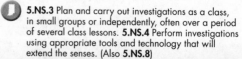

UNLOCK THE BIG ?

I will know the different ways that organisms interact in an ecosystem.

Words to Know

predator	consumer
prey	decomposer
producer	

Interactions in Ecosystems

Ecosystems are made up of living and nonliving things. The living things in ecosystems interact with each other in a variety of ways. Some organisms help one another meet their needs. Some organisms may eat other organisms and get energy or nutrients from them. Some organisms compete with one another for space or food.

In some ecosystems, birds may flock near larger animals. The animals may disturb insects in high grasses. As the insects fly or jump away, the birds are able to catch them for food. The birds are helped by this relationship, but the larger animal is not affected.

Some animals in an ecosystem must hunt other organisms to fill their energy needs. In this type of interaction, only one organism is helped. An animal that hunts and eats another animal is called a **predator.** Any animal that is hunted by others for food is called **prey.** The predator gets energy from the prey when the predator eats the prey.

1. **Classify** Use the picture below to classify the animals as predator or prey. Explain their roles.

....

....

....

....

....

....

These plants make their own food. They are producers.

The moose eats the plants. Moose are herbivores.

Bears are omnivores. They eat plants and animals.

Energy Roles in Ecosystems

Perhaps the most common interaction in an ecosystem occurs when organisms get energy. All organisms need energy to live. How an organism gets its energy determines its energy role. An organism's energy role makes up part of its niche in an ecosystem. Each organism in an ecosystem fills the energy role of producer, consumer, or decomposer.

Producers

Plants, some protists, and other microorganisms are producers. **Producers** make their own food for energy. Most producers use energy from the sun to make food. Some producers use chemicals from their environment for energy. Producers either use the energy to grow or store it for later. The food they make is often a source of energy for other organisms.

Consumers

Many organisms depend on producers to get energy. **Consumers** are organisms that cannot make their own food. They get energy from producers or other consumers. All animals, some fungi, and some microorganisms are consumers.

There are several kinds of consumers. They are classified by what they eat. Herbivores, such as moose, eat only plants. Carnivores eat only other animals. One example of a carnivore is a lion. Omnivores eat both plants and animals. Black bears are omnivores.

Some carnivores feed on dead animals. These consumers are called *scavengers*. Vultures and hyenas are two examples of scavengers.

2. **Give an Example** Write two examples of consumers. Tell whether they are herbivores, omnivores, carnivores, or scavengers.

....

....

....

....

Decomposers

Producers and consumers take in nutrients from the environment as they use energy and grow. **Decomposers** are organisms that get their energy by breaking down wastes and dead organisms. During this process, decomposers return materials to an ecosystem. In turn, other organisms reuse these materials for their own needs. Most decomposers are too small to see without a microscope.

3. **Classify** Read the caption to the right about the organisms shown. Use the key to label the organisms.

Key

C = consumer   **P** = producer   **D** = decomposer

The plant gets its energy from sunlight. The hummingbird sips nectar from the plant's flower for food. The mushrooms get energy from the dead tree.

These decomposers are too small to be seen without a microscope. They are breaking down the dead leaf.

243

Lightning Lab

You in the Food Chain
Think about a fresh food you ate or drank yesterday, such as an apple or a glass of milk. Make a food chain to show the path of energy from sunlight to you.

Food Chains

Energy passes through an ecosystem when food is eaten. This energy often begins as the sunlight that plants use to make food. The energy can take many different paths in an ecosystem. This movement of energy through an ecosystem can be shown in food chains. A food chain is a series of steps by which energy moves from one type of living thing to another. The shortest food chains involve only a plant and a decomposer. Other food chains involve a carnivore or an omnivore too. Arrows on a food chain show the path in which energy moves.

4. Fill in the Blanks Write a word that best describes each part of the Prairie Food Chain diagram below.

Prairie Food Chain

Grass is an example of a

....

Deer eat grass. They are

....

Coyotes eat deer. They are

....

5. ◉ **Sequence** Water oak trees are a source of food for termites. Black bears often look in rotting logs for insects such as termites to eat. Make a food chain for these organisms.

Food Webs

Relationships among organisms in an ecosystem can be complicated. There are many food chains in an ecosystem, but a food chain can only describe one way energy flows in an ecosystem. To see how these food chains are all connected in an ecosystem, you can use a food web. A food web is a diagram that combines many food chains into one picture. Like a food chain, a food web uses arrows to show the energy relationships among organisms.

6. ⊙ **Main Idea and Details** <u>Underline</u> the main idea in the paragraph about food chains. (Circle) the supporting details.

7. (Circle) Use different-colored crayons to show two food chains in this food web.

This food web shows the complex flow of energy in a salt marsh ecosystem.

kudzu

Competition

Every organism in an ecosystem has a niche, or role in that ecosystem. A niche includes the type of food the organism takes in, how it gets its food, and which other species use the organism as food. An organism may compete for the things it needs. Plants may compete for sunlight, soil, or water. Animals may compete for territory, water, light, food, or mates. For example, male black bears will compete with each other for territory and mates. Rabbits, mice, and other animals of a desert community compete with one another for plants to eat. An animal that cannot compete may die or be forced to move away.

8. **Infer** Kudzu is a vine that quickly grows and covers other plants. What is one resource for which kudzu competes with other plants?

....

Do the math!

Read a Graph

The graph shows how the population sizes of a hunter, such as an owl, and the animal it hunts might change over time. Use the graph to answer these questions.

1 Which is a reasonable estimate for the difference between the greatest and the least number of hunters?

A. 5 **B.** 16 **C.** 22 **D.** 40

2 What happens after the hunter's population becomes greater than the hunted animal's population?

A. This never happens.

B. The hunter's population decreases to zero.

C. The hunter's population decreases.

D. The hunted animal's population increases.

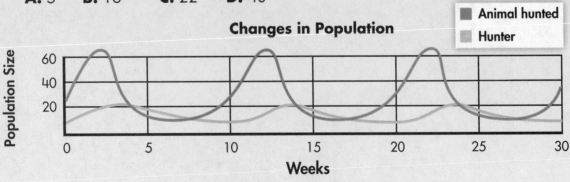

Changes in Population

Legend: Animal hunted, Hunter

mysaienceonline.com | Got it? | 60-Second Video

Symbiosis

A long-term relationship between two different organisms is called symbiosis. One organism is always helped. The other organism might be harmed, helped, or not affected. A *parasite* is an organism that lives on or inside of another organism. Parasites take nutrients away from the organisms where they live, which harms organisms.

In other relationships, both organisms are helped. For example, the cleaner shrimp eats parasites from the eel's mouth. The shrimp gets food and the eel keeps its teeth clean and free of parasites.

9. CHALLENGE Think about the interaction between bees and apple trees. How is this an example of symbiosis?

....

....

moray eel with cleaner shrimp

Got it?

5.3.1, 5.3.2, 5.NS.7

10. **Compare** How are food chains and food webs alike and different?

....

....

11. **Describe** What are the roles of producers, consumers, and decomposers in a food chain?

....

....

....

☐ **Stop!** I need help with ....

❚❚ **Wait!** I have a question about ....

▶ **Go!** Now I know ....

How do some Indiana organisms interact?

5.3.1 Observe and classify common Indiana organisms as producers, consumers, decomposers, predator and prey based on their relationships and interactions with other organisms in their ecosystem. (Also 5.3.2)

Envision It!

Tell how these organisms are interacting.

Inquiry **Explore It!**

How do food webs show relationships?

☐ **1.** Choose a card. Hold it so it can be seen. Stand in a circle with your group. Look for organisms that your organism eats or that eats you. Toss the ball of yarn to one of them but hold onto the end of the yarn.

☐ **2.** Take turns until everyone is connected. You have made a **model** of a food web.

☐ **3.** Lay down the yarn and the cards. Using the names of the organisms, draw your food web in the space to the right.

Materials

Food Web Cards   yarn

Explain Your Results

4. Interpret Data   Look at your food web. Explain the relationships the web shows. Give examples.

....

....

....

myscienceonline.com | **Explore It!** Animation

5.NS.3 Plan and carry out investigations as a class, in small groups or independently, often over a period of several class lessons. (Also 5.NS.7)

UNLOCK THE BIG ?

I will know how to classify Indiana organisms based on how they interact.

Words to Know
deciduous plant
evergreen plant

Indiana Organisms

When you look around outside, what sort of organisms do you see? Indiana is home to many organisms that are common in many parts of the United States. Some common Indiana plants, such as the tulip poplar, are deciduous trees. A **deciduous plant** loses all of its leaves for a part of the year. In Indiana, deciduous plants lose their leaves in the winter. Another Indiana tree is the eastern hemlock. This tree is an example of an **evergreen plant**, or a plant that keeps green leaves on its branches all year. Other plants that are found throughout the state include the serviceberry, common buttonbush, dogwood, goldenrod, and aster.

Of course, in addition to plants, Indiana is also home to many animals. Fish, such as the northern pike and yellow perch, and mammals, such as the red fox and Indiana bat, all live in Indiana. Just as in other ecosystems, the plants and animals of Indiana interact with one another in food chains, food webs, competition, and symbiotic relationships.

1. ◎ **Main Idea and Details** Read the first paragraph above. **Underline** the main idea of the paragraph. (Circle) three details.

Decomposers

Indiana is home to many decomposers as well. Decomposers are an important part of all ecosystems because ecosystems have limited resources. Living things compete for food, water, light, and space. By consuming dead plants and animals, decomposers add usable resources to the air and soil. Fungi, bacteria, and animals can all be decomposers.

Have you ever seen a brown spot on a ripe peach? If you left it for a few days, the brown spot would get larger. Decomposers, such as fungi and bacteria, cause these spots as they break down the peach. Rot, or decay, is very important to the health of an ecosystem. If nothing decayed, dead organisms and wastes would pile up and interfere with habitats. Nutrients would not be recycled.

Fungi

Molds and yeasts are two categories of fungi. Some fungi can break down the tough chemical substances in wood and other plants. You may have seen moldy bread. Mold can grow on foods such as bread and cheese. The mold gets energy from the foods.

2. Hypothesize
Suppose you have a piece of moldy bread or a moldy strawberry. What happens to the food over time? Why do you think it changes?

Mushrooms are a type of fungus. They help break down dead plants and material in soils. Some mushrooms can be toxic, but others, such as the portabella, are edible.

myscienceonline.com | THE BIG ? | I Will Know...

Bacteria

Some decomposers are so small you cannot see them without a microscope. Many of these microscopic organisms are called bacteria. Bacteria are everywhere. Some types of bacteria live in soil. When other organisms die, some of these bacteria get the nutrients they need to live from these dead organisms. In the process of getting nutrients, these bacteria break down the dead organisms into other nutrients that plants and animals can use. Other bacteria can take the materials broken down by fungi and break them down further into nutrients that plants and animals can also use.

Animal Decomposers

Some animals, such as earthworms and crabs, are decomposers. The red wiggler worm is an earthworm that can be found in Indiana. Animal decomposers break down dead plant and animal remains. They use nutrients left over from these dead organisms to live and grow.

3. ◉ **Sequence** Write three steps to show how nutrients return to the environment.

bacteria

red wiggler worms

fungus

Bacteria, fungi, and animals help turn yard waste into compost.

Go Green

Trees and Your Community Make a poster to show where you would plant trees in your community. Explain how planting these trees would help your community and the environment.

Interactions in Indiana Ecosystems

As in all ecosystems, Indiana ecosystems have organisms that can be classified as producers, consumers, and decomposers. They also have predators and prey.

Producers, Consumers, and Decomposers

If you look outside, you may see some common producers, such as grass, flowering plants, and oak trees. These plants are where the food chains in Indiana begin.

4. Give an Example Do you see other producers outside? List an example.

....

Consumers feed on producers or other consumers. In Indiana, a common example of a consumer is the gray squirrel. Throughout the state, the gray squirrel eats acorns, seeds, tree bark, and sometimes insects or birds' eggs.

Decomposers are commonly found throughout Indiana. Mushrooms are fungi that often grow on wet soil or on dead trees. The mushrooms get energy from the decaying trees and return some nutrients to the ecosystem.

5. Classify Look at the organisms in the Indiana Food Chain diagram. In the box below each, write whether it is a producer, consumer, or decomposer.

oak tree

....

gray squirrel

....

Cooper's hawk

....

Predators and Prey

Recall that a predator is a consumer that gets energy from eating other animals. Many birds are predators. In Indiana, Cooper's hawks and peregrine falcons hunt mice and other small animals. Eastern bluebirds hunt insects and spiders. Many fish are also predators. The brown trout, a fish found in some Indiana streams, eats mayflies, other insects, and some smaller fish.

6. **Determine** (Circle) the types of prey listed in the paragraph. Are these organisms producers, consumers, or decomposers? How do you know?

....

....

....

....

brown trout

Got it?

🎧 **5.3.1, 5.3.2**

7. **Decide** Classify each of the following organisms: sweetgum tree, groundhog, puffball mushroom, lake trout

Producer	Consumer	Decomposer
....	....	....
....	....	....

8. **UNLOCK THE BIG ?** Give one example of predators and prey interacting in an Indiana ecosystem.

....

....

⬜ **Stop!** I need help with ....

⏸ **Wait!** I have a question about ....

▶ **Go!** Now I know ....

How do organisms get and use energy?

5.3.1 Observe and classify common Indiana organisms as producers, consumers, decomposers, predator and prey based on their relationships and interactions with other organisms in their ecosystem. (Also 5.NS.9)

Envision It!

Tell how you think plants get the energy they need to live.

my planeT DiaRY
for Indiana

DISCOVERY

What comes to mind when you think of corn? You might think of corn on the cob, popcorn, or cornbread. However, corn is not just food. Scientists have discovered that it can also be used to produce a liquid fuel called ethanol. Ethanol is a type of biofuel. Biofuels are fuels made from living things. Other plants used to make biofuel are soy and sugarcane. Biofuels are more environmentally friendly than other fuels, such as gasoline. Because gasoline-powered vehicles produce air pollution, using biofuels instead might help preserve Earth's environment.

How do you think biofuels might affect your life?

mYscienceonLine.com | my planeT DiaRY

I will know how plants use energy from the sun.

Words to Know

photosynthesis
cellular respiration

Energy Sources

What is your favorite type of green salad? You might like one made of spinach. Perhaps you choose iceberg lettuce or crispy romaine lettuce. Spinach, iceberg lettuce, and romaine lettuce are all types of leaves. A leaf is a major plant part. Unlike animals, plants make their own food. Most of the food that a plant makes is made in the plant's leaves.

When you eat spinach or lettuce leaves, your body gets their energy. Your body cells need this energy to carry out its many functions. The energy you get is stored in the leaves. Where did the leaves get this energy? It came from the sun in the form of sunlight. The sun is Earth's primary energy source. The plant used the sunlight's energy to make its food, which it uses to grow. This form of energy passes on to you when you eat the leaves.

cabbage

1. **Identify** Where does the stored energy in these cabbage leaves come from?

_____

2. **Explain** How does a plant get its food?

_____

_____

Photosynthesis

Most plants make food in their leaves. Leaves and other plant parts are green because their cells contain chlorophyll. Chlorophyll is a green substance that traps energy from the sun. The sun's energy is transformed into chemical energy in the food that plants make. Chlorophyll is stored in the chloroplasts of plant cells.

Photosynthesis is the process that plants use to make sugar for food. During photosynthesis, plants use energy from sunlight, carbon dioxide from the air, and water absorbed by plant roots to make sugar. Oxygen is given off by the plant during this process. The sun's energy is transformed and then stored in the sugar. The process can be summarized in this equation:

$$\textbf{carbon dioxide} + \textbf{water} \xrightarrow[\textbf{chlorophyll}]{\textbf{light energy}} \textbf{sugar} + \textbf{oxygen}$$

The equation shows that plants produce oxygen during photosynthesis. The plant does not use photosynthesis to make oxygen, but it is given off during the process. Most organisms, including animals, could not live without the oxygen and sugar that plants make.

3. Describe What is the process of photosynthesis?

....

....

....

4. Fill in the Blank Look at the illustration of the chloroplast. Fill in each blank of the captions with the correct word or words.

5. [CHALLENGE] How do trees that lose their leaves in the fall survive all winter?

....

....

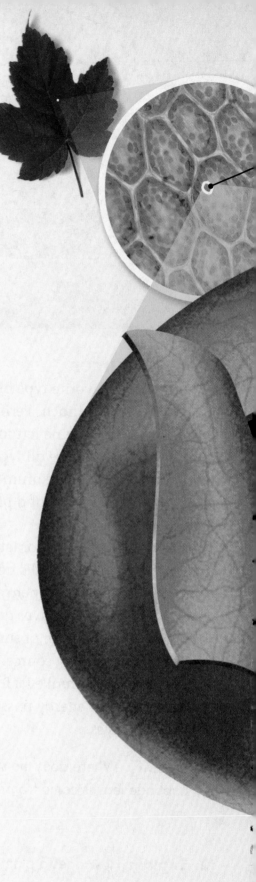

mYscienceonLine.com | THE BIG ? | I Will Know...

chloroplast

Sunlight

Chlorophyll in the chloroplasts absorbs sunlight. This is the source of energy used to make sugar

from ....

and ....

Carbon Dioxide

Carbon dioxide from the air enters the chloroplasts. Small holes on the surface of the leaf let carbon dioxide in.

Water

Water enters the chloroplast. Most often this water has been absorbed from soil by the plants' roots.

When the chloroplast absorbs more sunlight, more .... can be made.

During photosynthesis, ... is produced. The plant gives off some of this through holes on the surface of the leaf.

The large drawing is a chloroplast. The structures that look like stacked up plates contain chlorophyll. The small inset is an image of plant cells containing these plates from a microscope.

Lightning Lab

Do Plants Breathe?

Place a plastic bag over the end of a leafy branch. Seal the end of the bag with a twist tie. Observe the bag. Check back after 24 hours. What changed in the bag?

Respiration

Plant and animal cells need energy to do their work and grow. Plant cells use the food they make to get this energy. Animal cells use the food the animals have eaten to get energy. The process by which cells break down sugar to release energy is called **cellular respiration.**

During cellular respiration, sugar starts to be broken down through a series of chemical reactions. This process happens mostly in the mitochondria. Mitochondria are present in every cell and are the cell's power producers. The process makes carbon dioxide and water, and it releases energy. The process of cellular respiration can be summarized by this equation:

sugar + oxygen ⟶ energy + carbon dioxide + water

6. **Identify** Label the diagram to show the materials needed for and the products of cellular respiration.

Materials Needed

Cellular Respiration

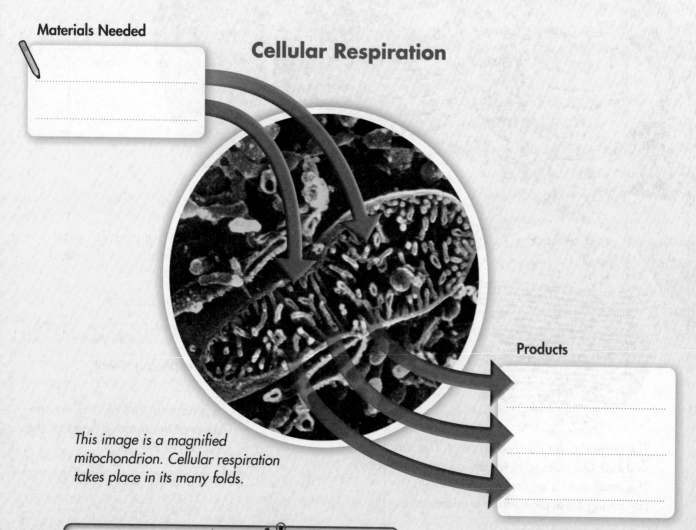

Products

This image is a magnified mitochondrion. Cellular respiration takes place in its many folds.

Plants can make more sugar than they need. This extra sugar is changed into other kinds of sugars and starches, which are stored in the plant. When plants need energy, they can break down the stored food to release its energy. This stored energy is also a source of food for animals and some other organisms.

7. ⦿ **Compare and Contrast** Complete the chart to compare the processes of photosynthesis and respiration.

Questions	Photosynthesis	Respiration
What is used?		
What is produced?		

Got it?   ⏸ 5.3.1, 5.NS.9

8. **Identify** What is Earth's primary energy source?

....

9. **Describe** What are the processes of photosynthesis and cellular respiration in plants?

....

....

....

....

⏹ **Stop!** I need help with ....

⏸ **Wait!** I have a question about ....

▶ **Go!** Now I know ....

How do people impact ecosystems?

 5.3.1 Observe and classify common Indiana organisms as producers, consumers, decomposers, predator and prey based on their relationships and interactions with other organisms in their ecosystem.

Tell how you think this factory might affect the environment.

Inquiry Explore It!

Which materials break down fastest?

Materials

water   soil   4 plastic straws

plastic cup   newspaper

4 plastic bags   facial tissue

plastic foam   plastic wrap

☑ **1.** Put a cup of soil into each of 4 plastic bags. Add water to dampen the soil.

> **Be careful!** Wear gloves.
> Wash your hands when finished.

☑ **2.** Place a piece of tissue into one bag. Insert a straw at one edge and seal. Repeat with the plastic wrap, newspaper, and plastic square.

☑ **3.** Place bags in a warm, dark place for 1 week.

☑ **4.** **Record** how each material changed after 1 week.

....

....

Explain Your Results

5. Examine your data. Identify any pattern you **observed.** Explain.

....

....

myscienceonline.com | **Explore It!** Animation

 5.3.2 Investigate the action of different decomposers and compare the role they play in an ecosystem with that of producers and consumers. **5.NS.8** Identify simple patterns in data and propose explanations to account for the patterns. (Also **5.NS.3**)

UNLOCK THE BIG ?

I will know how people can affect the environment and change ecosystems.

Words to Know

pollution
conservation

People Change Ecosystems

Organisms interact and can change their environments. Unlike most other organisms, people can change large parts of the environment. Changing the environment can upset the balance in ecosystems. People may cause pollution. People also change their environments by bringing new plants or animals into an ecosystem. They may also hunt and fish too much.

Pollution

Any substance that damages the environment is called **pollution.** Pollution can affect the air, water, and land. Cars and factories put gases that cause harm into the air. Chemicals that people use may end up in rivers and in the ocean. People also make trash. Some of it is dumped in landfills and then covered with soil. If the trash does not break down, it can cause pollution.

1. Infer Describe how chemicals dumped in a river might affect the organisms living in it.

....

....

2. Hypothesize What are three other items that should not be placed in trash and dumped in landfills?

....

....

....

Batteries contain metals that can harm the environment if the batteries are not disposed of properly.

3. **Infer** Describe how these zebra mussels might affect the clam they are growing on.

....

....

....

....

4. **Hypothesize** Why do you think the population of a species brought into a new area might grow quickly?

....

....

....

....

....

Nonnative Species

People may bring new plants and animals into ecosystems. New species often harm some populations in ecosystems. A nonnative species is a plant or animal that does not grow naturally in an ecosystem.

Zebra mussels are animals that people accidentally brought to the United States around 1988. They entered the Great Lakes attached to a ship that traveled from Russia. Once here, they spread throughout the lakes and then moved into rivers. They ate the food and took the space that other species needed. These events changed some ecosystems permanently.

Zebra-mussel populations grow quickly. These animals can cover almost any surface.

The garlic-mustard plant grew only in Europe and parts of Asia many years ago. People brought the plant to the United States to use as food and medicine. Since animals did not eat the plant, it spread quickly. Less space was left for other plants to grow. As a result, some animals had less to eat.

Garlic-mustard plants can spread over a forest floor.

myscienceonline.com | Got *it?* 60-Second Video

Regulation and Conservation

Too much hunting or fishing can also harm the environment. Regulation puts limits on how many animals a person can hunt and fish. Regulation is one way governments practice conservation. **Conservation** is an attempt to preserve or protect an environment from harmful changes. Towns, cities, states, and the government put aside large areas for conservation. People can go to these areas to enjoy nature.

5. [CHALLENGE] Describe how fishing licenses might help regulate overfishing?

....

....

....

FISHING LICENSE REQUIRED

Got it?

🅓 5.3.1

6. **Summarize** What are the ways that people can protect the environment?

....

....

7. **Describe** What is the consequence of bringing a nonnative species into an ecosystem?

....

....

⬜ **Stop!** I need help with ....

⏸ **Wait!** I have a question about ....

▶ **Go!** Now I know ....

What is inside an owl pellet?

Follow a Procedure

☑ **1.** Place an owl pellet on a sheet of paper. **Measure** its length. **Record.**

☑ **2. Observe** the pellet. Separate the contents of the pellet.

Materials

safety goggles

owl pellet

wooden probe

forceps

hand lens

sheet of paper   metric ruler

Inquiry Skill
You **infer** when you explain your observations.

 Wear safety goggles. Wash your hands when finished.

 5.3.1 Observe and classify common Indiana organisms as producers, consumers, decomposers, predator and prey based on their relationships and interactions with other organisms in their ecosystem. **5.NS.7** Keep accurate records in a notebook during investigations and communicate findings to others using graphs, charts, maps and models through oral and written reports. (Also **5.NS.8**)

☑ **3.** Fill in the chart to **classify** the contents of the pellet.

☑ **4.** Record your observations below.

Owl Pellet Observations					
	Pellet Length	Skull Bones	Other Bones	Teeth	Did you see fur? feathers? (describe)
Pellet data					

Analyze and Conclude

5. Interpret Data Make an **inference** about the types of food the owl consumed.

....

....

....

6. Draw a Conclusion You **observed** an owl pellet.
You saw parts of the organism the owl ate.
Make an inference about the relationship between
the owl and the other organisms.

....

....

7. UNLOCK THE BIG **?** What can scientists learn about the owl's
ecosystem by examining an owl pellet?

....

....

....

5.3.1

Ecologist

Do you enjoy exploring the outdoors? Then you might want to become an ecologist. Ecologists study how living things relate to their environment.

There are many fields of ecology in which to specialize. For example, if you are interested in environmental conservation, you could become an environmental consultant. If you want to help educate others about ecology, you could become a teacher. People who are especially interested in researching and solving ecological problems can become research scientists. They conduct research outdoors and in laboratories. Ecologists can also work for the government or organizations such as museums, zoos, and private companies.

Ecologists have strong backgrounds in life sciences such as biology, botany, and zoology. Math skills are important, as well as the ability to communicate clearly. Most professional ecologists hold at least a bachelor's degree from a university. Many have advanced degrees.

APPLY THE BIG ? What is one way an ecologist might interact with an ecosystem?

....

....

Vocabulary Smart Cards

ecosystem
habitat
population
community
predator
prey
producer
consumer
decomposer
deciduous plant
evergreen plant
photosynthesis
cellular respiration
pollution
conservation

Play a Game!

Cut out the Vocabulary Smart Cards.

Work with a partner. Choose a Vocabulary Smart Card. Do not show the term to your partner.

Give clues to help your partner guess what your term is.

Have your partner repeat with another Vocabulary Smart Card.

community

comunidad

ecosystem

ecosistema

predator

predador

habitat

hábitat

prey

presa

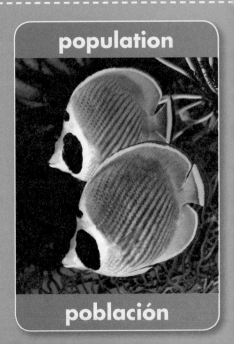

population

población

all the living and nonliving things in an area and their interactions

Write a sentence using this word.

....

....

....

todos los seres vivos y las cosas sin vida que hay en un área y sus interacciones

---

the group of all populations in an area

Write a word that is not an example.

....

....

....

....

grupo de todas las poblaciones de un área

Interactive Vocabulary

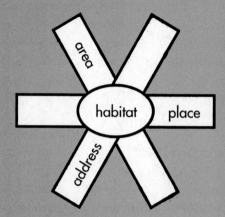

area
habitat   place
address

Make a Word Wheel!

Choose a vocabulary word and write it in the center of the Word Wheel graphic organizer. Write synonyms or related words on the wheel spokes.

---

a place that provides all the things an organism needs to live

Draw an example.

lugar que proporciona todas las cosas que necesita un organismo para vivir

---

an animal that hunts and eats another animal

Write a sentence using the plural form of this word.

....

....

....

animal que atrapa a otro animal y se lo come

---

a group of organisms of one species that live in an area at the same time

What is another meaning of this word?

....

....

....

grupo de organismos de la misma especie que viven en un área al mismo tiempo

---

any animal that is hunted by others for food

Write an example of this word.

....

....

....

cualquier animal que es cazado por otros para alimentación

cellular respiration

respiración celular

deciduous plant

planta de hoja caduca

producer

productor

pollution

contaminación

evergreen plant

planta de hoja perenne

consumer

consumidor

conservation

FISHING LICENSE REQUIRED

conservación

photosynthesis

fotosíntesis

decomposer

descomponedor

organism that makes its own food for energy

Draw an example.

organismo que hace su propio alimento para obtener energía

---

a plant that loses all of its leaves for a part of the year

Draw a picture that represents this term.

planta que pierde todas sus hojas durante una época del año

---

the process by which cells break down sugar to release energy

Write a sentence using this word.

....

....

proceso mediante el cual las células descomponen el azúcar para obtener energía

---

organism that cannot make its own food

Use this term in a sentence.

....

....

....

organismo que no puede hacer su propio alimento

---

a plant that keeps green leaves on its branches all year

Read the first word in this term. Write the two parts of the compound word.

....

....

planta cuyas ramas conservan sus hojas verdes todo el año

---

any substance that damages the environment

Draw an example.

cualquier sustancia que le hace daño al medio ambiente

---

organism that gets its energy by breaking down wastes and dead organisms

Draw an example.

organismo que obtiene su energía descomponiendo desechos y organismos muertos

---

the process that plants use to make sugar for food

Use a dictionary. What is the verb form of this word?

....

....

....

proceso por medio del cual las plantas producen azúcar para alimentarse

---

an attempt to preserve or protect an environment from harmful changes

Write a sentence using the verb form of this word.

....

....

....

intento de conservar o de proteger el medio ambiente de cambios dañinos

Chapter 6

Study Guide

REVIEW THE BIG **?** How do living things interact with their environments?

Lesson 1

What are the parts of an ecosystem?

- An ecosystem is made up of living and nonliving things.
- There are many different types of ecosystems.
- All the relationships among parts of an ecosystem keep it balanced.

Lesson 2

How do organisms interact?

- Food chains and food webs show the movement of energy.
- Organisms interact in ecosystems through competition and predator-and-prey relationships.

Lesson 3

How do some Indiana organisms interact?

- Indiana is home to many types of organisms, including deciduous and evergreen trees.
- Ecosystems in Indiana have producers, consumers, and decomposers.

Lesson 4

How do organisms get and use energy?

- The primary source of energy in ecosystems is the sun.
- Plants make food during the process of photosynthesis.
- Plants and animals get energy from food through cellular respiration.

Lesson 5

How do people impact ecosystems?

- People may cause pollution that affects the air, water, and land.
- People may bring new species into an ecosystem that harm it.
- Too much hunting and fishing can negatively affect the environment.

Lesson 1 5.3.1, 5.NS.7, 5.NS.8

What are the parts of an ecosystem?

1. **Identify** Which of the following is an example of a community?
   A. squirrels, blue jays, and oak trees
   B. a group of twenty sandhill cranes
   C. a school of tuna
   D. rocks, soil, and air

2. **Write About It** How are an organism's niche and habitat related?

Lesson 2 5.3.1, 5.3.2, 5.NS.7

How do organisms interact?

3. ◉ **Main Idea and Details**
   Underline the main idea and ⟨circle⟩ the details in the following paragraph.

   An organism may compete for the things it needs. Plants may compete for sunlight, soil, or water. Animals may compete for territory, water, light, food, or mates.

Lesson 3 5.3.1, 5.3.2

How do some Indiana organisms interact?

4. **Vocabulary** Which of the following best describes the role of a decomposer in an ecosystem?
   A. use energy from the sun to make food
   B. produce food for consumers
   C. return nutrients to the environment
   D. serve as prey for predators

5. **Classify** What type of organism is a raccoon? ⟨Circle⟩ all that apply.

   Producer   **Consumer**   **Decomposer**
   Predator   **Prey**

Lesson 4 5.3.1, 5.NS.9

How do organisms get and use energy?

6. **Explain** How are photosynthesis and cellular respiration related?

Lesson 5 5.3.1

How do humans impact ecosystems?

7. Explain Why must pollution be regulated?

....

....

8. Predict How might hunting too many rabbits affect the balance of an ecosystem?

....

....

....

....

9. Apply Purple loosestrife is a plant that people brought from Europe. It grows thickly in wetlands. How might this plant harm the wetlands ecosystem?

....

....

10. **APPLY THE BIG ?** **How do living things interact with their environments?**

Describe an ecosystem near you. Discuss how the living things interact. Use the terms *food chain, producer,* and *consumer.*

....

....

....

....

....

....

....

....

....

....

....

....

....

....

Multiple Choice

1 What is the role of this organism in a food chain?

A. It breaks down wastes and dead organisms.
B. It uses the sun's energy to make food.
C. It eats other organisms.
D. It cannot make its own food.

 5.3.1

Constructed Response

2 What are three things an animal gets from its habitat?

....

....

....

....

5.3.1

Extended Response

3 List two examples of decomposers.

....

....

What is the role of these decomposers in an ecosystem?

....

....

....

What would happen to the ecosystem if these decomposers did not live there?

....

....

....

....

....

....

5.3.2

Create a Compost Pile

Go Green!

5.3.2

Food waste and yard clippings make up 24 percent of solid waste in the United States. You can help reduce this waste by putting food waste such as apple cores, stale bread, and eggshells into a compost pile.

A compost pile is a mixture of food scraps, wood products, yard trimmings, soil, and worms. The worms, which are decomposers, eat the food scraps and break them down into "worm castings," or rich, fertile soil.

Composting can be simple and fun. It can be done indoors or outdoors. To make a compost pile, start with a wood, plastic, or brick bin. Fill it with shredded cardboard or clean paper. Add water and soil. Then add some worms. Bury food scraps, tea bags, dry leaves, and grass under the paper. Avoid composting meat and dairy products. Keep the compost pile moist and turn it over every week or so. The worms and natural processes will do the rest. Soon you will have nutrient-rich soil that can be used to fertilize a garden. So the next time you finish an apple, don't put it in the trash. Compost it!

APPLY THE BIG ? How do worms interact with a compost pile?

....

....

275

How are these HAIRS like a fence?

Human Body

Indiana

Chapter
7

Try It! How do parts of the body
work together like a system?

Lesson 1 What is the circulatory system?
5.NS.8

Lesson 2 What is the respiratory system?
5.NS.4

Lesson 3 What are the skeletal and muscular
systems?
5.4.1

Lesson 4 What is the nervous system?
5.NS.1, 5.NS.9

Lesson 5 What are some other systems?
5.NS.3

Lesson 6 How do physical structures compare in
living things?

Investigate It! How much air can you exhale?

Some animals, such as cats, have sensitive hairs called
whiskers that help them respond to change. The human
hairs in this picture are magnified many times. These
hairs act like whiskers and can cause a protective reflex.

Predict What structure do you think these hairs
protect?

....

....

THE BIG ? How are living things organized?

How do parts of the body work together like a system?

☐ **1.** Follow the directions on each activity card.

☐ **2. Communicate** your results.

Observations of Body Systems	
Card	Result
A	
B	
C	
D	

Materials

Card A—Balancing Act
1. Stand with your feet 30 cm apart and your arms down next to your sides.
2. Bend your left knee. Lift your left foot about 10 cm ab...
3. Stand next to a w... and right shoulde...
4. Bend your left kn... foot about 10 cm...
5. **Communicate** body worked tog... bala...

Card B—The Dominant Eye
1. Point to a corner of the room with both eyes open.
2. Keep pointing. Close your right eye. Open it.
3. Did your finger seem to shift away from pointing at the corner? If it did, your right...

Card C—Wiggling Fingers
1. Place your hand flat on the table.
2. Lift each finger one at a time and wiggle it.
3. Put each finger down before you lift and wig...
4. Ob... mo...
5. Co... ha... yo...

Card D—Standing in the Dark
1. Stand on one foot for 1 minute.
2. Close your eyes and stand on one foot for 1 minute.
3. **Communicate** Tell how your eyes worked with your body to help you balance.

Activity Cards A–D

Inquiry Skill
When you communicate your findings, you and others can make sound **inferences.**

Explain Your Results

3. 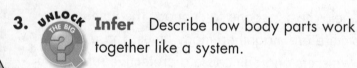 **Infer** Describe how body parts work together like a system.

....

....

....

....

....

....

5.NS.3 Plan and carry out investigations as a class, in small groups or independently, often over a period of several class lessons. **5.NS.7** Keep accurate records in a notebook during investigations and communicate findings to others using graphs, charts, maps and models through oral and written reports.

Text Features

Text features, such as headings, pictures, and captions, give you clues about what you will read.

A **heading** tells what the page is about.

highlight

A **picture** shows what the reading is about.

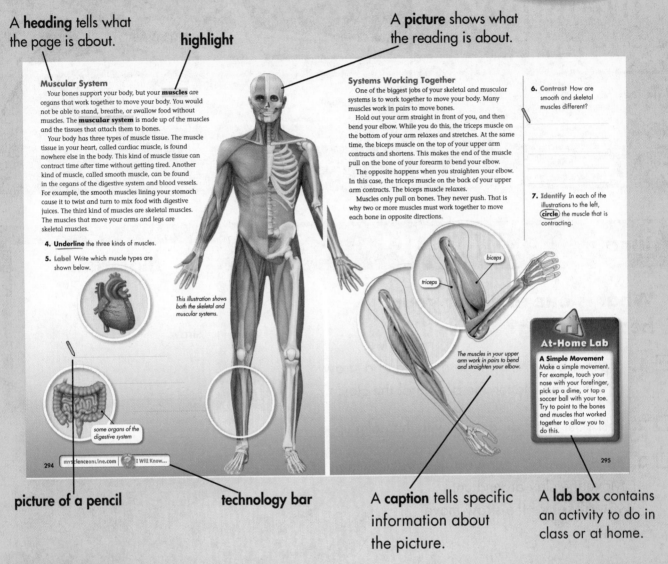

Muscular System

Your bones support your body, but your **muscles** are organs that work together to move your body. You would not be able to stand, breathe, or swallow food without muscles. The **muscular system** is made up of the muscles and the tissues that attach them to bones.

Your body has three types of muscle tissue. The muscle tissue in your heart, called cardiac muscle, is found nowhere else in the body. This kind of muscle tissue can contract time after time without getting tired. Another kind of muscle, called smooth muscle, can be found in the organs of the digestive system and blood vessels. For example, the smooth muscles lining your stomach cause it to twist and turn to mix food with digestive juices. The third kind of muscles are skeletal muscles. The muscles that move your arms and legs are skeletal muscles.

4. Underline the three kinds of muscles.

5. Label Write which muscle types are shown below.

This illustration shows both the skeletal and muscular systems.

some organs of the digestive system

Systems Working Together

One of the biggest jobs of your skeletal and muscular systems is to work together to move your body. Many muscles work in pairs to move bones.

Hold out your arm straight in front of you, and then bend your elbow. While you do this, the triceps muscle on the bottom of your arm relaxes and stretches. At the same time, the biceps muscle on the top of your upper arm contracts and shortens. This makes the end of the muscle pull on the bone of your forearm to bend your elbow.

The opposite happens when you straighten your elbow. In this case, the triceps muscle on the back of your upper arm contracts. The biceps muscle relaxes.

Muscles only pull on bones. They never push. That is why two or more muscles must work together to move each bone in opposite directions.

6. Contrast How are smooth and skeletal muscles different?

7. Identify In each of the illustrations to the left, (circle) the muscle that is contracting.

biceps

triceps

The muscles in your upper arm work in pairs to bend and straighten your elbow.

At-Home Lab

A Simple Movement Make a simple movement. For example, touch your nose with your forefinger, pick up a dime, or tap a soccer ball with your toe. Try to point to the bones and muscles that worked together to allow you to do this.

294 myscienceonline.com I Will Know...

295

picture of a pencil

technology bar

A **caption** tells specific information about the picture.

A **lab box** contains an activity to do in class or at home.

Practice It!

Read the text features in the chart below. Find the text features in the textbook pages shown above. Write a clue each one gives you about the content.

Text feature	What it tells me
yellow highlight	
picture of a pencil	
technology bar	

What is the circulatory system?

5.NS.8 Identify simple patterns in data and propose explanations to account for the patterns.

Envision It!

Tell how you think this highway system is like your blood vessels.

Inquiry Explore It!

What is one effect of your heart beating?

☑ **1.** Make a ball of clay. Push one end of a straw into the ball. Flatten the bottom of the clay.

☑ **2.** Rest your hand on a table with the palm up.

☑ **3.** Set the clay on your wrist near your thumb. Move the clay around until you **observe** the straw move.

☑ **4.** Describe the movements of the straw.

Materials

straw

clay

Explain Your Results

5. Infer what made the straw move.

myscienceonline.com **Explore It!** Animation

5.NS.4 Perform investigations using appropriate tools and technology that will extend the senses. (Also 5.NS.3)

UNLOCK THE BIG ?

I will know that the circulatory system moves blood through the body.

Words to Know

tissue   circulatory
organ   system
system   heart

Cells to Organs

The smallest part of your body that is alive is a cell. Cells are the basic units of all living things. The tiniest organisms are made of only single cells. Larger organisms are made of many cells, maybe trillions of them.

Have you ever noticed that teamwork is a great way to get work done? Cells in larger organisms often work together in tissues. A **tissue** is a group of the same kind of cells that work together to do the same job.

Tissues join with other types of tissues to form organs. An **organ** is a group of different tissues that join together into one structure. These tissues work together to do a main job in the body. Your heart, eyes, ears, and stomach are all organs. Organs that work together are called an organ system. A **system** is a set of things that work together as a whole.

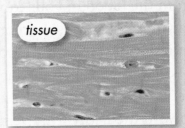

tissue

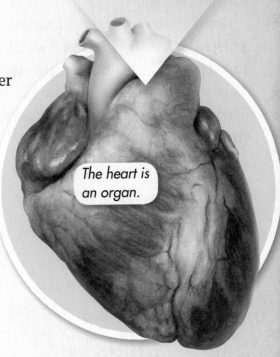

The heart is an organ.

1. ◉ **Text Features** Fill in the chart below. Use the first row as an example.

Text feature	What it tells me
Heading	This section tells how groups of cells form organs.
Highlight	

Circulatory System

The **circulatory system** moves blood through the body. It includes the heart, blood, and blood vessels. Blood vessels are like highways for blood cells. The three kinds of blood vessels are arteries, capillaries, and veins.

Most arteries carry blood with lots of oxygen. Arteries are blood vessels that carry blood away from the heart to other parts of the body. Arteries have thick, muscular walls. These walls stretch as the heart pushes blood through them. Arteries branch many times into smaller and smaller tubes.

The smallest arteries branch to become capillaries. A *capillary* is the smallest kind of blood vessel. Capillary walls are only one-cell thick. Oxygen and nutrients move from the blood in your capillaries through the thin walls to your body's cells. Carbon dioxide and other wastes move from cells to the blood in the capillaries.

Capillaries join together to form your smallest veins. Veins are blood vessels that transport blood toward the heart. Tiny veins join many times to form larger veins.

Unlike arteries and capillaries, veins have valves. Valves are flaps that act like doors to keep blood moving in only one direction. Valves open to let blood flow to the heart. They close if the blood starts flowing away from the heart.

2. Look at the diagram of the circulatory system to the right. (Circle) the organ that pumps blood through your body.

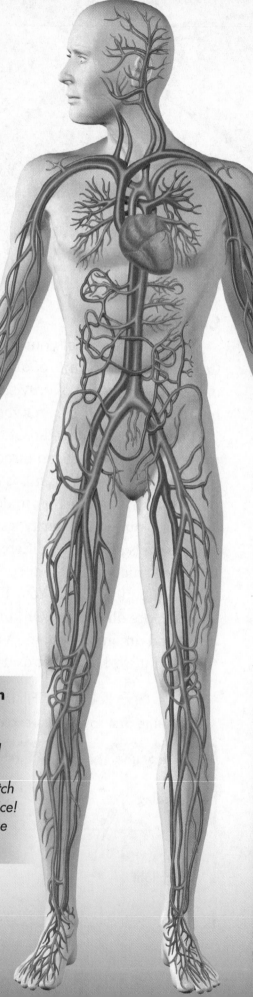

The Circulatory System
Huge numbers of blood vessels form a network throughout your body. If all the blood vessels were laid end to end, they would stretch around Earth more than twice! This picture shows only some of the larger blood vessels.

myscienceonline.com | THE BIG ? | I Will Know...

Veins and Arteries
Veins have thinner walls than arteries but thicker walls than capillaries.

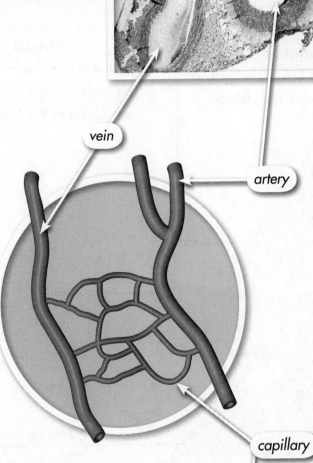

vein

artery

capillary

Capillaries
Side by side, ten capillaries would be barely as thick as one hair! Some capillaries are so narrow that red blood cells must flow through them in a single-file line.

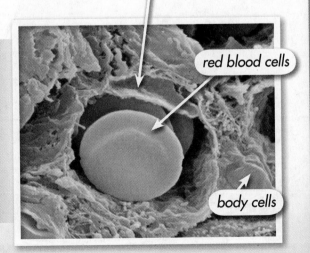

red blood cells

body cells

3. ◉ **Compare and Contrast** How are the jobs of a vein and an artery the same? How are they different?

....

....

....

....

4. Interpret Your body has about ten billion capillaries. Write this number in standard form.

....

At-Home Lab

Read the Label
Read the food labels on a variety of foods. Foods contain fats. Too much fat may clog your arteries. Record the fat content of each food. Compare. What surprised you? How could you reduce the amount of fat in your diet?

Parts of the Heart

Your heart began pumping before your were born. It will keep pumping as long as you live. The **heart** is a muscular organ that pumps blood throughout your body. The right and left atria and the right and left ventricles are the four chambers of the heart.

Usually, illustrations of the circulatory system show most veins colored blue and most arteries colored red. In this drawing of the heart, the veins from the lungs are colored red because they contain oxygen-rich blood. Arteries going to the lungs are colored blue because they contain blood with less oxygen.

5. **Describe** Look at the picture below. Label the chambers of the heart from 1 to 4 to show the order in which blood flows.

6. CHALLENGE Why do you think it is important that the heart pumps oxygen-rich blood to the body?

....

....

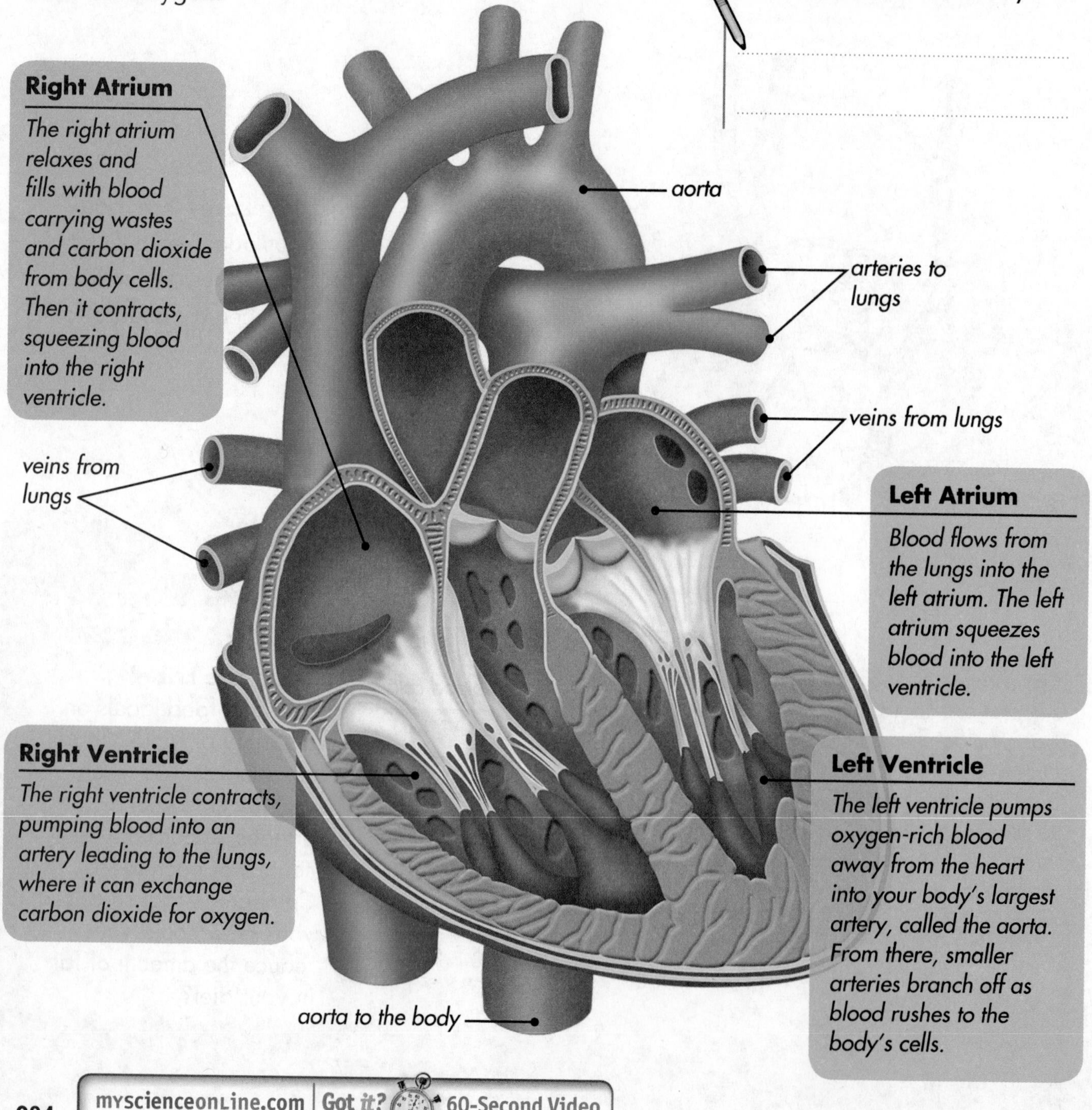

Right Atrium

The right atrium relaxes and fills with blood carrying wastes and carbon dioxide from body cells. Then it contracts, squeezing blood into the right ventricle.

aorta

arteries to lungs

veins from lungs

veins from lungs

Left Atrium

Blood flows from the lungs into the left atrium. The left atrium squeezes blood into the left ventricle.

Right Ventricle

The right ventricle contracts, pumping blood into an artery leading to the lungs, where it can exchange carbon dioxide for oxygen.

Left Ventricle

The left ventricle pumps oxygen-rich blood away from the heart into your body's largest artery, called the aorta. From there, smaller arteries branch off as blood rushes to the body's cells.

aorta to the body

myscienceonline.com | Got it? | 60-Second Video

Blood Flow Through the Heart

Your heart is divided into right and left sides. Each side of the heart works as a separate pump and sends blood along different paths. Blood enters the heart in the right atrium. Next, it flows to the right ventricle. The right ventricle pumps blood to the lungs. In the lungs, the blood gets oxygen and gets rid of carbon dioxide. Then, blood returns from the lungs and flows into the left atrium. Finally, blood flows to the left ventricle. The left ventricle pumps the oxygen-rich blood through arteries to the entire body.

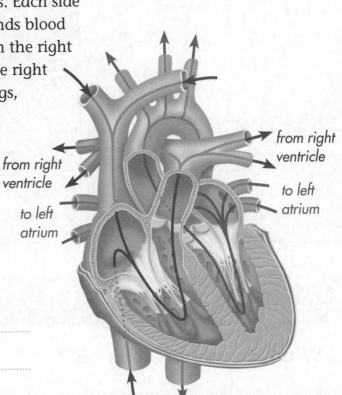

from right
ventricle

to left
atrium

from right
ventricle

to left
atrium

7. ◉ **Text Features** Write a caption to tell about the picture of the heart.

....

....

Got it? 🕐 **5.NS.8**

8. **Summarize** What is the main organ of the circulatory system? What is its function?

....

9. **UNLOCK THE BIG ?** Tell the order of vessels a blood cell travels through starting from the heart.

....

....

⬜ **Stop!** I need help with ....

⏸ **Wait!** I have a question about ....

▶ **Go!** Now I know ....

What is the respiratory system?

5.NS.4 Perform investigations using appropriate tools and technology that will extend the senses.

Envision It!

Tell how this man is using his respiratory system.

Inquiry Explore It!

What do you breathe out?

Water with BTB will change from blue to pale yellow if carbon dioxide is added.

☑ **1.** Fill a cup $\frac{1}{3}$ full of water with BTB. Cover it with plastic. Push a straw through the plastic.

☑ **2.** Gently breathe OUT through the straw into the water. **Observe.**

Explain Your Results

3. Infer Was there carbon dioxide in the air you breathed out? Explain using your **observations.**

....

....

....

....

....

Materials

safety goggles

2 plastic cups

straw

plastic wrap

water with BTB

Be careful!

Wear safety goggles.
Do not drink the BTB water.
Use the straws to breathe OUT only.
Do not share straws.

---

myscienceonline.com | **Explore It!** Animation

5.NS.3 Plan and carry out investigations as a class, in small groups or independently, often over a period of several class lessons.

I will know that the respiratory system is made up of the lungs and other structures. Blood moves oxygen through the body.

Words to Know

respiratory   lungs
  system   trachea
diaphragm

The Respiratory System

Take a long, slow breath. Can you feel your respiratory system at work? The **respiratory system** is the system of the body that helps you breathe. You take in air through your nose and mouth. Several muscles work together when you breathe. When you inhale, a dome-shaped muscle called the **diaphragm** moves down, making more space in your chest for air. Your rib muscles may also pull your rib cage up and out, making still more space. Air quickly rushes into your lungs and fills the space. The **lungs** are organs that help the body exchange oxygen and carbon dioxide with the air outside the body. When you exhale, your diaphragm and rib muscles relax, move up, and push air out of the lungs.

1. **Identify Underline** two ways that your chest makes room for the air you breathe.

2. **Label** Complete the captions on the diagrams to the right.

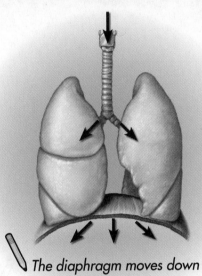

The diaphragm moves down when you _____.

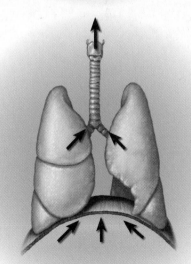

The diaphragm moves up when you _____.

Lightning Lab

Breathe It In
Slouch forward in your chair. Take a deep breath and then exhale. Now sit up straight. Take a deep breath and then exhale. In which position could you take a deeper breath? Explain.

Parts of the Respiratory System

When you breathe, air comes in through your nose or mouth. Hairs and a layer of mucus in the nose trap dust, germs, and other things that may be in the air. Mucus is a sticky, thick fluid. Many parts of the respiratory system are coated with mucus.

From the nose, air passes through the nasal cavities. The nasal cavities warm and moisten the air. Then, the air moves to the back of the throat and into the larynx. The larynx contains the vocal cords, where the voice is produced. The sound of your voice is the result of your breath making the vocal cords vibrate. When muscles stretch the vocal cords tighter, your voice gets a higher pitch.

From the larynx, a tube called the **trachea** carries air to the lungs. The trachea leads to two branches called bronchi that go into the lungs. In the lungs, the bronchi branch into smaller and smaller tubes called bronchioles. Asthma is a disease in which these tubes may become swollen. This keeps air from moving easily through the lungs.

The bronchioles end in clusters of tiny, thin-walled air sacs in the lungs. The air sacs are where oxygen enters the blood and carbon dioxide leaves the blood.

3. ⊙ **Sequence** List the parts of the respiratory system the air passes through.

....

....

4. CHALLENGE Your left lung is smaller than your right lung. Why do you think this is so?

....

....

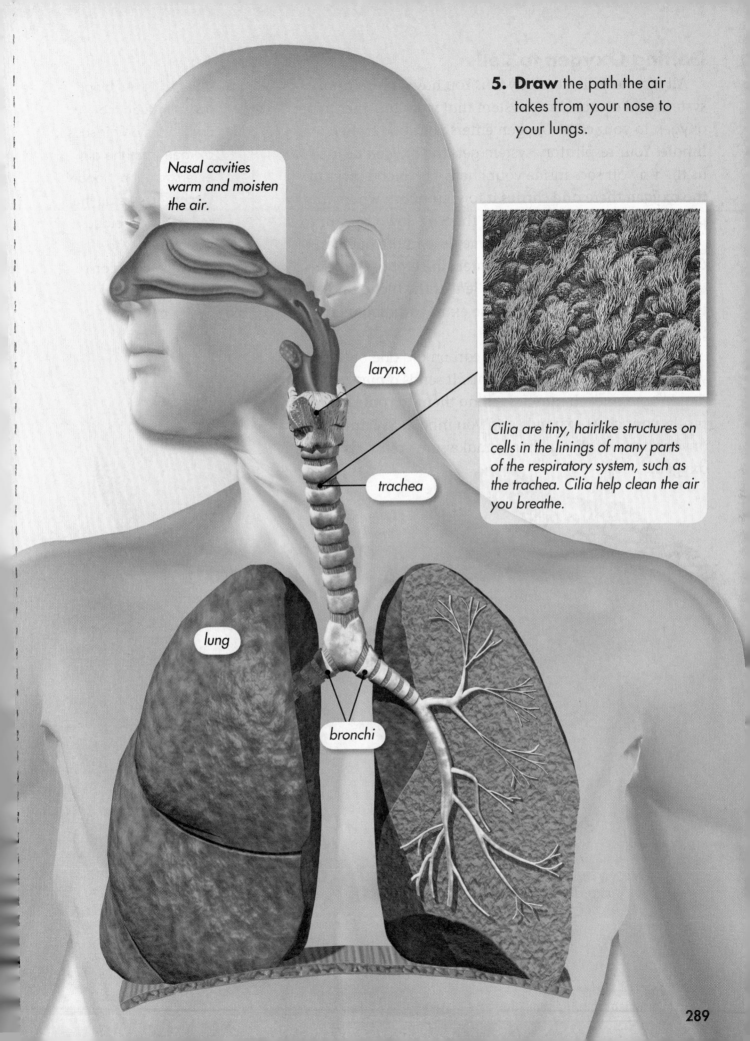

Nasal cavities warm and moisten the air.

5. Draw the path the air takes from your nose to your lungs.

Cilia are tiny, hairlike structures on cells in the linings of many parts of the respiratory system, such as the trachea. Cilia help clean the air you breathe.

larynx

trachea

lung

bronchi

289

Getting Oxygen to Cells

All of your cells need oxygen. You have a respiratory system and a circulatory system that work together to get oxygen to your cells. Oxygen enters your body when you inhale. Your respiratory system gets the oxygen as far as the tiny air sacs inside your chest. The blood picks up the oxygen there and carries it to your heart, where it is pumped to all of your cells—all the way down to your toes!

Two things happen at the same time in the air sacs. Oxygen leaves the lungs and enters the blood. Carbon dioxide moves the other way. It leaves the blood and enters the lungs. When you exhale, the extra carbon dioxide leaves your body.

When you hold your breath, carbon dioxide builds up in your blood. Your brain senses this. It sends a message to the diaphragm and rib muscles telling them to contract. As a result, your chest expands and you inhale. Several systems of your body work together to make sure your cells get oxygen.

6. Diagram As blood flows through the capillaries on air sacs, oxygen from the air enters into the blood. **Draw** arrows on the red and blue blood vessels below to show the direction of blood flow.

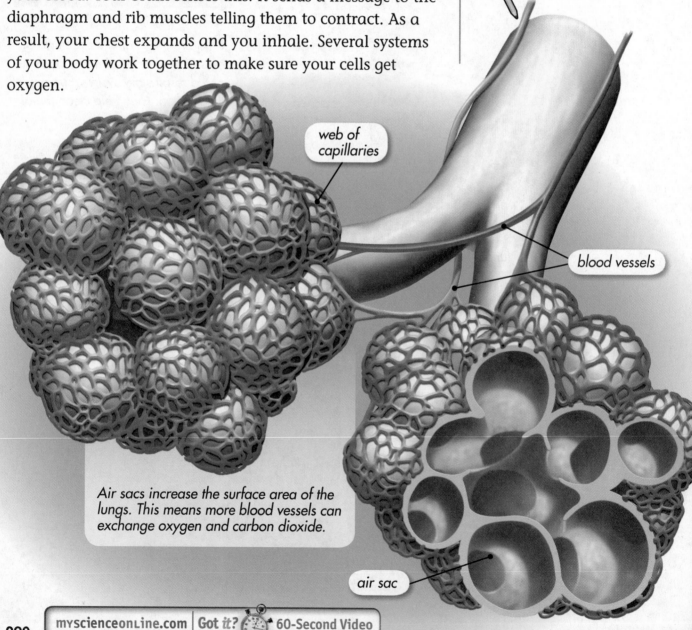

web of capillaries

blood vessels

Air sacs increase the surface area of the lungs. This means more blood vessels can exchange oxygen and carbon dioxide.

air sac

myscienceonline.com | Got it? | 60-Second Video

Surface Area

The air sacs in your lungs have a large surface area. Surface area is the measure of the area on the outside of a shape. Look at the pictures of the blocks. The first picture shows the blocks placed together in a cube. The second shows the blocks separately.

At first glance, it may seem like the surface area would be the same whether the blocks were placed together or they were separated. Let's find out if that is true.

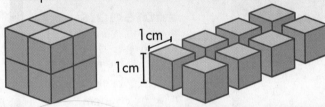

1cm
1cm

1 Find the surface area of the cube.

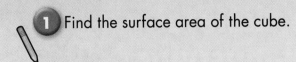

Find the surface area of all the blocks after they have been separated.

2 Was there a difference in the surface areas? Explain why you think that is true.

Got it?

7. **Summarize** What is the main organ of the respiratory system? What is its function?

8. **UNLOCK THE BIG ?** What is the order of structures that oxygen passes through between your nose and your bloodstream?

⬜ **Stop!** I need help with ....

⏸ **Wait!** I have a question about ....

▶ **Go!** Now I know ....

Lesson 3

What are the skeletal and muscular systems?

5.4.1 Investigate technologies that mimic human or animal musculoskeletal systems in order to meet a need.

Tell how this structure works.

Inquiry **Explore It!**

How do the parts of the skeletal system fit together?

☑ **1. Make a Model** Cut out each part from the Human Skeletal System. Put each part in the correct position.

☑ **2.** Glue each part in place. Label the parts you know.

Materials

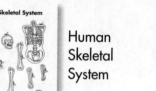

Human Skeletal System

glue

paper

scissors

Explain Your Results

3. Communicate How is your **model** alike and different from a real human skeleton?

....

....

....

....

4. How do you think your skeletal system helps you?

....

....

....

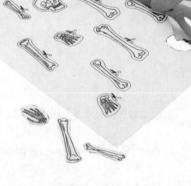

5.4.3 Design a solution to a problem in the context of musculoskeletal body systems. Using suitable tools, techniques and materials, draw or build a prototype or model of a proposed design. **5.NS.7** Keep accurate records in a notebook during investigations and communicate findings to others using graphs, charts, maps and models through oral and written reports. (Also **5.NS.3**)

myscienceonline.com | **Explore It!** Animation

Words to Know

skeletal system
skeleton
muscles
muscular system

Skeletal System

Think about what your body would be like without any bones. How would you move? What would you look like? Each of your bones is an organ. Your **skeletal system** is made up of bones that support your body and help you move. Different kinds of bones perform different functions.

Bones have several functions. Your **skeleton** is made up of all the bones in your body. It supports your body and gives you height. Bones of the skull, rib cage, and back protect important organs. Some bones form new blood cells. Bones also store minerals, such as calcium and phosphorus. Small amounts of stored minerals are released when the body needs them. These same minerals make bones hard and strong.

1. **Underline** three functions of bones.

2. CHALLENGE Why do you think it is important that you have so many bones in your skeleton?

....

....

....

3. **Identify** Look at the skeleton. Circle some bones that protect organs such as the heart and lungs.

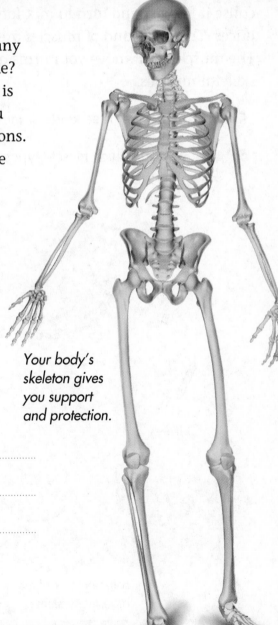

Your body's skeleton gives you support and protection.

myscienceonline.com | Envision It!   293

Muscular System

Your bones support your body, but your **muscles** are organs that work together to move your body. You would not be able to stand, breathe, or swallow food without muscles. The **muscular system** is made up of the muscles and the tissues that attach them to bones.

Your body has three types of muscle tissue. The muscle tissue in your heart, called cardiac muscle, is found nowhere else in the body. This kind of muscle tissue can contract time after time without getting tired. Another kind of muscle, called smooth muscle, can be found in the organs of the digestive system and blood vessels. For example, the smooth muscles lining your stomach cause it to twist and turn to mix food with digestive juices. The third kind of muscles are skeletal muscles. The muscles that move your arms and legs are skeletal muscles.

4. **Underline** the three kinds of muscles.

5. **Label** Write which muscle types are shown below.

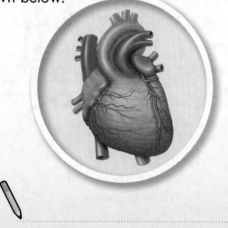

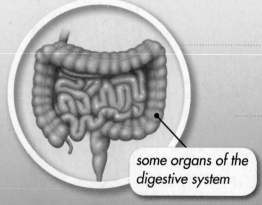

some organs of the digestive system

This illustration shows both the skeletal and muscular systems.

Systems Working Together

One of the biggest jobs of your skeletal and muscular systems is to work together to move your body. Many muscles work in pairs to move bones.

Hold out your arm straight in front of you, and then bend your elbow. While you do this, the triceps muscle on the bottom of your arm relaxes and stretches. At the same time, the biceps muscle on the top of your upper arm contracts and shortens. This makes the end of the muscle pull on the bone of your forearm to bend your elbow.

The opposite happens when you straighten your elbow. In this case, the triceps muscle on the back of your upper arm contracts. The biceps muscle relaxes.

Muscles only pull on bones. They never push. That is why two or more muscles must work together to move each bone in opposite directions.

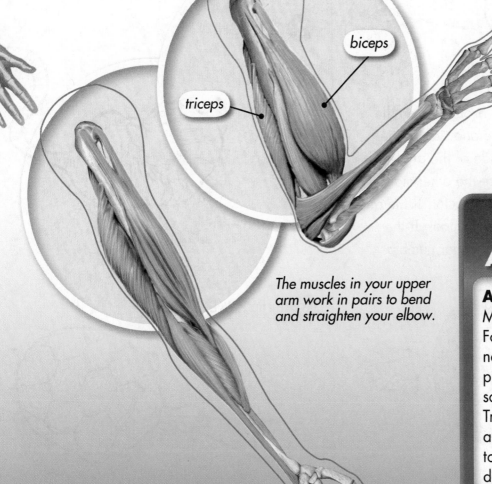

triceps

biceps

The muscles in your upper arm work in pairs to bend and straighten your elbow.

6. Contrast How are smooth and skeletal muscles different?

....

....

....

....

....

7. Identify In each of the illustrations to the left, (circle) the muscle that is contracting.

At-Home Lab

A Simple Movement
Make a simple movement. For example, touch your nose with your forefinger, pick up a dime, or tap a soccer ball with your toe. Try to point to the bones and muscles that worked together to allow you to do this.

295

Measuring Angles

You can use a protractor to measure angles. Angles are measured in degrees. The symbol ° indicates degrees. An angle that is less than 90° is acute. An angle that is greater than 90° is obtuse.

Example

An owl's neck has a greater range of motion than a human's neck. You can see the range of motion by looking down on an animal's head. Use your protractor to measure ∠ABC.

Place the center of the protractor on the angle's vertex, B. Place one side of the bottom edge on one side of the angle. Read the number where the other side of the angle crosses the protractor. If the angle is acute, use the smaller number. If the angle is obtuse, use the larger number.

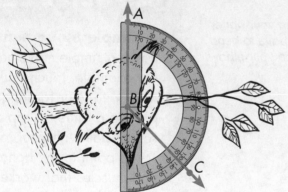

The measure of ∠ABC is 135°.

Measure the angles below. Tell whether the angle is acute or obtuse.

1 Human ∠DEF

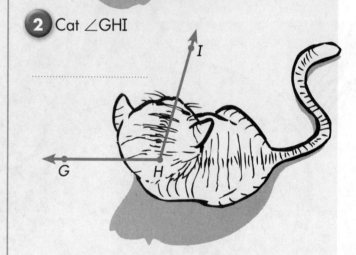

2 Cat ∠GHI

3 Turtle ∠JKL

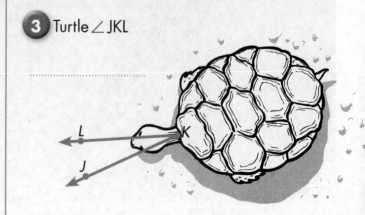

Muscle- and Bone-Building Materials

Your muscles are very strong. However, they can become injured or develop other problems. It is important to protect your muscles against overworking or overstretching. Healthful foods such as fruit and pasta provide your muscles with energy they need to do work.

Bones grow while you are young. As you get older, your bones may be more likely to weaken. Foods such as milk and spinach contain calcium that helps your bones grow and stay strong. Rest and exercise are important to keep both muscles and bones healthy.

8. **Suggest** Make a list of at least three things you do to keep your bones and muscles healthy.

....

....

....

Got it?   ⬤ 5.4.1

9. **Summarize** What are the main organs of the skeletal and muscular systems? What are their functions?

....

....

....

....

10. **Clarify** How do muscles work in pairs to move a bone?

....

....

◼ **Stop!** I need help with ....

⏸ **Wait!** I have a question about ....

▶ **Go!** Now I know ....

What is the nervous system?

5.NS.1 Make predictions and formulate testable questions. 5.NS.9 Compare the results of an investigation with the prediction.

Envision It!

Circle the square that you think is darker. Then cover all the other squares with paper. Is your answer the same?

Inquiry Explore It!

What is your reaction time?

1. Hold out your hand, slightly open. Have a partner hold a meterstick so that the end is even with your thumb.

2. Watch the meterstick.
As soon as your partner lets go of it, catch it.

3. Read the number closest to the top of your thumb. On the Reaction Time Bar Graph, color in the bar for Trial 1 to **record** your data.

4. Repeat 9 more times.

Explain Your Results

5. Compare your results to other groups' results.

....

....

6. **Infer** Based on your data, how does practice affect reaction time?

....

....

Materials

meterstick

Reaction Time Bar Graph

Reaction Time Bar Graph

You use the number of centimeters as a simple way to measure reaction time.

5.DP.9 Present evidence using mathematical representations (graphs, data tables). 5.NS.7 Keep accurate records in a notebook during investigations and communicate findings to others using graphs, charts, maps and models through

myscienceonline.com

Explore It! Animation

UNLOCK THE BIG ?

I will know that the nervous system includes the brain, spinal cord, nerves, and sense organs. It tells your body how to react to its environment.

Words to Know

nervous system
brain

Nervous System

In order to stay healthy, comfortable, and safe, your body needs information about your environment. It needs to know whether it is too cold or too hot, whether you are sitting down or standing up, and whether or not something hurts. Your body also needs to react appropriately, based on this information. Maybe you need to walk faster because you saw a bicycle heading your way. Or maybe you decide to eat because you are feeling hungry.

The system that receives information from your environment and controls how you react to it is the nervous system. The **nervous system** tells you what is going on in the world around you. It also tells your muscles how to contract to move the bones of your body. The nervous system includes nerves, the spinal cord, the brain, and sense organs.

1. **List** What are some different ways the juggler is using his body systems?

....

....

....

....

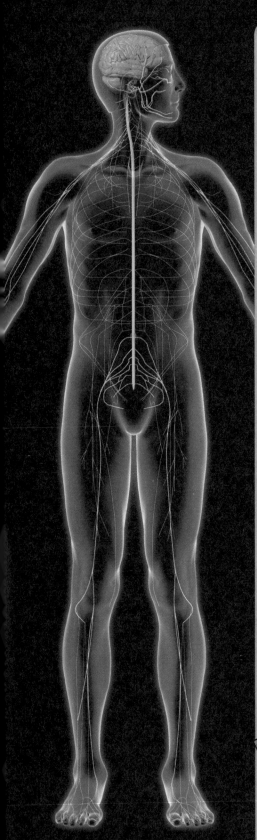

The nervous system is a system of structures that send information throughout the body.

Nerves

Nerve cells are also called neurons. Neurons pass messages throughout your body. Neurons are made of three parts: a cell body, an axon, and one or more dendrites. The cell body is the main part of the neuron. Dendrites receive messages from other neurons. The axon sends messages from the cell body to other neurons.

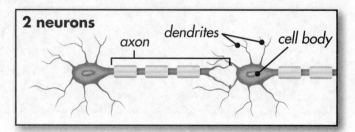

2 neurons

axon   *dendrites*   *cell body*

Messages can only travel in one direction between neurons. Most messages travel along neurons to the brain, which controls almost everything you experience and do. The brain interprets the message and responds by sending messages through neurons to different parts of the body telling them to act.

2. **Analyze** Draw an arrow on the neuron showing the direction a message travels through the axon.

Spinal Cord

Another important part of your nervous system is your spinal cord. Messages received and sent by the brain pass through your spinal cord. This long bundle of nerves runs down your back and is protected by your backbone. Parts of the spinal cord carry messages to the brain. Others carry messages from the brain.

3. **Describe** What is the function of the spinal cord?

....

....

....

Brain Functions

Performing tasks, such as remembering, pretending, and feeling, are functions of the brain. So are running, playing games, and listening to music. The **brain** is the main organ, or control center, of the nervous system.

Your brain is made up of three major parts. The largest part of your brain is the cerebrum. This part of your brain learns, reasons, decides, stores memories, and feels fear and joy. Another part of your brain is the cerebellum. The cerebellum controls balance and posture. A third part of your brain is the brain stem. Your brain stem controls your blood pressure, heartbeat, breathing, and digestion.

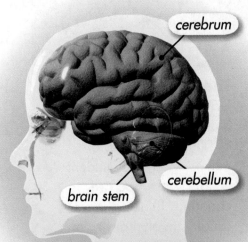

cerebrum

cerebellum

brain stem

4. **Analyze** If a person has a head injury and the cerebellum is damaged, what might the consequences be?

Voluntary Actions

A major function of your nervous system is to control voluntary actions. Voluntary actions are actions you decide to do, such as chewing, walking, or talking. The part of your brain that controls voluntary actions is the cerebrum.

Involuntary Actions

Another major function of your nervous system is to control involuntary actions. You do not need to think about starting and stopping involuntary actions. Your brain stem controls some involuntary actions, such as the beating of your heart.

Some messages that the body receives do not pass to the brain at all. One example is the response of your body when you touch your hand to a hot surface. The response to that action is a reflex, a response that happens automatically without the brain "thinking" about it.

5. **Hypothesize** Why are reflexes important?

6. **Fill in** the captions with the correct type of action.

Kicking a ball is a(n)

.... *action.*

Sneezing is a(n)

.... *action.*

Lightning Lab

The Blink of an Eye
How often do people blink? Count the number of blinks a classmate makes when that student is not aware you are counting. Blinking is usually involuntary.

Senses and Sense Organs

You walk outside. The smell of freshly cut grass fills the air. A cool breeze blows against your forehead. The sound of birds singing echoes through the air. You use your senses to know what is happening around you.

The nervous system is constantly collecting information both inside and outside your body. It allows you to speak, think, taste, hear, and see. It helps the body stay balanced by processing and responding to the information it receives.

Sight *The eyes have parts that sense light and send signals to the brain.*

Hearing and Balance *Ears have sensors that detect vibrations in sound waves. They also have sensors that help you control your balance.*

Smell *Sense organs in the nose read chemicals in odors. Impulses from these organs are read by the brain.*

Touch *Special sensors in the skin help you feel touch, changes in temperature, and sometimes pain.*

Taste *Taste buds are small sense organs located on the tongue.*

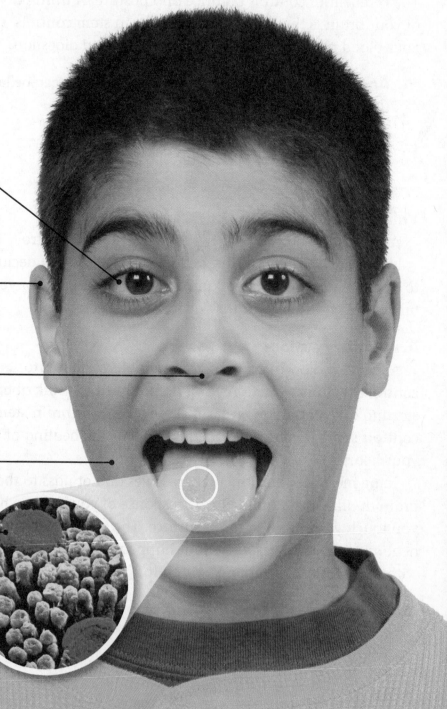

myscienceonline.com | Got it? 60-Second Video

7. **Describe** Your alarm clock rings. Name the senses that are used while turning your alarm off. Tell how each of these senses helps you turn the alarm off.

8. [CHALLENGE] Why is it that sometimes it takes longer to go through the steps of turning off your alarm?

Got it?

5.NS.1, 5.NS.9

9. **Group** What three main parts make up the nervous system? What are their functions?

10. **Contrast** How are the three parts of the brain different?

■ **Stop!** I need help with

❚❚ **Wait!** I have a question about

▶ **Go!** Now I know

What are some other systems?

5.NS.3 Plan and carry out investigations as a class, in small groups or independently, often over a period of several class lessons.

Envision It!

Tell how this kitchen tool is similar to your digestive system.

Inquiry Explore It!

What can speed digestion?

☑ **1.** Place a sugar cube in a bag. Gently crush it with your foot.

☑ **2.** Fill two cups about half full with water.

☑ **3.** Drop a whole sugar cube in one cup. Stir it with a spoon until dissolved. **Record** how long it takes to dissolve. ....

☑ **4.** Repeat step 3 with the crushed cube in the other cup. **Record** how long it takes to dissolve. ....

Explain Your Results

5. Compare the dissolving times of both cups.

....

....

6. **Infer** how the size of pieces of food might affect digestion time.

....

....

Materials

2 sugar cubes

water

plastic bag

spoon

2 plastic cups

timer, stopwatch, or clock with second hand

5.NS.5 Use measurement skills and apply appropriate units when collecting data.
5.NS.8 Identify simple patterns in data and propose explanations to account for the patterns.

myscienceonline.com | **Explore It!** Animation

UNLOCK THE BIG ?

I will know the parts and the functions of several other body systems.

Words to Know
....

digestive system	excretory system
stomach	kidneys
intestines	bladder
	skin

Digestive System

Food must be changed before your body can use it for energy. The **digestive system** breaks down food into very small parts that the body can use. Food can then be carried in the blood to your cells. Many organs work together to digest food. This process is called digestion.

Digestion starts in the mouth. When you chew, your teeth, tongue, and salivary glands work together to make the food easy to swallow. Chewing grinds the food down, and saliva helps to make a soft paste. Saliva also begins to break down starches in the food. These changes begin the process of digestion.

The esophagus is a tube that carries food to the stomach. Gravity alone does not move food to the stomach. The esophagus moves the food by squeezing rings of muscles in a pattern. Muscles behind the food contract as the lump of food passes each ring of muscle. This pushes the food through the esophagus to the stomach.

1. **Visualize** When food "goes down the wrong pipe," people can choke. Look at the picture. (Circle) what you think is the "wrong pipe." Tell what the tube is and where it leads.

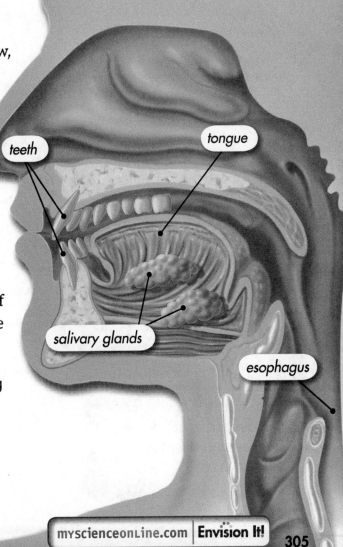

teeth

tongue

salivary glands

esophagus

Stomach

The lower end of your esophagus is kept closed by a tight ring of muscle. When you swallow, this muscle relaxes and opens to let food into your stomach. The muscle then closes to keep the food from moving back into your esophagus.

The **stomach** is the organ where food begins to break down after swallowing. Your stomach is under your ribs on the lower left. The walls of the stomach can stretch to store all of the food from a meal. The stomach releases acids that help break down food. As strong muscles in the stomach wall squeeze, the food and acids mix. The mixture becomes a soupy paste and is now ready to leave the stomach.

2. **Describe** What role does the stomach play in digestion?

....

....

....

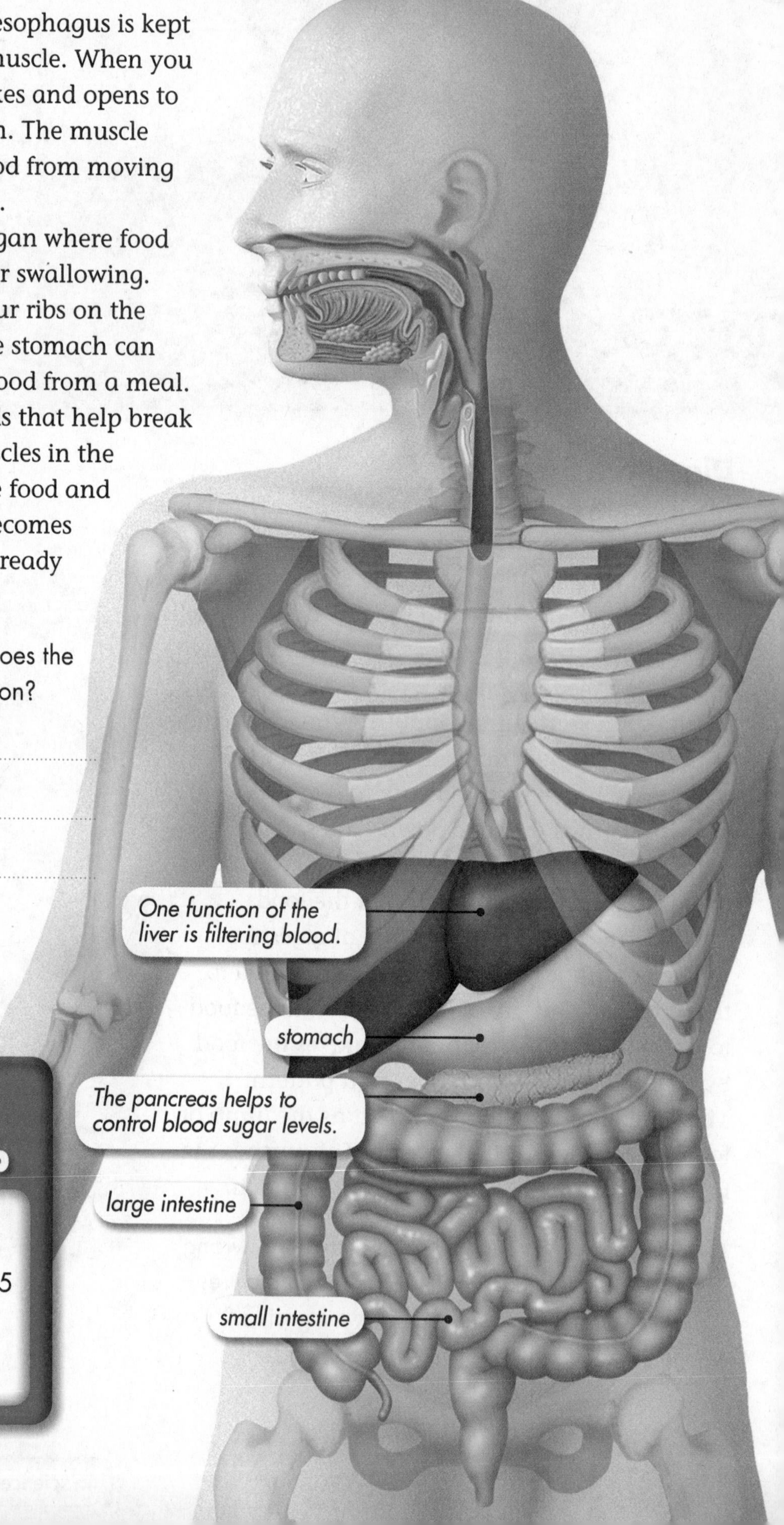

One function of the liver is filtering blood.

stomach

The pancreas helps to control blood sugar levels.

large intestine

small intestine

At-Home Lab

Chew Your Food
Put a saltine cracker in your mouth. Chew it for 5 minutes or so, but do not swallow it. Tell what you observe.

Intestines, Liver, and Pancreas

Partly digested food is squeezed from the stomach into the small intestine. The **intestines** are tube-shaped organs through which most nutrients and water are absorbed from food. The small intestine is about 7 meters long. In the small intestine, food is made less acidic and is broken down into small particles that the blood can absorb. Muscles of the small intestine move food in one direction. Your liver and pancreas are organs that send chemicals to the small intestine to help you digest food.

During digestion, most nutrients move into blood vessels in the walls of the small intestine. Tiny finger-shaped structures called *villi* cover the inside walls of the small intestine. Villi give the small intestine more surface area to absorb food.

Food that cannot be digested in the small intestine moves into a wider tube called the large intestine. Sections of the large intestine perform different jobs. One part recovers some water from the indigestible parts of food. Another part stores this waste until the waste is ready to leave the body.

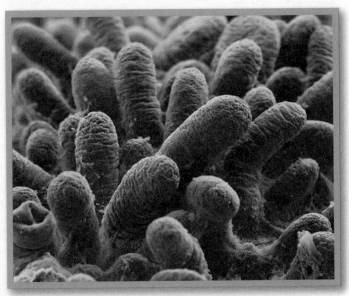

Villi help your body get more nutrients from your food.

3. **Summarize** How do the villi help the small intestine digest food?

4. **Calculate** There are about 3.3 feet in 1 meter. About how long is the small intestine in feet?

5. **Hypothesize** Look at the picture to the left. Beneath these villi's thin walls is a web of capillaries. Why is it helpful to have capillaries here?

Excretory System

Your body cells make wastes that enter your blood. Wastes can become toxic. For this reason, organisms have structures that remove waste from the blood. In your body, this job is done mostly by the **excretory system.**

Your **kidneys** are a pair of organs that remove waste from your blood. Kidneys have the shape and dark red color of kidney beans. The kidneys take out some water with the wastes. This mix of wastes and water is urine. A tube carries urine away from each kidney to the urinary bladder. The **bladder** is a hollow organ that collects and stores urine formed by the kidneys. At the bottom of the bladder is a tight round muscle that keeps urine inside until it is removed from the body by urination.

In addition to the kidneys and bladder, your **skin** also helps you get rid of wastes from the blood. The wastes are released through sweat glands along with water and salt. Skin also covers and protects the outside of your body.

When you sweat, wastes are removed through the skin and the body is cooled.

6. **Compare and Contrast** Tell how kidneys, lungs, and sweat glands are alike. Tell how they are different.

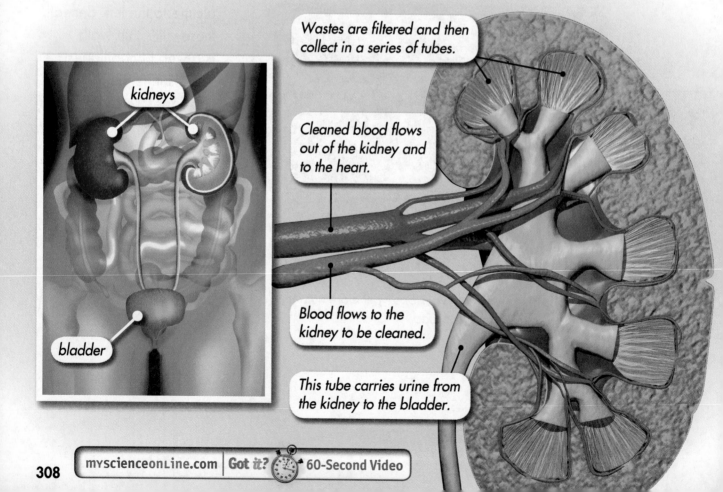

kidneys

bladder

Wastes are filtered and then collect in a series of tubes.

Cleaned blood flows out of the kidney and to the heart.

Blood flows to the kidney to be cleaned.

This tube carries urine from the kidney to the bladder.

myscienceonline.com | Got it? 60-Second Video

Reproductive System

Humans, like other organisms, have body structures that make it possible to reproduce and have offspring. Different types of sex cells are made by organs in males and females. Sex cells from a male and a female join to form an offspring. The body structures that make it possible for an organism to reproduce make up the reproductive system.

7. Describe What is the function of the reproductive system?

....

....

....

8. Fill in the crossword puzzle below.

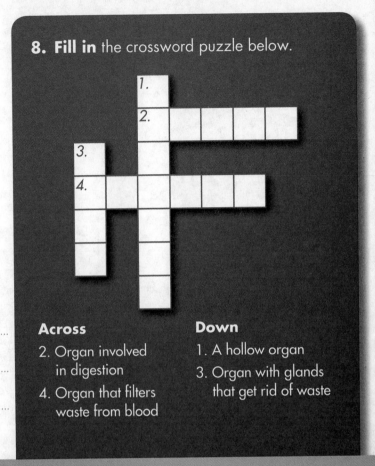

Across

2. Organ involved in digestion
4. Organ that filters waste from blood

Down

1. A hollow organ
3. Organ with glands that get rid of waste

Got it?

○ 5.NS.3

9. ◉ **Sequence** Food travels from the mouth to the end of the large intestine during digestion. List the structures food passes through in order. Choose one and tell its function.

....

....

....

10. **UNLOCK THE BIG ?** What system removes waste from the body?

....

■ **Stop!** I need help with ....

❙❙ **Wait!** I have a question about ....

▶ **Go!** Now I know ....

How do physical structures compare in living things?

The skin of the glass frog is very translucent. **Circle** the parts of the frog's body that you can see through its skin.

mY pLaneT DiaRY

Science Stats

A blue whale lives much longer than a mouse.

What do a mouse and a blue whale have in common? Well, among other things, they are both mammals, and their hearts will beat about 1 billion times during their lifetimes.

As a general rule, a mammal's heart beats about 1 billion times before the animal dies. The larger the animal, the slower its heart rate, and the longer it lives. A mouse, with a fast heart rate, lives about 2 years. A blue whale, with a much slower heart rate, may live to be 80. Humans are an exception to this pattern. Because we mature more slowly, our hearts beat closer to 3 billion times during our lifetimes.

Give an Example Name three mammals. Which do you think is more likely to live the longest? Explain.

....

....

....

UNLOCK
THE BIG
?

I will know similarities and differences in the structures and functions of parts of plants and animals.

Word to Know
....
exoskeleton

Physical Structures

Have you ever seen a tree with bark that was peeling? Some trees shed their bark as a normal part of their growth. The tough outer covering of bark peels away so that new tree growth can expand outward. In a similar way, snakes shed their skins as they grow. All living organisms have structures that help them grow, get energy, and stay healthy. Sometimes structures can be very similar even though the organisms are different.

Other times, physical structures can be very different even if they do similar jobs. For example, an animal egg may be very delicate and may need to be hidden from predators. By contrast, many plant seeds have tough coverings and easily survive being swallowed by an animal. The seeds develop inside tasty fruits that animals like to eat. The seeds benefit because an animal can carry them to places where they may grow better.

paperbark maple tree

1. ⦿ **Text Features** Find two text features on this page. Write a clue each one gives about the content.

....

....

garter snake

2. **Compare** How are a snake shedding its skin and a tree losing bark alike?

....

....

Structures for Support

Some animals, such as fish and humans, have internal skeletons. An internal skeleton supports the body. It also protects organs such as the brain and the heart.

Other animals have **exoskeletons,** which are hard skeletons on the outside of their bodies. Exoskeletons give structure and protection.

Plants have stems that stretch toward the sunlight and can hold the weight of leaves and fruit. Some plants, such as trees, have wood in their stems and branches for additional support.

4. Justify Many stems hold leaves high. Higher leaves are more likely to get sunlight. How is this helpful to a plant?

The skull is like a strong cage that protects the brain.

3. Draw some organs that are protected by the rib cage.

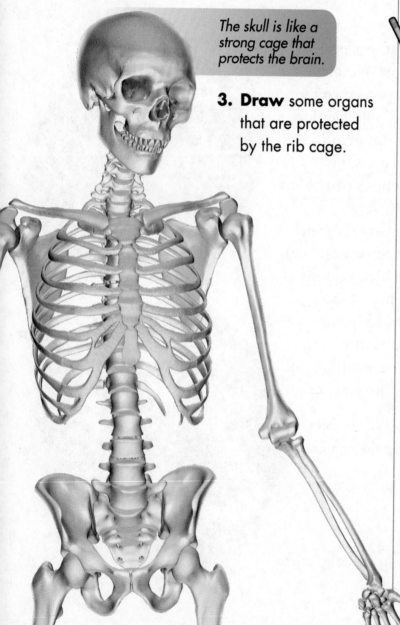

Insects, such as the cicada, have a hard exoskeleton. In order to grow, insects usually need to shed their old exoskeleton and grow a new one.

5. Compare and Contrast How is an exoskeleton similar to an internal skeleton? How is it different?

myscienceonline.com | THE BIG ? | I Will Know...

Structures for Reproduction

Living things can make other living things similar to themselves. This process is called reproduction.

Many plants reproduce using flowers. For example, when pollen from a cherry flower is carried to another cherry flower, the receiving flower becomes fertilized. It grows into a cherry with a seed inside. The seed has a source of nutrition and a protective covering. If this seed lands on good soil, a new cherry plant may grow.

Animals reproduce in different ways. For example, some female fish lay eggs on underwater rocks. Then males fertilize the eggs. An organism grows inside of each egg, which has a source of nutrition and a protective cover. In other animals, such as mammals, males have structures to fertilize eggs within the body of the female.

seedling

shark egg sac

6. Diagram On the flower below, (circle) where a seed will develop.

7. Label Write the correct letter in each circle above.

A organism

B protective cover

C nutrition source

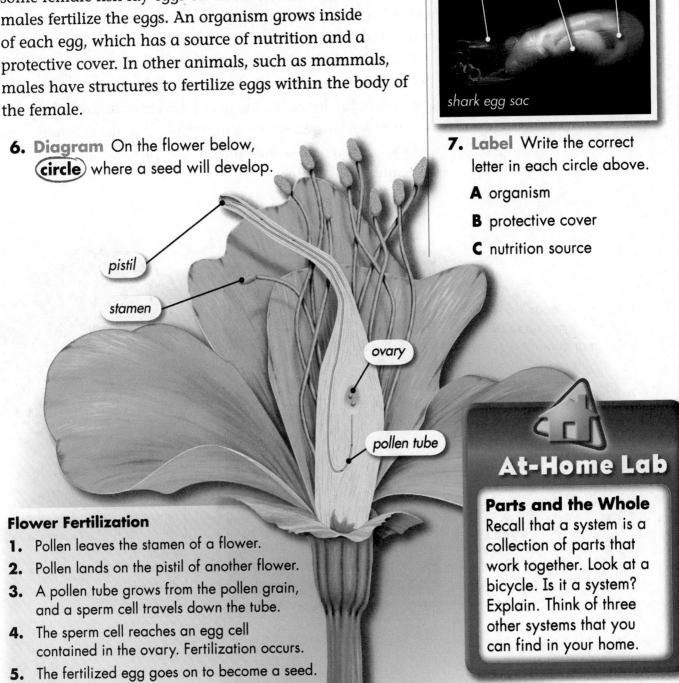

pistil

stamen

ovary

pollen tube

Flower Fertilization

1. Pollen leaves the stamen of a flower.
2. Pollen lands on the pistil of another flower.
3. A pollen tube grows from the pollen grain, and a sperm cell travels down the tube.
4. The sperm cell reaches an egg cell contained in the ovary. Fertilization occurs.
5. The fertilized egg goes on to become a seed.

At-Home Lab

Parts and the Whole
Recall that a system is a collection of parts that work together. Look at a bicycle. Is it a system? Explain. Think of three other systems that you can find in your home.

8. Draw a picture of one other animal that breathes using lungs and a picture of an animal that breathes with gills. Explain your choices.

Structures for Respiration and Circulation

In order for plants and animals to live, they need to exchange gases with their environments. Animals such as turtles and humans take in air through the mouth or nose and breathe using lungs. Some other animals, such as insects, take air in through structures called spiracles. These are holes in the insect's body. Most fish take in oxygen from water through their gills.

Lungs, spiracles, and gills are three ways animals can get oxygen. A spiracle often allows oxygen to go directly to body tissue. But with lungs and gills, oxygen entering the animal is transported through a circulatory system to the body's cells.

Plants have structures that are similar to spiracles on insects. These microscopic holes are called stomata and are located on the leaves of the plant. During photosynthesis, a plant uses carbon dioxide from the air to make sugar, or food. Oxygen is formed during this process and exits through the stomata.

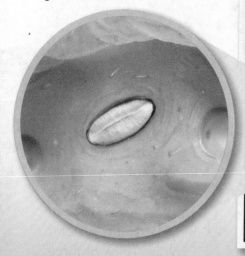

Spiracles on the skin of a caterpillar open up to let gases in or out.

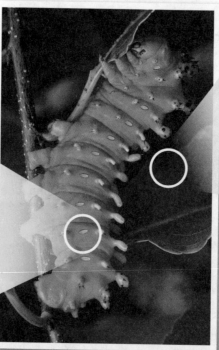

Like the spiracles of insects, stomata on the surface of a leaf open up to let gases in or out.

myscienceonline.com | Got it? ⏱ 60-Second Video

Some plants also have a circulatory system. These plants are called vascular plants. The tissues in the vascular system act similar to arteries and veins. The plant uses the vascular tissue to transport sugar made in the leaves to the roots for storage.

Tube structures within a plant stem transport water and nutrients to and from the leaves, roots, and rest of the plant.

9. **Compare and Contrast** How is the function of a plant's vascular system similar to the function of your arteries and veins? How is it different?

Got it?

10. **Rank** List the terms *organ system*, *tissue*, *cell*, and *organ* in order from largest and most complex to smallest and simplest.

11. **UNLOCK THE BIG ?** What are some organs in plants and animals that serve a similar purpose?

☐ **Stop!** I need help with ....

❙❙ **Wait!** I have a question about ....

▶ **Go!** Now I know ....

How much air can you exhale?

Follow a Procedure

☑ **1.** Lay a trash bag over the top of a desk or table. Remove as many wrinkles as possible. Tape down the edges.

☑ **2.** Pour about 50 mL of bubble solution onto the bag.

Materials

tape

ruler

bubble solution

graduated cylinder (or measuring cup)

straws

trash bag

Be careful! Do not inhale through the straw. Do not share straws.

☑ **3.** Spread the solution around on the bag with the ruler. Dip a straw in the jar of bubble solution. Touch the straw to the wet bag. Take a deep breath and slowly blow as much breath as you can into the straw. **Observe** a bubble forming.

Inquiry Skill

Scientists make careful observations and **measurements.** They record data accurately and use it to help make inferences.

5.NS.3 Plan and carry out investigations as a class, in small groups or independently, often over a period of several class lessons.
5.DP.9 Present evidence using mathematical representations (graphs, data tables). (Also **5.NS.8**)

4. Pop the bubble. **Measure** and **record** the diameter of the ring left on the bag. Use the Volume Chart to estimate the volume of air you exhaled.

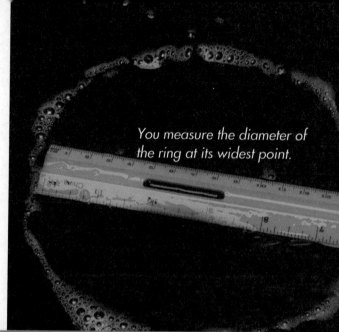

You measure the diameter of the ring at its widest point.

5. Record data for each student in your group.

Data Table					
Name of Student	Diameter of Ring (cm)	Volume of Air (L)	Name of Student	Diameter of Ring (cm)	Volume of Air (L)

Analyze and Conclude

6. When you blew into the straw, what happened to the air you breathed out?

....

....

7. **Infer** Why did different students have rings of different diameters?

....

....

....

....

....

Volume Chart	
Diameter of Ring (cm)	Volume of Air (L)
14	0.7
15	0.9
16	1.1
17	1.3
18	1.5
19	1.8
20	2.1
21	2.4
22	2.8
23	3.2

Charles Drew

Around the world, people owe their lives to the work of Dr. Charles Drew. He found ways of preserving blood in blood banks.

After graduating from medical school, Dr. Drew became interested in studying blood. In particular, he studied the problem of storing blood. Healthy people gave their blood to be stored until a patient needed it. The problem was that blood spoiled in a matter of days. Dr. Drew learned that plasma could be stored longer than whole blood and could sometimes be given to a patient instead of whole blood.

During World War II, Dr. Drew headed a program that sent blood and plasma to Great Britain. It was his idea to have "bloodmobiles," which were refrigerated trucks that went to locations where blood was donated. Later, Dr. Drew directed the first American Red Cross Blood Bank.

APPLY THE BIG Q How did Charles Drew's knowledge of the characteristics of blood help him find ways of helping people?

....

....

....

....

Vocabulary Smart Cards

tissue
organ
system
circulatory system
heart
respiratory system
diaphragm
lungs
trachea
skeletal system
skeleton
muscles
muscular system
nervous system
brain
digestive system
stomach
intestines
excretory system
kidneys
bladder
skin
exoskeleton

Play a Game!

Cut out the Vocabulary Smart Cards. Choose a word. Draw a picture of the word. Have a partner guess which word your picture shows. Take turns.

circulatory system
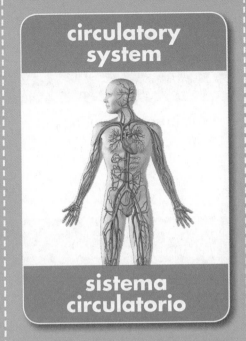
sistema circulatorio

tissue
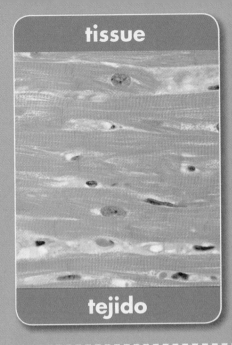
tejido

heart
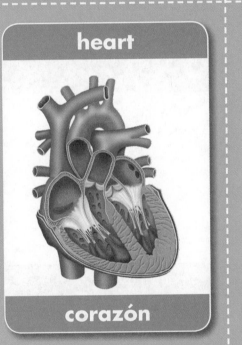
corazón

organ
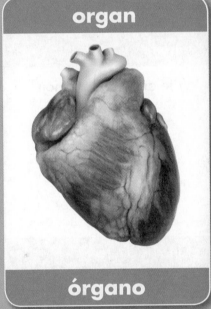
órgano

respiratory system
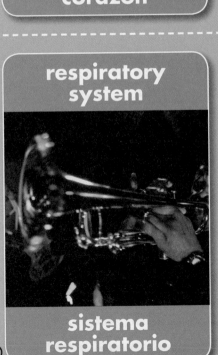
sistema respiratorio

system

sistema

a group of the same kind of cells that work together to do the same job

Write another definition for this word.

....

....

grupo de células del mismo tipo que trabajan en conjunto para realizar una misma función

a body system that moves blood through the body and includes the heart, blood, and blood vessels

Write a sentence using this term.

....

sistema del cuerpo que lleva la sangre por todo el cuerpo e incluye el corazón, la sangre y los vasos sanguíneos

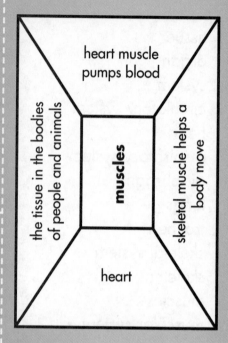

heart muscle pumps blood

the tissue in the bodies of people and animals

muscles

skeletal muscle helps a body move

heart

Make a Word Frame!

Choose a vocabulary term and write it in the center of the frame. Write details about the vocabulary term.

a group of different tissues that join together into one structure

Write another definition for this word.

....

....

grupo de diferentes tejidos que se unen en una estructura

a muscular organ that pumps blood throughout your body

Write three compound words using this word.

....

....

....

órgano muscular que bombea sangre por todo el cuerpo

a set of things that work together as a whole

Write three related words.

....

....

....

objetos que funcionan como una unidad

the system of the body that helps you breathe

Draw a picture.

sistema del cuerpo que te ayuda a respirar

muscular system	**skeletal system**	**diaphragm**
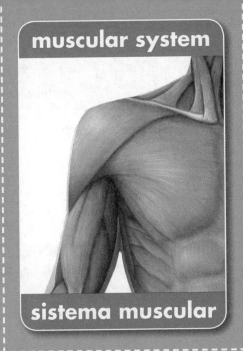	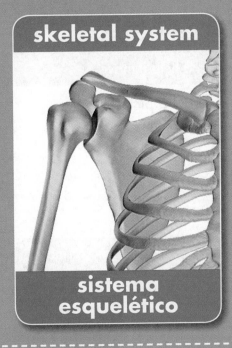	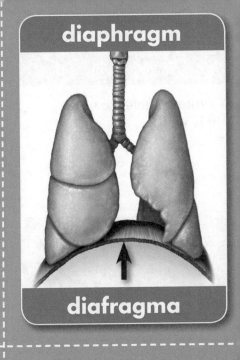
sistema muscular	**sistema esquelético**	**diafragma**
nervous system	**skeleton**	**lungs**
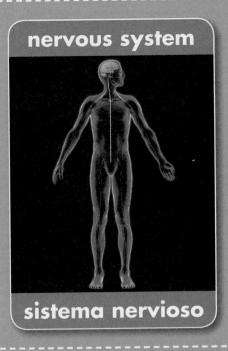	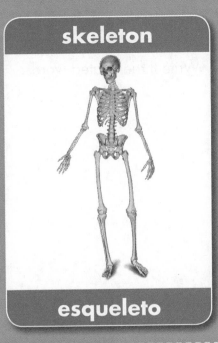	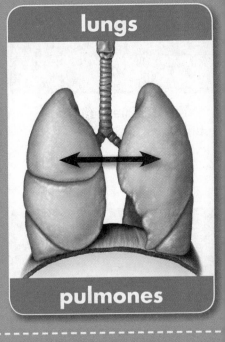
sistema nervioso	**esqueleto**	**pulmones**
brain	**muscles**	**trachea**
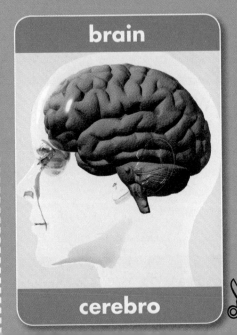	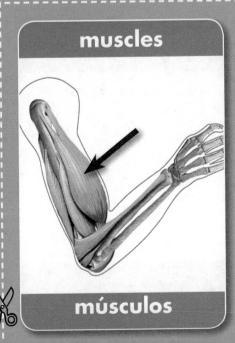	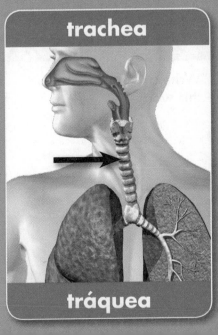
cerebro	**músculos**	**tráquea**

a dome-shaped muscle that moves down to make more space in your chest for air

Write a sentence using this word.

....

....

músculo en forma de cúpula que se mueve hacia abajo, haciendo más espacio en tu pecho para que entre el aire

---

a body system made up of bones that support the body and help it move

Draw a picture.

sistema del cuerpo formado por huesos que sostienen el cuerpo y lo ayudan a moverse

---

a system of the body that is made up of muscles and the tissues that attach them to bones

Write a sentence using this term.

....

....

sistema del cuerpo formado por músculos y los tejidos que unen los músculos a los huesos

---

organs that help the body exchange oxygen and carbon dioxide with the air outside the body

Write a sentence using this term.

....

órganos que ayudan a que el cuerpo intercambie oxígeno y dióxido de carbono con el aire fuera del cuerpo

---

all the bones in the body

Write three related words.

....

....

....

....

....

todos los huesos del cuerpo

---

a system of the body that tells you what is going on in the world around you

Draw a picture.

sistema del cuerpo que te dice qué está ocurriendo a tu alrededor

---

a tube that carries air to the lungs

Write a synonym of this word.

....

....

....

tubo que lleva aire hacia los pulmones

---

organs that work together to move the body

Write three examples.

....

....

....

....

órganos que funcionan como una unidad para mover el cuerpo

---

the main organ, or control center, of the nervous system

Write three compound words using this word.

....

....

....

órgano principal, o centro de control, del sistema nervioso

skin	excretory system	digestive system
	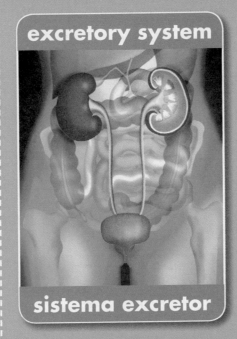	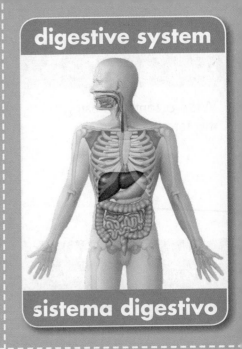
piel	sistema excretor	sistema digestivo

exoskeleton	kidneys	stomach
	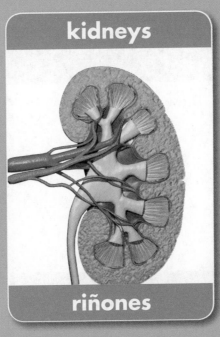	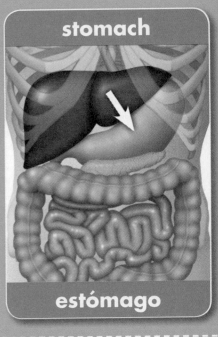
exoesqueleto	riñones	estómago

	bladder	intestines
		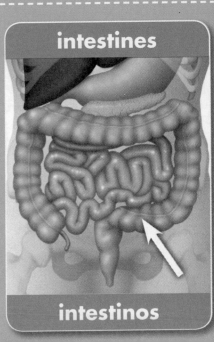
	vejiga	intestinos

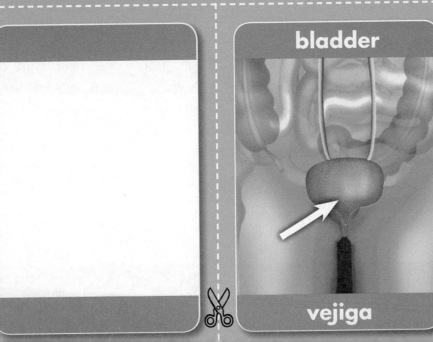

the body system that breaks down food into very small parts that the body can use

Write a sentence using this term.

....

....

sistema del cuerpo que descompone los alimentos en trozos pequeñitos que el cuerpo puede usar

---

a system of the body that removes waste from the blood

Write a sentence using this term.

....

....

....

sistema del cuerpo que elimina los desechos de la sangre

---

an organ that covers and protects the body and releases wastes from the blood through sweat glands

Write a sentence using this word.

....

órgano que cubre y protege el cuerpo y elimina los desechos de la sangre a través de las glándulas sudoríparas

---

organ where food begins to break down after swallowing

Draw a picture.

órgano donde los alimentos comienzan a descomponerse después de que los tragamos

---

a pair of organs that remove waste from the blood

Draw a picture.

par de órganos que eliminan desechos de la sangre

---

a hard skeleton on the outside of the body of some animals

Write the prefix of this word.

....

Write what the prefix means.

....

esqueleto duro en el exterior del cuerpo de algunos animales

---

tube-shaped organs through which most nutrients and water are absorbed from food

Write a sentence using this word.

....

órganos de forma tubular a través de los cuales se absorbe la mayoría de los nutrientes y el agua de los alimentos

---

a hollow organ that collects and stores urine formed by the kidneys

Write another meaning for this word.

....

....

....

órgano hueco que acumula y almacena la orina que se forma en los riñones

Lesson 1

What is the circulatory system?

- The circulatory system moves blood through the body.
- The circulatory system includes the heart, blood, and blood vessels.

Lesson 2

What is the respiratory system?

- The respiratory system exchanges gases between air and the blood.
- The respiratory system includes the nose, mouth, trachea, bronchi, and bronchioles and air sacs in the lungs.

Lesson 3

What are the skeletal and muscular systems?

- The skeletal and muscular systems support your body and help it move.
- These systems include the bones and muscles.

Lesson 4

What is the nervous system?

- The nervous system gathers information about the environment and tells the different parts of the body what to do.
- The nervous system includes the brain, sense organs, and nerves.

Lesson 5

What are some other systems?

- The digestive system changes food into forms the body can use.
- The excretory system removes wastes from the body.
- The reproductive system makes it possible to form offspring.

Lesson 6

How do physical structures compare in living things?

- Sometimes the structures of organisms can be similar even though the organisms are different.
- Structures can be different even if they do similar jobs.

Chapter Review

 How are living things organized?

Lesson 1   5.NS.8

What is the circulatory system?

1. **Analyze** Blood entering the heart is pumped to the lungs before being pumped back out to the body. Why is this important?

2. **Text Features** Use the following paragraph to answer the question.

> Tissues join with other types of tissues to form organs. An **organ** is a group of different tissues that join together into one structure. These tissues work together to do a main job in the body.

Why is the word *organ* in a yellow highlight?

Lesson 2   5.NS.4

What is the respiratory system?

3. **Infer** What might happen if the cilia in the trachea were damaged?

Lesson 3   5.4.1

What are the skeletal and muscular systems?

4. **Explain** Why are two or more muscles needed to move each bone?

Lesson 4   5.NS.1, 5.NS.9

What is the nervous system?

5. Infer How do reflexes keep your body safe?

....

....

....

....

....

....

Lesson 5   5.NS.3

What are some other systems?

6. Compare What different jobs do the small and large intestines do?

....

....

....

....

....

Lesson 6

How do physical structures compare in living things?

7. Vocabulary A(n) _____ is a hard skeleton on the outside of some animals that gives structure and protection.
  A. internal skeleton
  B. exoskeleton
  C. vascular tissue
  D. system

8. Compare How is the vascular system of a plant similar to the circulatory system of an animal?

....

....

9. **ANSWER THE BIG ?** **How are living things organized?**

Choose two systems of the human body. How do they work together?

....

....

....

....

....

....

327

Extended Response

1 Robots are often used to perform tasks that are too difficult or dangerous for humans to do. Miguel designed two robots to move heavy bags of pet food in his pet supply store. Robot A uses one large robot arm and Robot B uses two smaller robot arms. Data from a test of the two robots is shown in the table.

Time Needed to Move Bags of Food

Size of Pet Food Bag	Robot A	Robot B
10 kg	15 sec	30 sec
20 kg	60 sec	45 sec
30 kg	120 sec	60 sec
50 kg	300 sec	90 sec

Miguel wants to sell robots to other pet supply stores. Using the data given, should he make more units of Robot A or of Robot B?

....

Explain why he should use the robot you chose.

....

....

....

How has Miguel used technology based on the human muscular and skeletal systems to solve a problem?

....

....

....

....

5.4.1

Occupational therapists can reteach basic tasks.

Occupational therapists help patients relearn how to perform daily tasks.

Occupational therapists can help refine motor skills.

Occupational Therapist

Occupational therapists help people do the things they need to do each day. The goal of an occupational therapist is to help his or her patients lead productive and independent lives.

Patients' muscular, skeletal, or nervous systems may have suffered damage during an accident or a stroke. The occupational therapist determines the needs of a patient. Then, the therapist makes a list of exercises or tasks that will best help the patient.

A person who wants to become an occupational therapist will need four years of college. States may require therapists to pass certain tests before they are licensed to work. Occupational therapists need more than just medical knowledge. They need to be friendly and able to work with people.

APPLY THE BIG ?

How does knowledge of the way different body systems work together help occupational therapists do their jobs?

329

Materials

masking tape

5 clear plastic cups

plastic spoon

hand lens

pouring container with water

measuring cup

noniodized salt

flat toothpick

brine shrimp eggs

Inquiry Skill

You **control variables** when you make sure the conditions you are not testing remain the same. Controlling variables helps you make sure your experiment is a fair test.

How can salt affect the hatching of brine shrimp eggs?

Brine shrimp are tiny animals that live in salt water. They are in the same group of animals as crabs and lobsters.

Ask a question.

How does the amount of salt in the water affect how many brine shrimp eggs hatch?

State a hypothesis.

1. Write a **hypothesis** by circling one choice and finishing the sentence.

If brine shrimp are put in water with different amounts of salt, then the most eggs will hatch in the cup with (a) *no salt,* (b) *a low salt level,* (c) *a medium salt level,* (d) *a high salt level,* or (e) *a very high salt level* because

Identify and control variables.

2. When you conduct an **experiment,** you must change only one variable. The **variable** you change is the **independent variable.** What will you change?

3. The **dependent variable** is the variable you observe or measure in an experiment. What will you observe?

4. Controlled variables are the factors you must keep the same to have a fair test. List 3 of these factors.

5.NS.1 Make predictions and formulate testable questions. 5.NS.2 Design a fair test. 5.NS.9 Compare the results of an investigation with the prediction. (Also 5.NS.4, 5.NS.7)

Design your test.

☑ **5.** Draw how you will set up your test.

☑ **6.** List your steps in the order you will do them.

Do your test.

☑ **7.** Follow the steps you wrote.

☑ **8.** Make sure to **record** your results in the table.

Collect and record your data.

☑ **9.** Fill in the chart.

Interpret your data.

☑ **10.** Analyze your data. Think about the level of salt. Think how many brine shrimp were moving after 4 days.

In which level of salt did you observe the most brine shrimp moving after 4 days?

....

....

....

State your conclusion.

11. Communicate your conclusion.
Compare your **hypothesis** with your results.
Compare your results with those of other groups.

....

....

....

....

....

....

Soil Survival

Find a large clump of dry soil. If it is not dry, let it dry for a few days. Put it in a jar and add enough water to moisten it. Close the jar to keep the moisture in. After a few days, look at the soil closely. Are there any signs of life? Are there plants germinating? Are there small worms or insects? Record your observations.

🌑 5.3.1, 5.3.2, 5.NS.3

Your Job in the Ecosystem

Imagine that you are an experienced predator. You know the ecosystem you live in. You know where to find prey. Write a training brochure for new predators. Explain to them what they will find in the ecosystem. Tell them how their role in the ecosystem is important.

🌑 5.3.1

Make a Food Chain

Do research to find out about plants and animals that live in your area. You may want to interview an expert. Find out which animals eat which plants. Identify the predators and the prey. Make a diagram of a food chain that includes the plants and animals you researched. Share your findings with the class.

🌑 5.3.1

Using Scientific Methods

1. Ask a question.
2. State your hypothesis.
3. Identify and control variables.
4. Make a plan.
5. Test your hypothesis.
6. Collect, record, and interpret your data.
7. State your conclusion.
8. Do repeated trials.

Measurements

Metric and Customary Measurements

The metric system is the measurement system most commonly used in science. Metric units are sometimes called SI units. SI stands for International System. It is called that because these units are used around the world.

These prefixes are used in the metric system:

kilo- means *thousand*
1 kilometer = 1,000 meters

milli- means *one thousandth*
1,000 millimeters = 1 meter, or 1 millimeter = 0.001 meter

centi- means *one hundredth*
100 centimeters = 1 meter, or 1 centimeter = 0.01 meter

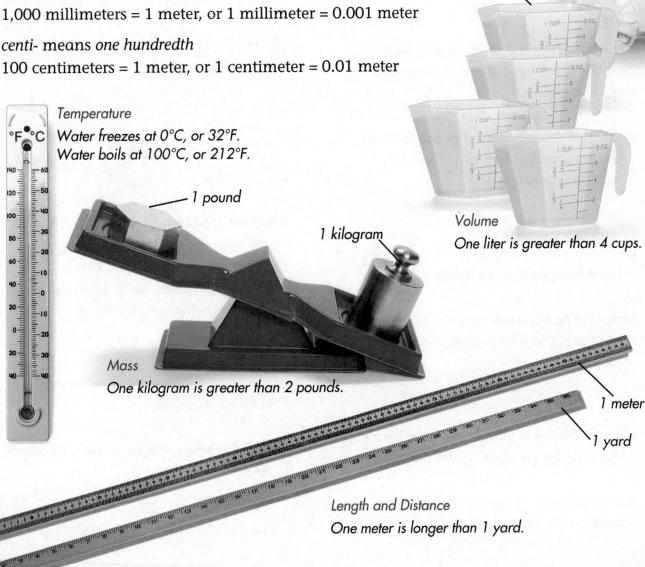

1 liter

1 cup

Temperature
Water freezes at 0°C, or 32°F.
Water boils at 100°C, or 212°F.

1 pound

1 kilogram

Volume
One liter is greater than 4 cups.

Mass
One kilogram is greater than 2 pounds.

1 meter

1 yard

Length and Distance
One meter is longer than 1 yard.

Glossary

The glossary uses letters and signs to show how words are pronounced. The mark ′ is placed after a syllable with a primary or heavy accent. The mark ′ is placed after a syllable with a secondary or lighter accent.

To hear these vocabulary words and definitions, you can refer to the AudioText CD, or log on to the digital path's Vocabulary Smart Cards.

Pronunciation Key

a in hat	ō in open	sh in she
ā in age	ȯ in all	th in thin
â in care	ô in order	ᴛʜ in then
ä in far	oi in oil	zh in measure
e in let	ou in out	ə = a in about
ē in equal	u in cup	ə = e in taken
ėr in term	u̇ in put	ə = i in pencil
i in it	ü in rule	ə = o in lemon
ī in ice	ch in child	ə = u in circus
o in hot	ng in long	

A

accuracy (ak′ yər ə sē) ability to make a measurement that is as close to the correct value as possible

exactitud capacidad de hacer una medición que se aproxime como sea posible al valor verdadero

atom (at′ əm) the smallest part of an element that has the properties of the element

átomo la partícula más pequeña de un elemento, que todavía tiene las propiedades de ese elemento

atomic theory (ə tom′ ik thē′ ər ē) the idea that everything is made of small particles

teoría atómica la idea de que la materia está formada por partículas pequeñas

axis (ak′ sis) an imaginary line around which an object spins

eje línea imaginaria en torno a la cual gira un objeto

B

bladder (blad′ ər) a hollow organ that collects and stores urine formed by the kidneys

vejiga órgano hueco que acumula y almacena la orina que se forma en los riñones

brain (brān) the main organ, or control center, of the nervous system

cerebro órgano principal, o centro de control, del sistema nervioso

C

cellular respiration (sel′ yə lər res′ pə rā′ shən) the process by which cells break down sugar to release energy

respiración celular proceso mediante el cual las células descomponen el azúcar para obtener energía

chemical change (kem′ ə kəl chānj) a change of one or more types of matter into other types of matter with different properties

cambio químico cambio de uno o más tipos de materia a otros tipos de materia con propiedades diferentes

circulatory system (sėr′ kyə lə tôr′ ē sis′ təm) a body system that moves blood through the body and includes the heart, blood, and blood vessels

sistema circulatorio sistema del cuerpo que lleva la sangre por todo el cuerpo e incluye el corazón, la sangre y los vasos sanguíneos

community (kə myü′ nə tē) the group of all populations in an area

comunidad grupo de todas las poblaciones de un área

compound (kom′ pound) a type of matter made of two or more elements

compuesto tipo de materia formada por dos o más elementos

conservation (kon′ sər vā′ shən) an attempt to preserve or protect an environment from harmful changes

conservación intento de conservar o de proteger el medio ambiente de cambios dañinos

constellation (kon′ stə lā′ shən) a group of stars that forms a pattern

constelación grupo de estrellas que forma una figura

consumer (kən sü′ mər) organism that cannot make its own food

consumidor organismo que no puede hacer su propio alimento

control group (kən trōl′ grüp) a standard against which change is measured

grupo de control estándar que se usa para medir un cambio

data (dā′ tə) information from which a conclusion can be drawn or a prediction can be made

datos información de la cual se puede sacar una conclusión o hacer una predicción

deciduous plant (di sij′ ü əs plant) a plant that loses all of its leaves for a part of the year

planta de hoja caduca planta que pierde todas sus hojas durante una época del año

decomposer (dē kəm pō′ zər) organism that gets its energy by breaking down wastes and dead organisms

descomponedor organismo que obtiene su energía descomponiendo desechos y organismos muertos

design process (di zīn′ pros′ es) a set of steps for developing products and processes that solve problems

proceso de diseño serie de pasos para desarollar productos y procesos que resuelven problemas

diaphragm (dī′ ə fram) a dome-shaped muscle that moves down to make more space in your chest for air

diafragma músculo en forma de cúpula que se mueve hacia abajo, haciendo más espacio en tu pecho para que entre el aire

digestive system (də jes′ tiv sis′ təm) the body system that breaks down food into very small parts that the body can use

sistema digestivo sistema del cuerpo que descompone los alimentos en trozos pequeñitos que el cuerpo puede usar

eclipse (i klips′) an event in which one object in space gets between the sun and another object

eclipse fenómeno en el que un objeto del espacio se interpone entre el Sol y otro objeto

ecosystem (ē′ kō sis′ təm) all the living and nonliving things in an area and their interactions

ecosistema todos los seres vivos y las cosas sin vida que hay en un área y sus interacciones

evergreen plant (ev′ ər grēn′ plant) a plant that keeps green leaves on its branches all year

planta de hoja perenne planta cuyas ramas conservan sus hojas verdes todo el año

----

evidence (ev′ ə dəns) observations that make you believe something is true

evidencia observaciones que te hacen creer que algo es cierto

----

excretory system (ek′ skrə tôr′ ē sis′ təm) a system of the body that removes waste from the blood

sistema excretor sistema del cuerpo que elimina los desechos de la sangre

----

exoskeleton (ek′ sō skel′ ə tən) a hard skeleton on the outside of the body of some animals

exoesqueleto esqueleto duro en el exterior del cuerpo de algunos animales

----

experiment (ek sper′ ə mənt) the use of scientific methods to test a hypothesis

experimento uso de métodos científicos para poner a prueba una hipótesis

F

freezing (frē′ zing) the change of a liquid into a solid

congelación cambio de liquido a sólido

G

gas (gas) a substance without a definite volume or shape

gas sustancia que no tiene ni volumen ni forma definidos

H

habitat (hab′ ə tat) a place that provides all the things an organism needs to live

hábitat lugar que proporciona todas las cosas que necesita un organismo para vivir

----

heart (härt) a muscular organ that pumps blood throughout your body

corazón órgano muscular que bombea sangre por todo el cuerpo

----

hypothesis (hī poth′ ə sis) statement of what you think will happen during an investigation

hipótesis enunciado de lo que crees que ocurrirá en una investigación

I

inference (in′ fər əns) a conclusion based on observations

inferencia conclusión basada en observaciones

inner planet (in′ ər plan′ it) any of the four closest planets to the sun

planeta interior cualqiuera de los cuatro planetas más cercanos al Sol

intestines (in tes′ tənz) tube-shaped organs through which most nutrients and water are absorbed from food

intestinos órganos de forma tubular a través de los cuales se absorbe la mayoría de los nutrientes y el agua de los alimentos

K

kidneys (kid′ nēz) a pair of organs that remove waste from the blood

riñones par de órganos que eliminan desechos de la sangre

L

Law of Conservation of Mass (lȯ ov kon′ sər vā′ shən ov mas) a rule stating that in a chemical change, mass is not created or destroyed; it only changes from one form to another

Ley de la Conservación de la Masa regla que dice que en un cambio químico la masa no se crea ni se destruye solamente pasa de una forma a otra

liquid (lik′ wid) a substance that has a definite volume but no definite shape

líquido sustancia que tiene un volumen definido pero no una forma definida

lunar eclipse (lü′ nər i klips′) event in which the moon passes through Earth's shadow

eclipse lunar fenómeno en el que la Luna pasa por la sombra de la Tierra

lungs (lungz) organs that help the body exchange oxygen and carbon dioxide with the air outside the body

pulmones órganos que ayudan a que el cuerpo intercambie oxígeno y dióxido de carbono con el aire fuera del cuerpo

mass (mas) the amount of matter in a solid, liquid, or gas

masa cantidad de materia que tiene un sólido, líquido o gas

melting (mel′ ting) the change of a solid into a liquid

derretir cambio de sólido a líquido

microchip (mī′ krō chip′) a small piece of a computer that contains microscopic circuits

microchip pequeña pieza de computadora que contiene circuitos microscópicos

mixture (miks′ chər) different materials placed together, but each material keeps its own properties

mezcla unión de materiales diferentes durante la cual cada material mantiene sus propiedades

molecule (mol′ ə kyül) the smallest particle of a compound that still has the properties of that compound

molécula la partícula más pequeña de un compuesto, que todavía tiene las propiedades de ese compuesto

moon (mün) a natural object that revolves around a planet

luna satélite natural que orbita un planeta

muscles (mus′ əlz) organs that work together to move the body

músculos órganos que funcionan como una unidad para mover el cuerpo

muscular system (mus′ kyə lər sis′ təm) a system of the body that is made up of muscles and the tissues that attach them to bones

sistema muscular sistema del cuerpo formado por músculos y los tejidos que unen los músculos a los huesos

nervous system (nėr′ vəs sis′ təm) a system
of the body that tells you what is going on in the
world around you

sistema nervioso sistema del cuerpo que te
dice qué está ocurriendo a tu alrededor

observation (ob′ zər vā′ shən) something you
find out about objects, events, or living things by
using your senses

observación algo que descubres con tus
sentidos sobre los objetos, sucesos o seres vivos

....

orbit (ôr′ bit) the path an object takes as it
revolves around a star, planet, or moon

órbita el camino que sigue un objeto al girar
alrededor de una estrella, un planeta o una luna

....

organ (ôr′ gən) a group of different tissues that
join together into one structure

órgano grupo de diferentes tejidos que se unen
en una estructura

....

outer planet (out′ ər plan′ it) any of the four
planets in our solar system beyond Mars

planeta exterior cualqiuera de los cuatro
planetas de nuestro sistema solar que quedan
más allá de Marte

photosynthesis (fō′ tō sin′ thə sis) the process
that plants use to make sugar for food

fotosíntesis proceso por medio del cual las
plantas producen azúcar para alimentarse

....

physical change (fiz′ ə kəl chānj) a change
in some properties of matter without forming a
different kind of matter

cambio físico cambio en algunas de las
propiedades de la materia sin que se forme un
nuevo tipo de materia

....

planet (plan′ it) a large, round object that
revolves around a star and has cleared the
region around its orbit

planeta cuerpo grande y redondo que orbita
una estrella y que ha despejado la zona que
rodea su órbita

....

pollution (pə lü′ shən) any substance that damages the environment

contaminación cualquier sustancia que le hace daño al medio ambiente

population (pop′ yə lā′ shən) a group of organisms of one species that live in an area at the same time

población grupo de organismos de la misma especie que viven en un área al mismo tiempo

precision (pri sizh′ ən) the ability to consistently repeat a measurement

precisión capacidad de repetir una medición de manera consistente

predator (pred′ ə tər) an animal that hunts and eats another animal

predador animal que atrapa a otro animal y se lo come

prey (prā) any animal that is hunted by others for food

presa cualquier animal que es cazado por otros para alimentación

procedures (prə sē′ jərz) step-by-step instructions for completing a task

procedimientos instrucciones paso por paso para realizar una tarea

producer (prə dü′ sər) organism that makes its own food for energy

productor organismo que hace su propio alimento para obtener energía

prosthetic limb (pros thet′ ik lim) an artificial arm, hand, leg, or foot that replaces a missing one

prótesis brazo, mano, pierna o pie artificial que reemplaza el miembro o la parte que falta

prototype (prō′ tə tīp) a version of a solution to a problem

prototipo versión de la solución de un problema

R

respiratory system (res′ pər ə tôr′ ē sis′ təm) the system of the body that helps you breathe

sistema respiratorio sistema del cuerpo que te ayuda a respirar

revolution (rev′ ə lü′ shən) one full orbit around an object

traslación una órbita completa alrededor de un objeto

rotation (rō tā′ shən) one whole spin of an object on its axis

rotación una vuelta completa de un objeto en torno a su eje

S

skeletal system (skel′ ə təl sis′ təm) a body system made up of bones that support the body and help it move

sistema esquelético sistema del cuerpo formado por huesos que sostienen el cuerpo y lo ayudan a moverse

skeleton (skel′ ə tən) all the bones in the body

esqueleto todos los huesos del cuerpo

skin (skin) an organ that covers and protects the body and releases wastes from the blood through sweat glands

piel órgano que cubre y protege el cuerpo y elimina los desechos de la sangre a través de las glándulas sudoríparas

solar eclipse (sō′ lər i klips′) event in which the moon passes between the sun and Earth and casts its shadow on Earth

eclipse solar fenómeno en el que la Luna pasa entre el Sol y la Tierra, proyectando su sombra sobre ésta

solar flare (sō′ lər flâr) an explosive eruption of waves and particles into space

fulguración solar erupción explosiva de ondas y partículas emitidas hacia el espacio

solar system (sō′ lər sis′ təm) the sun and its planets, along with moons, asteroids, and comets

sistema solar el Sol y sus planetas, junto con las lunas, los asteroides y los cometas

solid (sol′ id) a subsance that has a definite shape and volume

sólido sustancia que tiene una forma y un volumen definidos

solution (sə lü′ shən) a mixture in which substances are spread out evenly and will not settle

solución mezcla en la cual una sustancia se dispersa de manera uniforme en otra sustancia y no se asienta

star (stär) a huge ball of very hot gas that gives off energy

estrella bola gigantesca de gas muy caliente que irradia energías

stomach (stum′ ək) organ where foods begin to break down after swallowing

estómago órgano donde los alimentos comienzan a descomponerse después de que los tragamos

system (sis′ təm) a set of things that work together as a whole

sistema objetos que funcionan como una unidad

T

technology (tek nol′ ə jē) the knowledge, processes, and products that solve problems and make work easier

tecnología conocimiento, procesos y productos que se usan para resolver problemas y facilitar el trabajo

tissue (tish′ ü) a group of the same kind of cells that work together to do the same job

tejido grupo de células del mismo tipo que trabajan en conjunto para realizar una misma función

trachea (trā′ kē ə) a tube that carries air to the lungs

tráquea tubo que lleva aire hacia los pulmones

variable (vâr′ ē ə bəl) something that can change in a test

variable algo que puede cambiar durante una prueba

volume (vol′ yəm) the amount of space an object takes up

volumen cantidad de espacio que un objeto ocupa

weight (wāt) the force of Earth's pull on an object

peso fuerza con que la Tierra atrae un objeto

Index

This index lists the pages on which a topic appears. Page numbers following a *p* refer to a photograph or illustration. Page numbers following a *c* refer to a chart or graph.

A

B

C

W

X

Y

Z

Credits

Staff Credits

The people who made up the *Interactive Science* team — representing composition services, core design digital and multimedia production services, digital product development, editorial, editorial services, manufacturing, and production — are listed below.

Geri Amani, Alisa Anderson, Jose Arrendondo, Amy Austin, Scott Baker, Lindsay Bellino, Charlie Bink, Bridget Binstock, Holly Blessen, Robin Bobo, Craig Bottomley, Jim Brady, Laura Brancky, Chris Budzisz, Mary Chingwa, Sitha Chhor, Caroline Chung, Margaret Clampitt, Kier Cline, Brandon Cole, Mitch Coulter, AnnMarie Coyne, Fran Curran, Dana Damiano, Nancy Duffner, Amanda Ferguson, David Gall, Mark Geyer, Amy Goodwin, Gerardine Griffin, Chris Haggerty, Laura Hancko, Jericho Hernandez, Autumn Hickenlooper, Guy Huff, George Jacobson, Marian Jones, Kathi Kalina, Chris Kammer, Sheila Kanitsch, Alyse Kondrat, Mary Kramer, Thea Limpus, Dominique Mariano, Lori McGuire, Melinda Medina, Angelina Mendez, Claudi Mimo, John Moore, Phoebe Novak, Anthony Nuccio, Jeffrey Osier, Julianne Regnier, Charlene Rimsa, Rebecca Roberts, Camille Salerno, Manuel Sanchez, Carol Schmitz, Amanda Seldera, Sheetal Shah, Jeannine Shelton El, Geri Shulman, Greg Sorenson, Samantha Sparkman, Mindy Spelius, Karen Stockwell, Dee Sunday, Dennis Tarwood, Jennie Teece, Lois Teesdale, Michaela Tudela, Oscar Vera, Dave Wade, Tom Wickland, James Yagelski, Tim Yetzina, Diane Zimmermann

Illustrations

100, 113, 115, 181, 245, 287, 292, 294, 306, 321 Precision Graphics; 201, 202, 203 Robert (Bob) Kayganich; 257, 313, 315 Jeff Mangiat; 282, 289, 290, 295, 305, 308, 319, 323 Leonello Calvetti; 293, 298, 312 Big Sesh Studios

All other illustrations Chandler Digital Art

Photographs

Every effort has been made to secure permission and provide appropriate credit for photographic material. The publisher deeply regrets any omission and pledges to correct errors called to its attention in subsequent editions.

Unless otherwise acknowledged, all photographs are the property of Pearson Education, Inc.

Photo locators denoted as follows: Top (T), Center (C), Bottom (B), Left (L), Right (R), Background (Bkgd)

COVER: ©Top-Pics TBK/Alamy Images

2 (C) ©Arthur Tilley/Jupiter Images; 6 (T) ©Alexis Rosenfeld/Photo Researchers, Inc., (CR) Deep Sea Photography; 7 (CR) Humminbird, (B) Stockxpert/Jupiter Images; 8 (B) ©Arctic Images/Alamy Images; 9 (T) ©Douglas Faulkner/Photo Researchers, Inc.; 10 (B) ©Stephen Frink Collection/Alamy Images; 11 (TR) ©Getty Images/Jupiter Images; 12 (T) ©culture-images GmbH/Alamy Images; 13 (CR) ©Chris Ryan/Getty Images; 14 (BL) ©Jim West/Alamy Images, (BR) The image of turbulent flow around a car is from computations by Murtazo Nazarov at the Computational Technology Laboratory at the School of Computer Science and Communication at KTH, with car geometry by courtesy of Volvo Car Corporation; 15 (B) ©Masterfile Royalty-Free; 18 (TR) ©Jaubert Bernard/Alamy Images; 20 (T) ©Priit Vesilind/Getty Images; 21 (BR) ©David R. Frazier/Photo Researchers, Inc.; 25 (B) Digital Vision; 26 (B) Jupiter Images; 27 (CR) Vicky Kasala/Getty Images; 28 (T) ©FogStock/PhotoLibrary Group, Inc., (TR) Jupiter Images; 29 (TC) ©Fedor Selivanov/Shutterstock, (B) ©James L. Amos/Peter Arnold Images/PhotoLibrary Group, Inc., (TL) ©Steve Byland/Shutterstock, (TR) Jupiter Images; 30 (B) ©John Beatty/Photo Researchers, Inc.; 31 (TR) ©James Ingram/Alamy Images; 34 (TR) ©Image Source ; 35 (BR) ©Chris Ryan/Getty Images, (TR) ©Douglas Faulkner/Photo Researchers, Inc., (BL) ©Jaubert Bernard/Alamy Images, (CR) ©Stephen Frink Collection/Alamy Images; 37 (TR) ©David R. Frazier/Photo Researchers, Inc., (CC) ©John Beatty/Photo Researchers, Inc., (TC) Vicky Kasala/Getty Images; 39 (B) ©Arthur Tilley/Jupiter Images; 40 (TR) ©Martin Shields/Photo Researchers, Inc.; 43 (CL) ©JPL/NASA, (Inset) JPL/NASA; 44 ©Yuriko Nakao/Reuters/Landov LLC; 47 (C) ©Bon Appetit/Alamy Images, (TR) ©Carl Keyes/Alamy; 48 (T) ©Julia Hiebaum/Alamy Images; 49 (CR) ©BSIP/Phototake; 50 (BL) ©AJPhoto/Hôpital Américain/Photo Researchers, Inc., (T) ©Karl Kost/Alamy, (BR) ©Mauro Fermariello/Photo Researchers, Inc., (TL) Photo Researchers, Inc.; 51 (TL) ©ALIX/PHANIE/Photo Researchers, Inc., (CR) ©Mark Clarke/Photo Researchers, Inc., (CL) ©TMI/Alamy Images, (TR) Steve Gorton/Old Operating Theatre Museum, London/©DK Images; 52 (CL) ©Clive Streeter/Courtesy of The Science Museum, London/DK Images, (TL) Robertstock; 53 (TR) ©Yuji Sakai/Getty Images; 54 (T) ©Alex Segre/Alamy Images, (BR) ©Market Wire/NewsCom; 55 (R) Mikey Siegel/MIT; 56 (C) ©David Eby/Shutterstock, (BR) Touch Bionics; 58 (BR) ©AP Images; 59 (T) ©Steffen Jaehde/NewsCom; 60 (T) ©Volker Steger/Photo Researchers, Inc.; 62 (TL) ©Gord Waldner/StarPhoenix , (B) ©Image Source ; 63 (C) Image used with permission from Ultreo, Inc.; 64 (B) ©Picture Partners/Alamy Images; 66 (TL) ©Bettmann/Corbis, (T) ©Oliver Leedham/Alamy; 70 Franck Camhi/Alamy Images; 71 (CR) ©Julia Hiebaum/Alamy Images, (BR) Robertstock, (TL) Touch Bionics; 73 ©Yuriko Nakao/Reuters/Landov LLC; 77 (Inset) ©David J. Green - Technology/Alamy Images, (CR) JFK Space Center/NASA; 78 (C) ©Linda Bucklin/Shutterstock; 83 (C) ©Linda Bucklin/Shutterstock; 84 (CL) ©HomeStudio/Shutterstock; 86 ©Carsten Peter/Speleoresearch & Films/National Geographic Image Collection; 89 (C) ©Judith Miller/333 Auctions LLC/©DK Images; 90 (T) ©Bill Kennedy/Shutterstock; 91 (BR) ©Stuart Hannagan/Getty Images; 92 (B) ©Andraz Cerar/Shutterstock, (BR) ©Comstock/Getty Images, (BL) ©iofoto/Shutterstock, (CR) ©vnlit/Shutterstock; 93 (TR) ©AnutkaT/Shutterstock, (BR) ©Sonya Etchison/Shutterstock, (C) Dave King/Courtesy of The Science Museum, London/©DK Images, DK Images, (BL) Stockxpert/Thinkstock; 94 (C) Photos to Go/Photolibrary; 95 (CL) ©KdEdesign/Shutterstock, (TR) ©Richard Megna/Fundamental Photographs, (C, BL) Andy Crawford and Tim Ridley/©DK Images; 96 (CL) ©DK Images, (CR, C) Andy Crawford and Tim Ridley/©DK Images, DK

Images; 97 (TR) Andy Crawford and Tim Ridley/©DK Images; 98 (T) ©M. Mesgleski/PhotoLibrary Group, Inc.; 100 (C) ©Tom Schierlitz/Getty Images; 102 (C) Getty Images; 103 (TL) ©Marika Eglite/Shutterstock; 104 (T) ©AP Images; 105 (CR) ©DK Images; 108 (Bkgd) ©Lawrence Naylor/Photo Researchers, Inc., DK Images; 112 (Bkgd) ©Mary Evans Picture Library/Alamy Images, (Inset) Thinkstock; 113 (BL) ©DK Images, (TL) Andy Crawford and Tim Ridley/©DK Images, (B) DK Images, (C) Photos to Go/Photolibrary; 115 (TR) ©DK Images; 117 ©Carsten Peter/Speleoresearch & Films/National Geographic Image Collection; 119 Colin Keates/Courtesy of the Natural History Museum, London/©DK Images; 121 (Inset) ©1Apix/Alamy, (Bkgd) ©Steve Gschmeissner/SPL/Getty Images; 122 NASA; 125 ©S Oleg/Shutterstock; 126 (T) ©M. Dykstra/Shutterstock; 132 (BL) ©Miles Boyer/Shutterstock, (TR) ©PhotoAlto/Alamy; 134 (TL) ©arteretum/Shutterstock, (B) ©Tischenko Irina/Shutterstock, (CL) STSci/NASA; 135 (CR) Trish Gant/©DK Images; 142 (T) ©fotohunter/Shutterstock; 143 (R) ©1996 Richard Megna/Fundamental Photographs, (T) ©Anthony Ise/Getty Images; 144 (CR) ©FoodCollection/SuperStock, (Bkgd) ©Olga Lipatova/Shutterstock; 145 (BR) ©Charles D. Winters/Photo Researchers, Inc., (Bkgd) ©Luminis/Shutterstock; 146 (Bkgd) ©Flashon Studio/Shutterstock, (BR) ©PeppPic/Shutterstock; 147 (BR) ©sciencephotos/Alamy Images; 148 (CR) ©Albert Lleal/Minden Pictures, (BL) ©GC Minerals/Alamy Images; 149 (T) ©irin-k/Shutterstock; 150 David Young-Wolff/PhotoEdit, Inc.; 155 (TR) ©1996 Richard Megna/Fundamental Photographs, (CR) ©Flashon Studio/Shutterstock, (B) NASA; 161 NASA; 168 ©AP Images; 170 (CR) ESA/NASA; 171 (Bkgd) ©Worldspec/NASA/Alamy Images, (CR) Library of Congress; 173 (R) Stephen & Donna O'Meara/Photo Researchers, Inc.; 174 (CR) ©Tony & Daphne Hallas/Photo Researchers, Inc., (B) STScI/AURA/Hubble Heritage/NASA; 175 (TR) JPL/NASA, (B) Robin Hunter/©DK Images; 176 (CL) Johannes Schedler / Panther-Observatory, (TL) NASA; 177 (T) ©Charles & Josette Lenars/Corbis; 178 (T) ©Eckhard Slawik/Photo Researchers, Inc., (B) Babak Tafreshi / Photo Researchers, Inc./Photo Researchers, Inc.; 179 (BL) JPL/NASA, (BC) NASA; 180 (TL) JPL/NASA; 181 (TL) JAXA/NASA; 182 (B) Gerard Lodriguss / Photo Researchers, Inc./Photo Researchers, Inc.; 183 (TR) ©Babk Tafreshi /Photo Researchers, Inc.; 184 (TL) ©Masterfile Royalty-Free; 185 (L) ©Andre Nantel/Shutterstock; 186 (BR) JPL-Caltech/T. Pyle/NASA, (C) NASA; 187 (BC) NASA; 188 (TR, CR) NASA; 189 (TR, CR) NASA; 190 (C) NASA, (TR) U.S. Geological Survey; 191 JPL/Cornell University/NASA; 192 (T) NASA; 193 (CR) ©Mehau Kulyk/Photo Researchers, Inc., (BR) NASA; 194 (T, CR, BR, B) NASA; 195 (B) JPL-Caltech/Keck/NASA, (C) NASA; 196 (BR) ©JPL/NASA, (TR) ES/Erich Karkoschka, University of Arizona/NASA; 197 (T) NASA; 198 (T) ©Olivier Blondeau/iStockphoto; 199 (CR) NASA; 205 (BL) GSFC/NASA, (BR) JPL/NASA; 206 (Bkgd) ©Detlev van Ravenswaay/Photo Researchers, Inc., (B) ©Larry Landolfi/Photo Researchers, Inc.; 207 (B) ©Larry Landolfi/Photo Researchers, Inc.; 208 (T) ©Alexey Stiop/Shutterstock; 209 ©blickwinkel/Alamy Images, (T) ©Eckhard Slawik/Photo Researchers, Inc.; 212 (Bkgd) National Science Foundation; 213 (CL) Gerard Lodriguss / Photo Researchers, Inc./Photo Researchers, Inc., (TR) JPL/NASA, (CR, BR) NASA, (TL) Stefan Seip; 215 (L) ©Alexey Stiop/Shutterstock, (B) ©AP Images, (BL)

©Eckhard Slawik/Photo Researchers, Inc., (TR, CR, BR) NASA; 219 (BL) Stocktrek Images/Getty Images; 228 ©Peter Arnold, Inc./Alamy Images; 231 (Inset) John Cancalosi/Alamy Images, (Bkgd) Robert Francis/Alamy Images; 232 (T) ©Doug Webb/Alamy Images, (B) ©Karl Ammann/Corbis; 233 (CR) ©Mark Conlin/Alamy Images; 234 (B) ©Mark Conlin/Alamy Images; 235 (BR) blickwinkel/Hecker/Alamy Images, (TR) Buddy Mays/Alamy Images, (CR) Jerry L. Ferrara / Photo Researchers, Inc./Photo Researchers, Inc., (T) Michael Dwyer/Alamy Images, (C) Rick & Nora Bowers/Alamy Images; 236 (B) ©David Tipling/Nature Picture Library, (CL) ©James McLaughlin/Alamy Images, (C) ©Marvin Dembinsky Photo associates/Alamy Images; 237 (CL) ©Bob Blanchard/Shutterstock, (BR) ©Corbis Super RF/Alamy, (B) ©David R. Frazier Photolibrary, Inc./Alamy Images, (C) ©Michael P. Gadomski/Photo Researchers, Inc.; 238 (TR) Anthony Mercieca / Photo Researchers, Inc./Photo Researchers, Inc.; 239 (TR) ©imagebroker/Alamy; 240 (T) David Keith Jones/Alamy Images; 241 (B) ©Bob Blanchard/Shutterstock; 242 (B) ©Photoshot Holdings Ltd./Alamy Images, (C) ©Rob Crandall/Alamy Images; 243 (CL) ©Eye of Science/Photo Researchers, Inc., (B) ©Spring Images/Alamy Images, (CR) Jupiter Images; 244 (R) ©Jack Milchanowski/age fotostock/PhotoLibrary Group, Inc., (L) ©Jeff Greenberg/Alamy Images, (C) Photos to Go/Photolibrary; 246 (CL) ©Inga Spence/Photo Researchers, Inc., (TL) Jim Strawser/Alamy Images; 247 (TR) ©Wolfgang Pölzer/Alamy Images; 248 (T) ©Peter Bisset/PhotoLibrary Group, Inc.; 249 (R) ©Georgette Douwma/Nature Picture Library; 251 (C) ©Andrew Syred/Photo Researchers, Inc., (L) ©Eye of Science/Photo Researchers, Inc., (B) ©LianeM/Shutterstock, (R) ©Wild Wonders of Europe/Falklind/Nature Picture Library; 252 (BL) ©blickwinkel/Alamy Images, (CL) ©Mircea Bezergheanu/Shutterstock, (BR) ©Rick & Nora Bowers/Alamy Images; 253 (TR) ©Sheila Terry/Photo Researchers, Inc.; 254 (T) ©Szfei/Shutterstock, (B) Wave Royalty Free / Photo Researchers, Inc./Photo Researchers, Inc.; 255 (R) ©Slowfish/Shutterstock; 256 (TR) ©John Durham/Photo Researchers, Inc., (TC) Stephen Oliver/©DK Images; 257 (BL) ©Sinclair Stammers/Photo Researchers, Inc.; 258 (B) ©Professors Pietro M. Motta & Tomonori Naguro/Photo Researchers, Inc.; 259 (B) Rod Planck / Photo Researchers, Inc./Photo Researchers, Inc.; 260 (T) Jupiter Images; 262 (C) Maximilian Weinzierl/Alamy Images, (B) Stephen J. Krasemann / Photo Researchers, Inc./Photo Researchers, Inc.; 263 (TR) ©Steve Shepard/iStockphoto; 266 (C) Mark Burnett/Alamy Images; 267 (CL, BL) ©Bob Blanchard/Shutterstock, (TR) ©Doug Webb/Alamy Images, (TL, CR) ©Mark Conlin/Alamy Images, (Inset, BR) ©Martin Strmiska/Alamy; 269 (TR, CR) ©Bill Coster / Alamy/Alamy Images, (BC) ©John Durham/Photo Researchers, Inc., (CC) ©Peter Bisset/PhotoLibrary Group, Inc., (TL) ©Professors Pietro M. Motta & Tomonori Naguro/Photo Researchers, Inc., (BC) ©Sinclair Stammers/Photo Researchers, Inc., (BL) ©Steve Shepard/iStockphoto, (CL) Jupiter Images, (BC) Stephen Oliver/©DK Images; 271 (B) ©Peter Arnold, Inc./Alamy Images; 273 Jupiter Images; 275 (Bkgd) Peter Anderson/©DK Images, (Inset) Stuart Kelly/Alamy Images; 276 (C) ©SPL/Photo Researchers, Inc.; 280 (T) ©JRC, Inc./Alamy; 281 (CR) ©Innerspace Imaging/Photo Researchers, Inc., (BR) medicalpicture/Alamy Images; 283 (T) ©CNRI/Photo Researchers, Inc., (B) ©SPL/Photo Researchers, Inc.; 284 (C)

This is your book.

You can write in it.

Take Note

This space is yours. It is great for drawing diagrams and making notes

This is your book.

You can write in it.

interactive
SCIENCE

This is your book.

You can write in it.